A
Present
of
Things
Past

BOOKS BY THEODORE DRAPER

The Six Weeks' War (1944)

The 84th Infantry Division in the Battle of Germany (1946)

The Roots of American Communism (1957)

American Communism and Soviet Russia (1960)

Castro's Revolution: Myths and Realities (1962)

Castroism, Theory and Practice (1965)

Abuse of Power (1967)

Israel and World Politics (1968)

The Dominican Revolt (1968)

The Rediscovery of Black Nationalism (1970)

Present History (1983)

A Present of Things Past

SELECTED ESSAYS

Theodore Draper

HILL AND WANG

A division of Farrar, Straus and Giroux • NEW YORK

The author is grateful to the following publications for
permission to reprint, in somewhat different form, previously
published material: *Dissent, The New Republic, The New York
Review of Books,* and *The New York Times*

Library of Congress Cataloging-in-Publication Data
Draper, Theodore.
    [Selections. 1990]
    A present of things past : selected essays / Theodore Draper. — 1st ed.
        p.   cm.
    Includes index.
    1. United States—Foreign relations—1945–
  2. United States—Foreign relations—Soviet Union.
  3. Soviet Union—Foreign relations—United States.
  4. Communism—Soviet Union.   5. Soviet Union—Foreign relations—1945–
  6. Communism—United States—1917–   I. Title.
  E806.D682   1990   89-11128
  327.73—dc20   CIP

For Dorothy and Jacob Rabkin
Affectionately

Contents

Preface

THE READER may well wonder about the diversity of subjects in this book. The explanation is unavoidably personal.

I have been writing professionally since 1935, a period of over fifty years. In that time I have worked on different, often exceedingly different, subjects, sometimes deliberately, sometimes fortuitously. In fact, looking back, I have rarely stayed with a single subject for more than five years. I get interested in a subject; I devote myself to it; I do what I can with it; I know—or think I know—as much as I want to know; I turn to something else.

Two five-year projects will illustrate how this cycle has worked out.

Sometime in the mid-1950s, I took it into my head that the country needed a straightforward, "traditional" history of American Communism, rather than the mainly tendentious treatments then in vogue. By chance, the Fund for the Republic, which had been set up by the Ford Foundation, wanted to make a large-scale study of the American Communist movement. I was taken on to do the history until 1945; five years and two volumes later, I had managed to reach 1929. My work was completed long afterward by someone else. Nevertheless, I had deliberately chosen this subject and gave it up only because the project's money gave out.

After I had finished these two books, I went on to *The Reporter* magazine as associate editor. One of my assignments was Latin America, I suppose because I knew some Spanish and had lived for some time in Mexico—or perhaps because no one else wanted to take the job. Fidel Castro had come to power in January 1959, and now it was 1960. For months, *The Reporter* had been looking for an authoritative article on Castro's Cuba without success. Despite all my efforts, I could not get one that satisfied me. In that period, Cuban experts were in very short supply in the United States.

So the editor, the late Max Ascoli, decided that I would have to go down to Cuba and do the article myself. I went; stayed a few weeks; wrote the article; and left the magazine soon after it had appeared. The article attracted some favorable attention; I continued to study and write about Cuba for the next five years and had two more volumes to show for them. Still, this is one subject I have never felt moved to return to, perhaps because I did not choose it in the first place.

The first and longest piece in this book represents a return to an old interest. My first book, *The Six Weeks' War*, published in 1944, dealt with the fall of France in 1940. As befitted the subject, it was largely military in nature, though, as in most of my work, I had no particular license to undertake it. During World War II, I served as historian of the 84th Infantry Division and wrote its official history, published in 1946. When I was asked to review David Eisenhower's book on his grandfather, I thought it would be gratifying to return to an old interest. The review, as my reviews will, took on a life of its own and turned out to be for the most part my own independent assessment of "Eisenhower's War."

The same course was followed in the section "From American Communism to Gorbachev." These pieces also represented a return to a subject that I had dropped many years earlier but felt compelled to reexamine as a result of new work in the field that happened to drag me into the discussion. I have included the piece "Soviet Reformers: From Lenin to Gorbachev," written at an early stage of Gorbachev's progress, for two reasons. One is that the Leninist phase is still poorly understood in many quarters. The other is that I have found little to change in it three years later. The reader may be interested to compare what I wrote with later views on the Gorbachev phenomenon.

Other parts of this book deal with new subjects and new problems. I am more attracted to problematic subjects that I do not fully understand at the outset and that send me seeking for an answer or explanation than to the reworking of something that has become familiar. I came to "The Mystery of Max Eitingon" in such a mood, the circumstances of which are related in the piece itself. This is the only one in which I have added some new material; the others have been edited slightly, if at all.

When I am asked what I am, I do not know what to answer. I am surely not an academic, because I do not hold an academic post. On the other hand, I doubt whether what I write can be called journalistic. I would like to think of myself as a historian of a special kind. As far as I know myself, I try to study a subject as seriously as a professional historian might. I usually write on the kinds of subjects that I have included in a previous collection called *Present History*, that is, subjects closer to the present than most historians deal with, yet treated from a larger historical perspective and with traditionally historical methods.

It will be seen that most of the contents of this book were originally published in *The New York Review of Books*. I owe a large debt of gratitude to its remarkable editor, Robert B. Silvers, with whom I have had a longer and more rewarding collaboration than with any other.

*It might be fitly said, "There are three times:
a present of things past, a present of things present,
and a present of things future."*

—SAINT AUGUSTINE, *The Confessions*,
Book XI, Chapter 20

FROM EISENHOWER TO REAGAN

Eisenhower's War

1

OF ALL AMERICAN WARS since the Revolution, the Second World War was fought with fewest regrets. Even now, after four decades, hardly anyone looks back at the war disapprovingly. Yet, in retrospect, it came to an end in a peculiarly double-edged way. That the world was rid of a Nazi tyranny will always be its proudest achievement. That it was replaced in almost half of Europe by a Communist tyranny will always darken that achievement. Any balance sheet of what the war finally accomplished cannot ignore the difference between what the war meant for Eastern and for Western Europe.

The most anguished question is whether the extension of Soviet power could have been avoided. It is a question that by its very nature can never be answered with any confidence. The war can be refought only as an exercise in speculation and hindsight, on paper. The way it—or any other war—was fought gives no reason to believe that it would have gone entirely right if it had been fought differently. What we can do now is to try to understand what hard choices had to be made and why they were made in a way that has shaped the world we live in. We may not agree on whether it was right for the Western Allies to stand by as the Red Army went into Vienna, Berlin, and Prague, but at least we can try to put ourselves back into that time and place, as if we had to face those hard choices as they arose.

Offhand, one might not imagine that a book on one Eisenhower

3

by another would offer the best available means for making such a retrospective effort. Anyone who starts reading *Eisenhower: At War* (Random House, 1986) by the general's grandson, David, must wonder how "objective" or unprejudiced it can be. I opened the book with this question in mind; I closed it satisfied that the author must have known that his readers would not respect anything that smacked of an apologia or glorification.

The work is largely based on a thorough study of existing sources, mixed with a few sidelights from personal interviews. Despite its bulk of almost a thousand pages, it mostly deals with the last eighteen months of the war—from the Allied invasion of Normandy to the German surrender. It is for the reader who wants to refight the war at the highest level of command, sometimes day by day, often in meticulous detail.

In one respect, the form of *Eisenhower: At War* is somewhat disconcerting. The reader immediately encounters an introduction of 17 pages that may well raise more questions than the following 825 pages of text. David Eisenhower has seen fit in his opening pages to put forward a number of theories or interpretations that hold out a claim to originality; he promises to show how Eisenhower met political and military challenges "in ways that have not been fully understood, if understood at all." The introduction tends to prepare the reader for a narrative that is more startling, and more tendentious, than it actually is.

Three of these novel interpretations stand out, and I will have more to say about them in due course. It may be well to state them at the outset, as David Eisenhower does, in order to keep them in mind as we go along.

1. Eisenhower's motives and decisions during the war were far more political than has been thought. The problems of the Allied-Soviet relationship made him "think and act as a politician." The political aspects of his job were what it "was mainly about."[1]

2. Eisenhower's political role led him "to cede Berlin and Prague to the Russians." Presumably he would have done otherwise if he had been less politically motivated.

---

[1] Here as elsewhere, the emphasis in the introduction is not always consistent with that in the body of the book. In his conclusion, David Eisenhower also writes: "To the end, Eisenhower's approach was military: defeating the German army and gaining an unconditional cease-fire" (p. 789).

3. On the British side of the alliance, David Eisenhower suggests—as no one to my knowledge has ever done before—that Churchill and Montgomery were not really serious about policies and strategies which they urged upon Eisenhower and which gave him so much trouble. The British proposal for a campaign in southeastern Europe "seems to have been made mainly for political reasons," not because it was considered to be militarily feasible. Montgomery did not actually believe in his scheme in September 1944 to get to Berlin and hoped that Eisenhower would turn it down flatly. Despite their pressure for such a move, the British were "in fact lukewarm if not opposed to a Berlin campaign" even in March 1945. In short, some of the greatest British-American controversies during the war were allegedly based on disingenuous or insincere British demands.

David Eisenhower's book stimulated me to reconsider the war in Europe, partly with his help and partly by going back to original sources. In what follows, I have tried to set forth this reconsideration in my own terms, with comments from time to time on his views. I have not always agreed with him, but I have always admired the thoroughness and seriousness of his effort.

2

The nominal head of the two-member coalition was the Supreme Commander, General Dwight D. Eisenhower. His previous career had made him an unlikely candidate for the job. As a West Point graduate in 1917, he had come on the scene too late to see action in France. He had spent the 1920s going through all the right training schools for upward assignments and promotions, only to land in 1933 as special assistant to the imperious General Douglas MacArthur, whom he served in Washington and in the Philippines for the rest of the decade. In the early months of the Second World War, he seemed doomed to remain a staff officer in Washington as chief of the War Plans Division and then the Operations Division in the office of the Chief of Staff, General George C. Marshall, another overshadowing superior.

After a decade in desk jobs, he was finally rescued from them in June 1942 by getting the appointment as commander in chief of the Allied forces in the European theater, which in practice put him in North Africa. This assignment indicated that he was Marshall's favorite and was being groomed for bigger things. Nevertheless it had its drawbacks. Three quarters of the troops under him were British. The two leading British commanders, Field Marshal Sir Harold Alexander and General Sir Bernard L. Montgomery, were nominally subordinate to him but far exceeded him in combat experience and actually took charge of the fighting while he was stuck away in Algiers far from the action. Eisenhower did not cover himself with glory in his Mediterranean role and still had to prove himself when he was named Supreme Commander of the Allied Expeditionary Force in Western Europe at the end of 1943.

In one way, his first experience as Allied commander later worked against him. It gave the British a precedent for treating him as titular chief while their generals largely conducted the war on the ground. The lesson was not lost on the other ranking American generals in the Mediterranean phase, Omar N. Bradley and George S. Patton, Jr. They came out of North Africa and Italy resentfully determined to take over real power in Europe and to put an end to the Mediterranean practice of using piecemeal American units to support major British forces in important operations. The American sensitivity in Europe to the issue of who was commanding whom and the suspicion of Eisenhower's susceptibility to British influence were outgrowths of his North African initiation as Allied commander.

Eisenhower took his directions from the Combined Chiefs of Staff, made up of the American Joint Chiefs of Staff and the British Chiefs of Staff Committee, at the head of which were General George C. Marshall for the Americans and Field Marshal Sir Alan Brooke for the British. They could overrule him, though they were usually hesitant to do so.

The institutional differences between the British and American command structures made for built-in complications. The British had three autonomous commanders in chief for ground, air, and sea forces. The Americans had only one, in ultimate command of all three services. Eisenhower as American commander had far more authority than as Allied commander. In fact, he "exercised only formalistic authority" over the British, as David Eisenhower puts it. As for the French generals, they took their orders from de Gaulle, and de Gaulle took his orders from no one.

These loose and nebulous arrangements made personal relations far more important than formal authority. In dealing with the British, Eisenhower needed professional prestige and respect. He especially needed them from the two leading British military figures, Brooke and Montgomery, the latter appointed commander of the British Army in Europe. To them, he was not only not supreme; he was not even a qualified commander.

Eisenhower did not come into his appointment as Supreme Commander with the necessary prestige, because he had never commanded soldiers in the field and had for so long been a staff officer. As Supreme Commander, he had been a last-minute replacement for Marshall, when President Roosevelt had decided that he could not do without Marshall in Washington. Without a record as a combat commander, Eisenhower was a novice compared with Montgomery, the latter already immortalized by the British press as the "hero of El Alamein." The only reason Eisenhower was chosen over Alexander or Montgomery was the recognition forced on the British that the Americans would not send a preponderance of manpower and matériel across the Atlantic unless an American was put in charge.

It helped that Eisenhower, despite his Middle Western and German Mennonite background, was something of an Anglophile. It did not help that he had to cope with Brooke, of a family of Northern Irish baronets, and Montgomery, the unwanted child of an Anglican bishop. The fate of Allied coalition warfare was largely in the hands of this odd trio—Brooke, Montgomery, and Eisenhower.

Brooke was a man of sharp intelligence and saturnine temperament. His most lovable trait was his passion for ornithology.[2] Otherwise, he was almost congenitally irascible and egocentric. Throughout the war, he kept a diary in which he confided his innermost thoughts about his Allied associates and others. Almost no one gets a good word except his protégé, Montgomery. Of all his victims, Eisenhower suffers the most. Brooke portrays him as a nice fellow who meant well but who had no strategical brain for commanding armies. "Eisenhower has got absolutely no strategical outlook . . . The main impression I gathered was that Eisenhower was not [a] real director of thought, plans, energy or direction . . . But it is equally clear that Ike knows nothing about strategy . . . Ike has

---

[2] The story is told by Sir John Kennedy, the Deputy Director of Military Operations of the British Army, that Brooke was one day tired and depressed. Kennedy thought it must have been caused by bad news in the war. He later found out that something else was bothering Brooke—"he was unable to identify some of the birds in the volumes of Levaillant he had acquired, for lack of a proper French dictionary of archaic bird names" (Sir John Kennedy, *The Business of War* [Morrow, 1958], p. 301).

the very vaguest conception of war!"[3] Others have kept equally in-
discreet diaries, but no military man of such eminence has had them
published while his erstwhile comrades-in-arms were still very much
alive.

Montgomery was even more trying. He was an authentic British
eccentric of the most extreme type. He dressed, ate, went to sleep,
and otherwise behaved eccentrically. He usually affected fur-lined
boots, baggy corduroy trousers, a gray turtleneck pullover or one
pullover on top of another, and a black beret, while everyone else
went about in regulation uniform. He lived much of the time isolated
in a trailer, accompanied by a few young aides who were the only
ones permitted to eat with him. He went to sleep no later than ten
in the evening, no matter what the circumstances or company. He
almost always refused to attend conferences with American generals
and sent his chief of staff, Major General Sir Francis de Guingand,
to represent him, with no authority to make decisions. He insisted
on meeting with Eisenhower alone and on doing almost all the talking. He once delivered such a bitter tirade that Eisenhower had to
stop him with "Steady, Monty! You can't speak to me like that. I'm
your boss."[4]

The other two ranking American generals, Bradley and Patton,
loathed Montgomery. His egotism was so monumental that Bradley
regarded it as "megalomania."[5] Montgomery habitually hectored the
Americans as if he were a Victorian schoolmaster addressing slightly
backward students. Relations became so strained that finally the
Americans and he were barely on speaking terms. Bradley acknowl-

---

[3] Brooke did not publish his diaries directly. Instead, he enabled the British historian
Arthur Bryant to use them *in extenso* in two books, *The Turn of the Tide* and *Triumph
in the West* (Doubleday, 1957 and 1959; the quotations above are from the latter, pp. 100,
139, 181). Brooke generally followed these disparagements with intended compliments,
such as this: "Just a co-ordinator, a good mixer, a champion of inter-Allied cooperation,
and in those respects few can hold a candle to him" (pp. 189–90).

[4] Chester Wilmot, *The Struggle for Europe* (London: Collins, 1952), p. 489. Wilmot, an
able journalist, whose book is still worth reading, first popularized the British view that
Eisenhower was a "military statesman rather than the generalissimo . . . open to persuasion
by the last strong man to whom he talked" (pp. 467–68). Wilmot's book was virtually
dictated by Montgomery in those passages dealing with strategic disputes and Eisenhower's
shortcomings.

[5] Omar N. Bradley and Clay Blair, *A General's Life* (Simon and Schuster, 1983), pp. 326,
340, 396. For good measure, Bradley also calls Montgomery "this arrogant egomaniac"
(p. 394). Bradley had published memoirs soon after the war in which he had treated
Montgomery gently (*A Soldier's Story* [Holt, 1951]). In his second version, *A General's
Life*, he really let loose what had been long suppressed; he mentions Montgomery twelve
times, almost always with unconcealed detestation.

edged that "friendly and intimate co-operation between him and the Field Marshal [Montgomery] was out of the question."[6] The long-suffering Eisenhower once dropped his guard sufficiently to say: "Montgomery had become so personal in his efforts to make sure that the Americans—and me, in particular—got no credit, that, in fact, we hardly had anything to do with the war, that I finally stopped talking to him."[7]

The third and last volume of Montgomery's official biography portrays him as a military genius of the highest order, alloyed with tragic flaws of character. He was a congenital "bully." Obsessiveness was a trait "ingrained in his character." He was "outrageous in his conceit, his egoism and self-righteousness." He "liked to dominate rather than to share." His "tactlessness and egocentricity" outraged almost everyone, including finally the Queen. He was "the square peg in the round hole." He treated his mother, his son, and some of his closest associates with a heartlessness and even cruelty that were pathological. The military historian Basil Liddell Hart called him "very small-boyish" and "a curious psychological case." Malcolm Muggeridge regarded his character as "bizarre." Goronwy Rees detected a touch of madness in him, mitigated only by the war. His son David spoke of his "overriding eccentricity." Yet he was the key British military figure with whom Eisenhower and the Americans had to work in this coalition.[8]

Then there was Churchill. Unlike Roosevelt, who did not consider himself to be a military expert and rarely interfered in strictly military matters, Churchill recognized no dividing line between his political and military roles. Because he was Minister of Defense as well as Prime Minister, he regularly ignored protocol by getting in touch with commanders in the field, as if he were a member of the Chiefs of Staff. His indefatigable brain hatched scheme after scheme, almost none of which ever came to fruition.[9] He was peculiarly oblivious to the well-being of the military staff, whom he habitually kept at meet-

[6] Lord Tedder, *With Prejudice* (London: Cassell, 1966), p. 658.

[7] Cornelius Ryan, *The Last Battle* (Simon and Schuster, 1966), p. 658.

[8] Nigel Hamilton, *Monty the Field-Marshal, 1944–1976* (London: Hamish Hamilton, 1986), pp. 246, 250, 265, 267, 565, 692, 708, 809, 941.

[9] Brooke's analysis of Churchill as a strategist rings truest: "In all his plans he lives from hand to mouth; he can never grasp a whole plan either in its width (i.e. all its fronts) or its depth (long-term projects)." The next two paragraphs dramatically illustrate Brooke's meaning (Bryant, *Triumph in the West*, pp. 98–99).

ings with him until two or three in the morning; they had to get up early, while he stayed in bed until noon. Brooke was the chief sufferer; Eisenhower noted in his understated way that "after about two o'clock, Brookey would get pretty tired."[10] Brooke's memoirs are full of vivid flashes on what fighting the war with Churchill was like.[11] Yet, unlike Montgomery, Churchill was always forgiven; he more than made up in morale what he cost in chasing after his strategic will-o'-the-wisps. Coalition warfare with him was not easy for the Americans; he rarely gave up even after an agreement had been reached; but he had a way in the end of making amends that seemed to leave very few permanent scars.[12]

The differences in the British-American coalition were by no means limited to British versus Americans. On some issues, Churchill was opposed as strenuously by his British advisers as by the Americans. Moreover, the British military staff was itself divided. All of Eisenhower's deputies at his Supreme Headquarters Allied Expeditionary Force (SHAEF) were British.[13] They almost always sided with Eisenhower against the British staff officers in London, who virtually considered the British at SHAEF to have sold out to the Americans. Air Chief Marshal Sir Arthur Tedder, the Deputy Supreme Commander at SHAEF, was distrusted so strongly that determined efforts were made in London to remove him. Montgomery took his revenge against Eisenhower, Tedder, and SHAEF as a whole by writing in the "Log," or record, of his 21st Army Group five days after the German surrender:

---

[10] *General Eisenhower on the Military Churchill* (Norton, 1970), p. 30.

[11] One example: "Winston related all his old reminiscences connected with various Cabinet appointments he has held, none of which have any bearing on the points under discussion. I remain very fond of him, but, by Heaven, he does try one's patience!" (*Triumph in the West*, p. 183).

[12] Bryant: "What upset Brooke and his colleagues was that, on his [Churchill's] being asked to approve the plans they had prepared for implementing the agreement made with the Americans at Cairo for future strategy against Japan, he had denied all knowledge of such an agreement. When they reminded him that he and the President had initialled it, he replied that he did not consider his doing so binding. Instead he reverted to his old project, rejected by both the British and American Chiefs of Staff, for a landing in Sumatra which he believed, entirely contrary to their opinion, would cut Japan's seaborne communications with Burma" (Ibid., p. 99).

[13] The four Deputy Chiefs of Staff, the Allied Naval Commander, and the Air Commander in Chief were British. Only the Chief of Staff, Lieutenant General Walter Bedell Smith, was American (for the entire roster at SHAEF, see Forrest C. Pogue, *The Supreme Command*, in the series *United States Army in World War II* [Washington, D.C.: Office of the Chief of Military History, Department of the Army, 1954], pp. 536–38).

The organization for command was always faulty. The Supreme Commander had no firm ideas as to how to conduct the war, and "was blown about by the wind" all over the place; at that particular business he was quite useless.

The Deputy Supreme Commander [Tedder] was completely ineffective; none of the [British] Army Commanders would see him and they growled if ever he appeared on the horizon.

The staff at SHAEF were completely out of their depth all the time.[14]

Montgomery frequently asked his military assistant, Lieutenant Colonel Christopher Dawnay: "Why are they so hostile to me at SHAEF? Who are my enemies?" Brigadier Sir Edgar Williams, Montgomery's intelligence officer, identified them as the four British deputies at SHAEF, Major Generals Strong, Gale, Whiteley, and Morgan.[15] The British could have used a good deal more coalition among themselves in their warfare.

The Americans had their own problems. Paradoxically, while Eisenhower almost never pleased Brooke and Montgomery, he displeased Bradley, Patton, and at times Marshall for being too pro-British. The smart thing to say at Patton's headquarters was that Eisenhower "is the best general the British have."[16] Patton agreed with Montgomery and Brooke about Eisenhower but for a different reason. "Ike is bound hand and foot by the British and does not know it. Poor fool," Patton wrote in his diary. "We actually have no Supreme Commander—no one who can take hold and say that this shall be done and that shall not be done."[17] Though Eisenhower saved Patton from disgrace at least twice, Patton was capable of being insubordinate and even of lying or, as a military historian has put it more gently, of "stretching the truth."[18] Yet Eisenhower kept him on, because he was his most aggressive field commander. Bradley was also convinced that Eisenhower had "a tendency to favor British plans and generals, often to our detriment."[19] To prevent what they considered pro-British decisions on Eisenhower's part, Bradley and Patton had to threaten to resign, an almost unheard-of act of des-

[14] Richard Lamb, *Montgomery in Europe 1943–45* (Franklin Watts, 1984), p. 394.

[15] Ibid., p. 378.

[16] Ladislas Farago, *Patton: Ordeal and Triumph* (Obolensky, 1963), p. 674.

[17] Martin Blumenson, *The Patton Papers 1940–1945* (Houghton Mifflin, 1974), Vol. 2, p. 480.

[18] Russell F. Weigley, *Eisenhower's Lieutenants* (Indiana University Press, 1981), p. 266.

[19] Bradley and Blair, *A General's Life*, p. 315.

peration on the part of the highest-ranking American generals, which would have smashed any semblance of coalition warfare and ruined Eisenhower's career. Yet Eisenhower survived even their revolts against his authority.

One cannot judge Eisenhower's performance as Supreme Commander fairly without understanding the conditions under which he worked. These conditions were understandably covered up during the war and often mythicized afterward. Eisenhower's chief of staff, General Walter Bedell Smith, was one of the mythmakers: "General Eisenhower commanded an Allied force in which nationality was of no importance."[20] Montgomery's chief of staff, "Freddie" de Guingand, pretended: "The relationship between the Allies in the Second World War was truly remarkable for the small amount of friction that occurred."[21] This pious humbug does serious injustice to whatever Eisenhower achieved by making it seem so simple and easy. In reality, the Allied setup for coalition warfare was so riven with rivalries and cross-purposes that it was a wonder Eisenhower was able to survive with his sanity intact.

3

The irony is that the trouble within the British-American coalition could have been much worse if Eisenhower had been a stronger or more willful commander. The issues that divided the British and Americans were far deeper and more irreconcilable than Eisenhower's style of command. What often passed for a disagreement with Eisenhower was really a clash between British and American interests and strategies. At the bottom of it all was a struggle for dominance that would have embroiled Great Britain and the United States with or without Eisenhower. On matters of grand strategy, he took his orders from Washington, where General Marshall was decisive. Eisenhower would not have held the job very long if he had not done what Marshall wanted him to do.

In its simplest terms, the main difference between the British and American conceptions of how to wage the war against Germany at

[20] Walter Bedell Smith, *Eisenhower's Six Great Decisions* (Longmans, Green, 1956), p. 167.

[21] Major General Sir Francis de Guingand, *Generals at War* (Hodder and Stoughton, 1964), p. 99.

first turned on a choice between a "peripheral" and a "frontal" strategy.

The British favored the peripheral. This implied that the only action for the foreseeable future would take place on the outskirts of Europe, particularly in the Mediterranean area, North Africa, and the Middle East. A direct attack on the German forces in Europe was not ruled out, but it was contemplated only if and when they had been so seriously weakened that no more than a short, relatively inexpensive, and final push was necessary. The campaigns in North Africa and Sicily in 1942–43 were products of the peripheral strategy.

The Americans favored the frontal approach. It meant the use of Great Britain itself as a staging area for an invasion of France such as took place on June 6, 1944, in Normandy. The Americans agreed reluctantly to the campaigns in North Africa and Sicily only because they were not as yet ready for the cross-Channel operation and did not wish to appear to be idle for over a year while waiting for it. Every time the British proposed still another peripheral action, however, the Americans regarded it with increasing distrust and disapproval.

"Had we had our way," admitted Sir John Kennedy, who was in a position to know, "I think there can be little doubt that the invasion of France would not have been done in 1944."[22] No one can tell when it might have been done. In effect, it would have depended mainly on the Russians to produce the conditions that would have permitted the Western Allies to move in for the kill—with far-reaching consequences for the future armed division of Europe.

On this score, Eisenhower was a typical American general. He believed devoutly in the frontal strategy and had, in fact, been chief of the Operations Division of the General Staff that had drawn up a plan for a cross-Channel invasion. Had the Americans had their way, it would have been planned for the spring of 1943. Once the decision was made in the autumn of 1942 to fight in North Africa, this plan was sidetracked, much to the disgust of American military planners, who complained bitterly of "periphery-pecking" and "scatterization."[23] The Americans at this stage saw themselves as apostles

---

[22] Kennedy, *The Business of War*, p. 305.

[23] Maurice Matloff, *Strategic Planning for Coalition Warfare 1943–1944* (Washington, D.C.: Office of the Chief of Military History, 1959), p. 14.

of the hallowed military principles of mass and concentration. Whether the forces assembled in Great Britain in 1943 could in any case have carried out a successful invasion of the Continent is questionable, though a British writer has argued forcefully that it could have been done and regretted that it was not.[24]

The British handling of the "second front" issue was more devious than outright rejection. Whenever the Americans insisted strongly enough on a course of action, the British usually went along in the end, whatever their misgivings. Churchill had agreed in principle to a cross-Channel invasion as early as April 1942 but had never really reconciled himself to it. Thereafter he had proposed one alternative after another, which had the practical effect of postponing an invasion to some indefinite hereafter. Every time the British thought up some other objective, such as bringing a reluctant Turkey into the war or moving into the Balkans, the Americans saw another furtive design to draw attention and resources away from the main prize on the Continent. As late as May 3, 1944, only a month before D day, Churchill told a meeting of Dominion prime ministers that he had wanted to wage the war in a different way by going into Europe from the southeast instead of the northwest. In his memoirs, Churchill was somewhat less than guileless. He reminds the reader that he "was always willing to join with the United States in a direct assault across the Channel," but that he "was not convinced that this was the only way of winning the war."[25] In fact, he was not convinced that this was any way of winning the war short of a virtually unopposed assault on a weakened Germany.

The British attitude toward the growing American predominance in the war came out most vehemently during the long wrangle in mid-1944 over the subsidiary landing in southern France, which the British opposed and the Americans favored. By this time, the Americans had over 11 million men in arms, the British 5 million. The British had exhausted their supply of replacements; the Americans were still sending over new divisions. Brooke noted in his diary: "The situation is full of difficulties; the Americans now begin to own the major strength on land, in the air and on the sea. They, therefore, consider that they are entitled to dictate how their forces are to be deployed." The British chiefs finally dropped their opposition by

[24] John Grigg, *1943: The Victory That Never Was* (Hill and Wang, 1980).
[25] Winston S. Churchill, *Closing the Ring* (Houghton Mifflin, 1951), p. 582.

adopting this line of reasoning: "All right, if you insist on being damned fools, sooner than fall out with you, which would be fatal, we shall be damned fools with you, and we shall see that we perform the role of damned fools damned well."[26]

The controversy over "Anvil," the code name for the landing in southern France, one of the longest and most divisive disputes of the entire war, tests David Eisenhower's thesis that Eisenhower's major decisions were at least as much political as military, or were primarily political. Even in his introduction, where so much emphasis is put on the political Eisenhower, it is admitted that his "crucial decision to back ANVIL rested on military factors." In the body of the book, we are told that Eisenhower resisted Churchill on the ground that he, Eisenhower, "lacked political authority" to recommend that the landing should be shifted from southern France to Brittany. In this case, Eisenhower had hardly seemed to "think and act as a politician."

Yet political factors had intruded into the Anvil controversy, as in most of these inter-Allied disputes. A landing in southern France in support of the cross-Channel invasion had been agreed on with Stalin at the Teheran Conference in November 1943. By mid-1944, after the successful landings in Normandy and a steady Russian advance toward the borders of East Prussia, Poland, and Romania, any proposal for the British and Americans in Italy to go into the Balkans or anywhere else in southeastern Europe carried with it the implication of competition with the Soviets for control of the region and a threat to Allied-Soviet military cooperation. Here again David Eisenhower produces a provocative interpretation of British motivation that makes it seem to be something other than the British claimed it was.

The issue was then raised by General Sir Henry Maitland Wilson, the British Supreme Commander in the Mediterranean, only about two weeks after the Normandy landings in June 1944; he wanted to use the forces in Italy for a campaign from Venice to Trieste and on through the Ljubljana Gap toward Vienna. David Eisenhower gives three reasons why Wilson's proposal was striking in its "unreality."

[26] Bryant, *Triumph in the West*, pp. 167–68. When Churchill lost a long argument over the abandonment or delay of the landing in southern France, he characteristically gave in, saying: "I pray God that you may be right. We shall of course do everything in our power to help you achieve success" (*Triumph and Tragedy* [Houghton Mifflin, 1953], p. 71).

Even the British Chiefs of Staff, he writes, knew that a Vienna strategy was not a practical alternative. From this he infers that it "was not so much a 'military' proposal to exploit an illusory Allied freedom of action but an attempt to influence policy months, perhaps years, hence."

It is an intriguing but implausible theory. Wilson was a professional military man. He made what appeared to be a strictly military proposal in the midst of a most difficult and dangerous period of the Normandy campaign. That he should have put his name to a plan that he did not intend at that time to be taken seriously and only wanted to draw attention to future Soviet domination of Eastern Europe strains credulity. The British generals in the Mediterranean were always trying with Churchill's encouragement to find a larger mission for their command and increased support for the British forces in Italy. There would never be any military failures if their "unreality" were enough to rule them out as real intentions. This theory also implies that the British were not really serious about blocking the Soviet incursion into Eastern Europe in 1944 and merely concocted a visionary plan to make a political point for "perhaps years, hence." It is hard to imagine responsible leaders during a war spending so much time and causing so much discord for a cause so remote.

Who was right in these typical British-American disagreements of World War II?

Each was right, it seems to me, to want to fight the war according to its best interests and optimal use of its resources. The imperial lifeline—when the British Empire was still more than a historical memory—extended across the Mediterranean to the Middle East. The Mediterranean front was the only one throughout the war in which the British had the preponderance of forces and superiority of command. Churchill was always seeking targets along the Mediterranean that seemed to offer maximum rewards with minimum expenditure of force. A frontal attack on German defenses in France brought back the nightmare of human sacrifices in the First World War. "The fearful price we had had to pay in human life and blood for the great offensives of the First World War was graven in my mind," wrote Churchill in explanation of his doubts about the advisability of a direct assault across the Channel.[27] It was only right

---

[27] Churchill, *Closing the Ring*, p. 582.

that this price should have been graven in his mind. Yet the Americans regarded this British preoccupation with scorn and took it to be a failure of nerve.

The Americans had had no such fearful experience in the First World War. They saw no reason to fight the war in behalf of British imperial interests. Roosevelt was a typical American in his desire that the war should end with the end of all the old-time empires, the French as well as the British. American resources seemed for a time to be limitless, though even they were eventually strained to the utmost to fight wars across the Atlantic and Pacific oceans. American military tradition and doctrine called for striking a decisive blow at the enemy's main force. The British preference for peripheral raids and incursions was regarded as a policy of pinpricks that promised to extend the war indefinitely or until the Russians had all but won it by themselves.

Eisenhower had insisted back in 1942 that "the full might of Great Britain and the United States could not possibly be concentrated in the Mediterranean," that "the best choice was invasion of northwest Europe, using England as a base," and that "no other operation could do more than peck at the outer perimeter of the German defense."[28] The best choice for the Americans was not necessarily the best choice for the British, though the British themselves were not always united on what the best choice was for them. Yet the recriminations on both sides went on endlessly, because neither side could bring itself to accept the fact that one strategy was just as legitimate as the other, depending on the vantage point from which the choice was made.

Of all the disagreements that beset the British-American coalition, those bearing on war aims were the hardest to reconcile. Each side was more interested in accusing the other of pursuing national interests than in recognizing that different national interests were natural and understandable in the circumstances. The reconciliation or accommodation of divergent national interests would have been difficult enough, but there does not seem to have been much thought given to it or recognition that it was necessary to make the effort. So long as the British had the upper hand, they dragged the Americans along; then the Americans gained the upper hand and dragged the British along.

---

[28] Dwight D. Eisenhower, *Crusade in Europe* (Doubleday, 1948), pp. 45–46.

4

David Eisenhower does well to show how the general grew into his role. It was not a steady, uniform advance. Eisenhower was, as David puts it, by nature "open-minded and conciliatory." His first impulse was always to "grope for compromise." Yet criticism of his disposition to compromise can be misplaced. If there are no compromises in coalition warfare, there may very well be no coalition. Still, there are compromises and compromises. Some of Eisenhower's compromises worked for the good of the whole enterprise; some did not.

An example of one of the better and easier compromises came early in the preparation for the Normandy landings. Eisenhower had insisted on his personal control of the strategic air forces in direct support of the invasion forces. The "air barons" resisted tenaciously. Eisenhower was so convinced of the necessity for total control of all the factors determining the success of the infinitely complex operation that he threatened to resign if he did not get what he thought he needed. The threat led to a British proposal to give him "supervision" of the bombers. The American side suggested "command." A compromise was reached to use the term "direction." Eisenhower was satisfied.

The actual command of the Normandy invasion was settled in a fashion that was far more troublesome. The two landing forces, one British, the other American, were put under the direct command of Montgomery, who for the time being doubled as both Allied and British ground commander. Once both forces were firmly implanted in Normandy, however, the arrangement provided for a takeover of the ground command of the British and Americans by Eisenhower, whose projected role was also double, but this time Allied and American. The changeover was scheduled for September 1, 1944, by which time Montgomery was determined to circumvent it. His next move was the beginning of months of the most intense and disruptive infighting at the top.

Beginning in August, Montgomery initiated a campaign that challenged Eisenhower's basic strategy and imminent assumption of personal battlefield command. The "broad-front" strategy was not peculiarly Eisenhower's; it was the unequivocal policy of Marshall and the Joint Chiefs of Staff. Eisenhower certainly believed in it; he was charged with carrying it out; and he had to take the brunt of the British effort to scuttle it. By that time, Paris had been liberated and the Seine crossed—by the 21st Army Group under Montgomery in the north and the 12th Army Group under Bradley in the center and south. Bradley was about to get the same status as Montgomery, with Eisenhower above both of them. Bradley had the American First Army under General Courtney H. Hodges in the center and the American Third Army under Patton in the south. The American 6th Army Group under General Jacob Devers was coming up from Marseilles to link up with Patton.

The problem at that moment was how to take advantage of the headlong German retreat and possibly end the war in 1944. By mid-August, Montgomery had a plan. In essence, it called for the abandonment of the broad-front strategy whereby all the forces all along the line pushed forward together, each sector looking for a weak spot in the enemy's lineup to exploit. Montgomery conceived of a "single thrust" in the northeast to capture the Channel ports, especially Antwerp; to seize the Ruhr; and to strike out for Berlin. To accomplish this feat, Montgomery reckoned that he needed the support of at least nine U.S. divisions from Hodges's First Army, with the leading role allotted to his own 21st Army Group. The practical consequences of his proposal were startling—that all other action all along the front should be brought to a halt; that he should be given complete command of the operation; that all available supplies should go to him; and that the previous command structure, which had put him in overall ground command, should remain unchanged instead of going to Eisenhower on September 1. Montgomery was virtually offering to win the war in the West all by himself, if only the Americans would give him the additional means to do so. After the peripheral-frontal dispute, the broad-front–single-thrust disagreement plagued the Allies the most to the end of the war.

As may be imagined, Montgomery's plan did not endear itself to the American commanders, least of all to Bradley and Patton, who would have been immobilized. All the Mediterranean resentments, from North Africa onward, broke loose. Montgomery's challenge tested Eisenhower's "supreme command" as never before. We need not now try to judge whether Montgomery's plan would have worked and shortened the war by at least six months, as he claimed it would have done; only speculation is possible, because it was never fully tried. Our interest is in how Eisenhower reacted to it, and how David Eisenhower reacts to his subject's reaction.

Eisenhower considered Montgomery's plan to be "fantastic."[29] Among other things, it implicitly cut Eisenhower out from direct command of an action intended to end the war. It faced Eisenhower with a revolt by Bradley and Patton, who had no intention of being stopped in their tracks for the greater glory of Montgomery and of being reduced to the status of spectators at the presumptive climax. It would have made a shambles of Eisenhower's established broad-front strategy. Montgomery's plan was so vulnerable from a strictly military point of view that even the official British military history stresses its "serious difficulties."[30] Montgomery's plan was based on the assumption that the Germans were so demoralized that they were incapable of defending themselves; Eisenhower believed that the enemy was capable of one more "all-out defensive battle in the West."[31] If Montgomery was right, the military risks of going seven hundred miles to Berlin with almost all the supplies still coming from the Normandy beaches were minimal; if Eisenhower was right, Montgomery's plan invited disaster.

Eisenhower and Montgomery seemed to be changing personas. Until now, Eisenhower had been complaining that Montgomery had not been aggressive enough. Caution had been Montgomery's outstanding attribute. He was, as Eisenhower later put it, the master of the "formal, set-piece attack," which required "careful, meticulous, and certain" preparation.[32] Risk taking was not in his nature, because he wished at all costs to avoid defeat. His own chief of staff has testified to his reluctance to take risks.[33] Now he was proposing to take such risks that the Americans were appalled. Paradoxically, Eisenhower in this case appeared to be the cautious one, Montgomery the compulsive gambler. The Americans had previously complained that the peripheral strategy of the British had violated the principles of mass and concentration; now the British complained that the broad-front strategy of the Americans was violating the same principles.

[29] Ibid., pp. 292–93, 305–6.

[30] John Ehrman, *History of the Second World War*, Vol. 5: *Grand Strategy* (London: Her Majesty's Stationery Office, 1956), pp. 379–81.

[31] Eisenhower to Montgomery, September 16, 1944, *The Papers of Dwight David Eisenhower* (Johns Hopkins University Press, 1970), Vol. 4, p. 2152. Hereafter *Eisenhower Papers*.

[32] Eisenhower, *Crusade in Europe*, pp. 211, 387.

[33] De Guingand, *Generals at War*, p. 76.

This incident—typical of others in the next few months—is treated by David Eisenhower in full detail and offers the reader a good idea of how he handles the most controversial issues. "As usual," he remarks, "Eisenhower groped for compromise." In effect, Eisenhower decided to meet Montgomery partway by giving him some American support to take Antwerp, while not yet approving the follow-up to Berlin and offering several alternative objectives to Berlin. Yet he assured Montgomery, "Clearly, Berlin is the main prize" and "There is no doubt whatsoever, in my mind, that we should concentrate all our energies and resources on a rapid thrust to Berlin."[34]

Nevertheless, David Eisenhower is convinced that "Eisenhower never considered the single-thrust idea—only ways to derail it." If so, Eisenhower went about the derailment in an uncharacteristically disingenuous fashion and satisfied no one. Montgomery for the rest of his life blamed Eisenhower for not giving him enough to do the job properly; Bradley and Patton railed that he had given away too much. David Eisenhower's account is, characteristically, both candid and charitable:

> Eisenhower assigned Montgomery the objective, but he did not assign the American troops to assist in taking the objective . . . In short, Eisenhower was giving Montgomery an opportunity to accomplish several things simultaneously: first, to satisfy a precondition for a Ruhr-Berlin offensive [by initially taking Antwerp]; second, to surmount Eisenhower's skepticism about Montgomery's plan as a whole.

It is hard to see how Montgomery could have surmounted Eisenhower's skepticism about his plan as a whole if Eisenhower did not give him the means that he had considered necessary to make good on the plan as a whole. In fact, Eisenhower gave Montgomery the means to do what Eisenhower wanted him to do—to capture Antwerp and open a port of entry for supplies—and not enough to do what Eisenhower did not want him to attempt—to drive on to Berlin in one swoop. It was the way Eisenhower dealt with the problem that so disturbed Montgomery. As David Eisenhower suggests, Eisenhower seemed to dare Montgomery to make good on his plan, but in a piecemeal fashion, whereas Montgomery's entire conception depended on cutting through a supposedly demoralized enemy in a single operation. To prove in that fashion that Montgomery was

[34] *Eisenhower Papers*, Vol. 4, p. 2148.

wrong did not betoken a strong-minded or strong-willed commander. Bradley commented scornfully that "a real military commander" would have behaved differently. David Eisenhower replies to Bradley: "But a 'real military commander' in Eisenhower's shoes would not have lasted two months in his job, as events would show." That was probably so, but it acknowledges that Eisenhower was not yet a real military commander—or might never be permitted to be one.

The denouement was costly. Antwerp was taken on September 4, but it was valueless as a port of entry unless the enemy was cleared out of the Scheldt estuary across some fifty miles of sea, with Arnhem the critical objective. Montgomery's misjudgment at this point— the only "bad mistake" he ever admitted committing[35]—ended in the almost total loss of the British 1st Airborne Division, one of the worst miscarriages of the war. Not until the end of November was the first ship unloaded at Antwerp, much too late to have done any good for Montgomery's grandiose plan. The delay and, even more spectacularly, the German breakthrough in the Ardennes the following month seemed to prove Eisenhower's point that the enemy was far from finished, but it is no credit to him that he had tried to prove a point in that halfhearted fashion.

Here again David Eisenhower casts doubt on the genuineness of Montgomery's stated motive for proposing to lead a march to Berlin in September 1944. In his introduction, he offers the thought that Montgomery's plan "did not represent Montgomery's actual belief" that he could get to Berlin and end the war. Instead, it appears to David Eisenhower that "the British were posing the issue of Russia and Eastern Europe in the guise of a strategic choice, and once again forcing Eisenhower to confront the political consequences of his military actions," namely, to stay with his broad-front offensive instead of agreeing to a "single thrust" to Berlin. David Eisenhower tells the story fairly, but his interpretation strikes me as farfetched.

Montgomery's plan assumed that the German defenses in the West were crumbling and that it was necessary to strike immediately to go through them all the way to Berlin. On this assumption, Montgomery was deadly serious about the strictly military merit of his plan. For the rest of his life, Montgomery accused Eisenhower of having needlessly lengthened the war by six months by not whole-

---

[35] *The Memoirs of Field Marshal the Viscount Montgomery of Alamein, K. G.* (World Publishing Co., 1958), p. 266. Hereafter *Montgomery Memoirs*.

heartedly embracing his strategy. Montgomery prided himself on his austere military professionalism; he was a notorious innocent politically. That he of all people should have actually disbelieved in his military proposal and merely wanted to pose a political issue in military guise borders on the incredible. In this case, David Eisenhower politicizes Montgomery too much as elsewhere he politicizes Eisenhower too much.

Montgomery and Brooke did not let up in their efforts to get rid of Eisenhower and his broad-front approach. The German counterattack in the Ardennes almost brought about a total breach in the top command. To Bradley's disgust, Eisenhower temporarily transferred his First and Ninth armies to Montgomery's command. As the crisis eased, Bradley wanted to get back at least the First Army; Montgomery opposed any change.

Again Eisenhower had difficulty choosing. As David Eisenhower tells the story, "Eisenhower characteristically found himself in sympathy with both Bradley and Montgomery." In the midst of the turmoil, Montgomery saw fit to demand "operational control" over the entire northern sector, again seeking to replace Eisenhower in direct command. Eisenhower reacted with such fury that he drafted a message to the combined Chiefs of Staff to choose between him and Montgomery and to replace Montgomery with Alexander—but never sent it. Bradley considered resigning.

Afterward Montgomery, oblivious to the rage he had inspired in the Americans, held a press conference at which he claimed personal credit for having stopped the Germans. In his memoirs, Eisenhower, not given to overstatement, acknowledged that "this incident caused me more distress and worry than did any similar one of the war."[36] Churchill had to step into the breach with a parliamentary speech in which he denied that the fighting in the Ardennes had been "an Anglo-American battle." He informed the British public, which had been led to believe that Montgomery had been the savior of the stricken Americans, that "in fact, however, the United States troops have done almost all the fighting, and have suffered almost all the losses." He pointedly referred to it as "the greatest American battle of the war."[37] Montgomery sent Eisenhower a personal letter of apology when he learned that Eisenhower was just about to demand

[36] Eisenhower, *Crusade in Europe*, p. 356.
[37] House of Commons, January 18, 1945.

his replacement by Alexander.[38] The crisis at the top passed, but just barely.

From Normandy to the Ardennes, Eisenhower seemed to react defensively to the indignities and defiances to which he was subjected almost without respite. He was caught between the British higher-ups, who did not bother to conceal their contempt for his generalship, and his American subordinates, who were contemptuous of his futile efforts to appease the British. Coalition warfare was, paradoxically, "warfare" within the highest echelons of the coalition. Of the internal struggle that had taken place at the time of the Normandy battle a previous study of Eisenhower's military career went so far as to make this observation: "The Allied generals seemed to be fighting one another more than the Germans."[39] It sometimes seemed a wonder that the Allied generals had any mind or energy left to fight the Germans.

A new Eisenhower appeared to emerge after the ordeal of the Ardennes. He had survived the greatest of his trials with both the German and Allied generals; he became, according to Bradley, "more forceful and commanding" than ever before."[40] This should be a caution that Eisenhower's career as Supreme Commander cannot be summed up in an easy or simple formula. He grew in the job; like the Presidency, it permitted only on-the-job training. Yet life as Supreme Commander was no easier for him after he had begun to make decisions more commandingly. Those who disliked his decisions before were apt to dislike them all the more afterward.

Eisenhower and Montgomery were the two extremes in this type of coalition warfare. If one believes much of British literature on the war, Eisenhower had only one thing going for him—that, as Montgomery's official biographer has put it, "there was really only one Allied soldier and leader who inspired a spirit of continuing Allied dignity and resolution."[41] If there was really only one, it is to be

---

[38] *Montgomery Memoirs*, p. 286.

[39] Stephen E. Ambrose, *Eisenhower: A Life* (Simon and Schuster, 1983), Vol. 1, p. 327. Eisenhower had anticipated just such infighting in 1943: "I am not so incredibly naive that I do not realize that Britishers instinctively approach every military problem from the viewpoint of the Empire, just as we approach them from the viewpoint of American interests. But one of the constant sources of danger to us in this war is the temptation to regard as our first enemy the partner that must work with us in defeating the real enemy" (*Eisenhower Papers*, Vol. 2, p. 928).

[40] Bradley and Blair, *A General's Life*, p. 373.

[41] Hamilton, *Monty the Field-Marshal, 1944–1976*, p. 530.

wondered what might have happened if he had not been there. Otherwise, the same opinion holds that Eisenhower was always wrong and Montgomery was almost always right in purely military matters. The debate over Eisenhower's military decisions will go on forever, partly because the facts are in dispute, but there is no dispute about his indispensability as the soul of the alliance.

If anyone was unfit for coalition warfare, it was Montgomery. Even if he was the military genius that his idolators claim he was, he did not have at his own command the forces needed to carry out his plans. Dogmatic, dictatorial, he often defeated his own purposes by refusing to adapt his ends to his means. Coalition warfare for him meant putting the entire resources of the coalition at his disposal. That Montgomery was so flagrantly miscast as a leading partner in a coalition suggests that too little thought had been given to the requirements of this type of warfare. Eisenhower raised the question for the British whether an aptitude for coalition warfare can compensate for alleged military ineptitude; Montgomery raised the question for the Americans whether disqualification for coalition warfare can be compensated for by alleged military brilliance.

One lesson to be learned from both Eisenhower and Montgomery would seem to be that a certain temperament, character, or personality is necessary in the top command to make coalition warfare work. Professional competence cannot be enough.

5

Once Germany neared defeat, the problems of the postwar era began. They brought on an acute crisis between the British and Americans and an incipient falling out between both of them and the Soviets, with such grave consequences that we are still living with them today.

The main difference between the British and Americans was that increasingly the British were interested in the future balance of power in Europe, and the Americans were more interested in first defeating Germany and Japan. The British concern had led Churchill to offer Stalin a deal in percentages in October 1944, whereby Great Britain and the Soviet Union would engage in a power-sharing arrangement in Eastern Europe. The Americans were by that time looking forward to the climactic phase of the war in the Far East and the organization of a more effective successor to the League of Nations. To President

Roosevelt, the only thing that could justify the sacrifices made in the war was a United Nations capable of guaranteeing the peace, a vision that had not yet been made into a mockery. Historically, the British had pursued a balance of power in Europe for centuries; it had long been a dirty word in the United States.

For better or worse, Roosevelt did not think that the country was ready to be permanently entangled in Europe. Until the atomic bomb put an end to the prospect of Japanese resistance, a large portion of the American forces in Europe had been designated for transfer to the Far East. The President could not in any case make binding commitments in Europe without congressional approval—a daunting condition at that time for any long-term engagements. Personal inclination and practical politics made Roosevelt and those around him prefer to hold the future open and deal with it when it came.

The American dilemma was that Roosevelt and the country at large knew what they didn't want far more clearly than what they did want. They knew that they did not want Hitler's Germany to win the war. They knew that they did not want Great Britain to go under. They knew that they did not want Soviet or Communist influence to expand. But they did not know what kind of world they wanted except in the vaguest and most ideal formulas. These inchoate impulses and ill-defined interests resulted in a virtual paralysis of postwar policy-making, despite some of the thought given to it in official and unofficial circles. When it came to making decisions, it was more prudent not to foreclose options than to choose between them. In comparison with the United States, Great Britain had well-defined interests and a balance-of-power policy to uphold in Allied negotiations, especially in the case of the traditionalist Churchill.

Here again, it was not a matter of which country was right or wrong. It was a matter of different countries with different interests, institutions, and traditions. If the United States had then been willing to take over the British imperial role or to help maintain Great Britain in that role, it would have been required to make an overnight transmutation of its old self into a new one. If the British and Americans had so much trouble agreeing on military policy, it was only to be expected that they would have even more trouble dealing with the postwar political world.

The hitch was that the future could not wait. The line between the military and the political, between the war and the postwar, increasingly narrowed. For Eisenhower, that line pointed in the direction of three European capitals—Vienna, Berlin, and Prague. And they in turn pointed toward the Soviet Union, out of which the Russian armies were inexorably advancing toward them.

One critical postwar decision was made before the war came to an end. Its political implications were apparently not fully realized at the time because it was thought of as merely the military partition of a defeated Germany into zones of occupation. A British-inspired plan was proposed as early as July 1943; it tentatively assigned northwest Germany to the British, southern Germany to the Americans, and everything to the east of the British area to the Soviets. Formal proposals along these lines were submitted by the British in January 1944 and by the Soviets the following month. So far the Americans had taken little initiative in the matter. Roosevelt, however, objected to a southern zone because he thought that it would make it necessary to "police" France, and possibly Italy, as well as the Balkans in order to safeguard supplies and communications. His effort to exchange zones with the British failed after months of negotiations; a final agreement between the three powers was not reached until the Yalta Conference in February 1945, with a fourth zone added for France in the southwest, carved out of the British and American zones. Berlin, which was well within the Soviet zone, was provided with a four-power administration.[42]

Ironically, none of this was what Roosevelt had previously wanted. In 1943, he had resisted the southwestern zone, for one reason because he believed that it was an area in which "the British would undercut us in every move we make," a remark that brought to the surface his limited tolerance of long-range British aims. In that year he also wanted Berlin to be included in the American zone. He once said that he wanted "United Nations [*sic*] troops to be ready to get to Berlin as soon as did the Russians." (The record apparently should have read "States" rather than "Nations.") He believed that there "would definitely be a race for Berlin" and suggested that "we may have to put the United States divisions into Berlin as soon as possible." His most intimate adviser, Harry Hopkins, had thought that "we [should] be ready to put an airborne division into Berlin two hours after the collapse of Germany."[43] These remarks show that

[42] John Ehrman, *History of the Second World War*, Vols. 5 and 6: *Grand Strategy* (London: Her Majesty's Stationery Office, 1956); Vol. 5, pp. 515–16, and Vol. 6, pp. 107–10.

[43] William M. Franklin, "Zonal Boundaries and Access to Berlin," *World Politics* (October 1963), pp. 7, 10–11.

there had been no prior disposition in principle to cede Berlin to the Russians. By 1945, these initial inclinations had been made moot by the movement of the Allied armies and the zonal agreement.

Eisenhower had had nothing to do with these zones. Agreement on them implied that, wherever the armies might stop in their advance across Germany, they would end by going back to the allotted zones of occupation. Military occupation was bound to have serious political, social, and economic consequences; they do not seem to have been taken very seriously in the planning stage. If anything foreclosed the immediate postwar fate of Germany, it was these zones of occupation, as long as they were supposed to be put into effect. The general who was put in the position of being damned if he did and damned if he didn't was Eisenhower.

6

Whenever the opportunity arises, David Eisenhower stresses how closely connected in Eisenhower's view were the western and eastern fronts against Germany. The idea is, of course, not original with him, but he has taken special pains to demonstrate how sensitive Eisenhower was to the symbiotic relationship. The Normandy landings themselves were predicated on a simultaneous Russian offensive, as agreed at the Teheran Conference at the end of 1943. Any movement of German divisions from the eastern to the western front would have jeopardized the invasion of France to the point of making it unfeasible. As David Eisenhower astutely points out, the great question was whether Hitler would prefer to take risks in France rather than in Russia. When he decided to hold fast in Russia he virtually sealed the fate of his forces in France. With a sixty-mile bridgehead only five miles deep at points in Normandy late in June, the British and Americans were lucky that Hitler had decided not to send reinforcements to France at the expense of his still-vast army in Russia.

After this, Eisenhower was immensely concerned with what was or was not happening or about to happen on the Russian front. It was not a one-way transaction. The only reason that Stalin was reconciled to the North African campaign in 1942, and why he later demanded a "second front" in Europe in 1943 or at latest in mid-1944, was his anxiety to relieve the German pressure in the east by keeping as many German divisions as possible busy in the west. Eisenhower could never afford to forget that the Russians were fighting about three quarters of the German armed forces, and that the burden on the eastern and western fronts was most unequal. If the percentages had been reversed, or even equal, the Western allies would probably not have stood a chance. One must try to put oneself back into the wartime reality to understand why 20 million Russian casualties constituted such a formidable bargaining counter.

The British-American "second front" in France had two lives. In public, the aim was to prevent the Germans from knocking out the Soviets or forcing them to make a separate peace. In private, the British and Americans knew that they had to put their forces on the Continent in order to compete in determining its destiny. By early 1943, as the battle of Stalingrad went in favor of the Soviets, "Roosevelt, Hopkins and Marshall all expressed a growing fear of the Soviet Union and a desire to place troops in Western Europe as soon as possible in order to block any attempted Soviet expansion and give the Western allies an equal voice at the peace conference."[44] One of the strongest arguments in favor of an early cross-Channel assault was that nothing less could achieve this purpose.

All this was easier said than done, for one reason because the second front was an inherently difficult and hazardous undertaking, and for another because the British and Americans could not agree for so long on whether it was the best thing to do. With another war going on in the Far East and with the British pulling for the Mediterranean strategy, the only way to satisfy everyone would have been to provide enough resources for everything everywhere. But resources were in such short supply that the war in the Far East had to take second place, and the Italian and French fronts competed for the same landing craft. Time was the main problem, if the Western allies were to get far enough on the Continent to block the expansion of postwar Soviet power—and time was running out.

The resolution of British-American differences and the preparation for the Normandy landings took so long that the continental competition on the ground with the Soviets began long after the survival of the Soviets was no longer in doubt and the defeat of Germany was only a question of time. From the Teheran Conference in late 1943 onward, both Churchill and Roosevelt were put in the position

---

[44] Mark Alan Stoler, *The Politics of the Second Front* (University of Wisconsin dissertation, 1971, p. 243; Greenwood Press, 1977). This work deserves to be better known; it is a model dissertation which breaks new ground and offers new insights.

of trying to win Stalin's goodwill, because they were not in a position to force him to do their will. A reader of the records of the wartime conferences cannot help being struck by the demanding tone adopted by the Soviet spokesmen and the defensive attitude of the Western leaders. Too much has been attributed to personal failings or political shortsightedness; the real trouble was that a second front in mid-1944 could not get the same results in any territorial competition with Russia as a second front in 1942 or 1943 might have done, when it had first been promised. The delay may have been unavoidable, but it was no less costly for that reason.

Fear that the Soviets would have the upper hand after the war grew with the course of the war. No one had a monopoly of clairvoyance—the British no more than the Americans. If Churchill was any more remonstrative than Roosevelt, it was only toward the end of the war, after it was too late to do much about it. One important reason for the earlier equanimity was a common assumption that after the war the Soviets would need the Western powers far more than they would need the Soviets. So long as this view prevailed on both sides of the Atlantic, there seemed to be no need to worry.

In January 1942, Churchill advised Foreign Secretary Anthony Eden on what to expect after the war:

> No one can foresee how the balance of power will lie or where the winning armies will stand at the end of the war. It seems probable however that the United States and the British Empire, far from being exhausted, will be the most powerfully armed and economic *bloc* the world has ever seen, and that the Soviet Union will need our aid for reconstruction far more than we shall then need theirs.[45]

A remarkably revealing discussion took place among the top British and American military in August 1943. The Chief of the Imperial General Staff, Field Marshal Sir Alan Brooke, led off with the opinion that there was little chance of the Germans succeeding in getting a negotiated peace with the Russians, which had long been the Western bugbear.

The American Chief of Staff, General George C. Marshall, spoke next.

> From reports he [Marshall] had received, it appeared that Russia was turning an increasingly hostile eye on the capitalistic world, of whom they were becoming increasingly contemptuous. Their recent "Second

---

[45] Winston S. Churchill, *The Grand Alliance* (Houghton Mifflin, 1950), p. 696.

Front" announcement, no longer born of despair, was indicative of this attitude. He would be interested to know the British Chiefs of Staff's views on the possible results of the situation in Russia with regard to the deployment of Allied forces—for example, in the event of an overwhelming Russian success, would the Germans be likely to facilitate our entry into the country to repel the Russians?

Brooke answered that

he had in the past often considered the danger of the Russians seizing the opportunity of the war to further their ideals of international communism. They might try to profit by the chaos and misery existing at the end of hostilities. He had, however, recently raised the point with Dr. [Eduard] Benes [President of the Czechoslovak government in exile], who had forecast the Russian order to international communist organizations [referring to the dissolution of the Comintern on May 15, 1943] to damp down their activities. Dr. Benes' view had been that since Russia would be terribly weakened after the war, she would require a period of recovery, and to speed up this recovery would require a peaceful Europe in which she could take advantage of the markets for her exports.

To which Brooke added that there would be

Russian demands for a part of Poland, at least part of the Baltic States, and possible concessions in the Balkans. If she obtained these territories, she would be anxious to assist us in maintaining the peace of Europe.[46]

These expressions of guarded optimism, typical of the early and middle war years, starkly contrast with the fear and hostility that came toward the end of the war. It was only with the approaching collapse of Germany and the menacing advance of the Russian Army into Eastern Europe that the British alarm signals went off. The changeover, which did not become marked until well into 1944, was largely restricted to the highest official circles, with little effect on Western public opinion.

For the British to react to the later mood, it was again necessary for them to manipulate the much stronger forces that the Americans commanded. Until 1943, the British had actually surpassed the Americans in armed strength. The two sides began to draw further and further apart in 1944. In March, British-controlled and American divisions in contact with the Germans were equal. In July, the figures

---

[46] *Foreign Relations of the United States: The Conferences at Washington and Quebec 1943* (Government Printing Office, 1970), pp. 910–11.

were thirty-eight British, forty-eight American; by the end of the year, forty-eight to seventy-eight. The disparity in total armed forces was even greater—4.9 million British and 11.2 million American in March 1944; 5 million to 11.8 million in July; 4.9 million to 12 million at the end of the year.[47] Military and industrial production drew even further apart. Coalition warfare with equal partners would have been difficult enough; with such unequal partnership it was vastly more trying—especially for the weaker partner. As the war progressed and their relative position deteriorated, the British felt increasingly that they were losing ground to the Americans instead of to the Russians or Germans.

There was, however, one respect in which the British always thought of themselves as superior. It was in the realm of political experience and military acumen. Nothing made the Americans so bitterly resentful as the barely disguised attitude of Brooke or Montgomery that Marshall, Eisenhower, and the Joint Chiefs of Staff were bumbling amateurs and that the British chiefs were seasoned professionals. Brooke never got over the sentiment which he put into his diary: "I despair of getting our American friends to have any strategic vision."[48] Montgomery thought so little of Eisenhower's intelligence that he charged even in his memoirs that "Eisenhower failed to comprehend the basic plan to which he had himself cheerfully agreed"—the plan having been nothing less than that of the Normandy operation.[49] To the Americans, the British were perfectly willing to provide the brains as long as the Americans supplied the brawn. Under such conditions, the manipulation of the stronger part of the coalition by the weaker was bound to be exasperating for both sides.

7

The fate of three European capitals was bound up with this relationship between the British and the Americans.

Vienna was the first of the three to come up for decision, because it was the earliest to be proposed as a Western military objective. The possibility seems to have been tentatively brought up first by

[47] Ehrman, *Grand Strategy*, Vol. 6, p. 19.
[48] Bryant, *Triumph in the West*, p. 49.
[49] *Montgomery Memoirs*, p. 229.

Churchill in July 1943, when he was still preoccupied with the Italian campaign. He threw out the suggestion to the British Chiefs of Staff that the forces in Italy, after reaching the Po River, might "attack westward in the South of France or northeastward towards Vienna."[50] At this time, Roosevelt was quite taken with the idea of going into the Balkans. None of his military advisers agreed with him, and the slow, painful progress in Italy as well as the increasing demands of the buildup in England put a temporary end to the idea of going into the Balkans or as far as Vienna. Nevertheless, it was a time both Churchill and Roosevelt could agree on getting into Europe from the southeast; there was no political inhibition against it; the opposition came from both the British and American military. If Vienna had been considered militarily feasible in 1943, it might well have been aimed at, and the Americans would not have been charged with thwarting a race to Vienna.

The British generals in the Mediterranean had brought up Vienna more seriously in June 1944, soon after the Normandy landings, when plans for the subsidiary landings in southern France—called Anvil— were still being debated. Instead of Anvil, they had suggested taking off from Italy across the Adriatic to Trieste, then through the Ljubljana Gap on the frontier of Austria and Yugoslavia, and on to Vienna. The plan never had a chance, because the Americans were totally opposed to it and the British were split on it. Churchill was for it, but Brooke sided with the Americans. The main argument against it was that it was bound to be a logistical nightmare and at best practicable only if the Germans were so far gone that they would offer little or no resistance. With Eisenhower still stuck in Normandy, and counting on Anvil for support, and with major German forces in the Balkans, the preconditions for success were most unpromising, as the German resistance at Arnhem and in the Ardennes later confirmed. In fact, the British-American forces in Italy were so hard-pressed that weakening them in order to go off to Vienna, about six hundred miles away across mountains in midwinter, soon became unthinkable.[51]

Thus Austria was again not ruled out for any political reason or Soviet opposition. Curiously, Stalin invited the Western Allies into

---

[50] Michael Howard, *The Mediterranean Strategy in World War II* (London: Weidenfeld and Nicolson, 1968), p. 45.

[51] The subject is fully treated in Trumbull Higgins, *Soft Underbelly* (Macmillan, 1968).

Austria on two occasions at the end of 1944. In October, during a Soviet-British meeting in Moscow, Stalin proposed a joint attack on Vienna.[52] He again made the same sort of suggestion the following month, to the American envoy, W. Averell Harriman.[53] Nothing came of Stalin's overture, for one reason because the British-American forces in Italy were not able to take advantage of it, even if he had meant it sincerely.

Vienna was never a likely Western military objective, yet Vienna came to mean for Churchill resistance to the dangerous spread of Russian influence in the heart of Europe. Churchill's wartime attitude toward the Soviet Union was so changeable and ambivalent that he can be made to be both confident and fearful about future relations, depending on the quotation attributed to him. In 1942, he was confident that the Soviet Union could be handled, because it would need the West more than the West would need it. In September 1944, he confronted the Americans *for the first time* with the thought that it would be necessary to prevent the Soviets from going too far. At the second British-American conference in Quebec, he made a plea for the plan to go from Italy to Trieste to the Ljubljana Gap all the way to Vienna, in order to give "Germany a stab in the armpit." But then he said that an added reason for the move was

> the rapid encroachment of the Russians into the Balkans and the consequent dangerous spread of Russian influence in the area. He preferred to get into Vienna before the Russians did as he did not know what Russia's policy would be after she took it.[54]

The Americans said nothing in opposition to the idea; they simply did not commit themselves to it. Roosevelt did not reply directly to Churchill's feeler. It was merely agreed to ask the British command in the Mediterranean to draw up a plan for a move into the Istrian Peninsula in northwest Yugoslavia, which was still a long way from Vienna, with the understanding that the operations had not been approved and "might, in fact, never take place."[55] Nevertheless, Churchill later put into his memoirs a rather farfetched version that

---

[52] Bryant, *Triumph in the West*, p. 228.

[53] W. Averell Harriman and Elie Abel, *Special Envoy to Churchill and Stalin, 1941–1946* (Random House, 1975), p. 379.

[54] *Foreign Relations of the United States: The Conference at Quebec 1944* (Government Printing Office, 1972), p. 314.

[55] Ibid., pp. 305, 322.

the Americans had fully accepted "the idea of our going to Vienna, if the war lasts long enough and if other people do not get there first."[56]

No plan was ever made, for one reason because the Chief of the Imperial General Staff, Brooke, was opposed to the whole idea for purely military reasons. He later wrote: "We had no plans for Vienna, nor did I ever look at this operation as becoming possible."[57] The Americans did not have to knock it down, because Churchill could not get his own high command to pick it up.

Only a month later, Churchill took a rather different line on the Russian menace. In October 1944, he talked to his physician, Lord Moran, about his dealings with the Russians:

> Of course, it's all very one-sided. They get what they want by guile or flattery or force. But they've done a lot to get it. Seven or eight million soldiers killed, perhaps more. If they hadn't, we might have pulled through, but we could not have had a foot in Europe.

Moran then said that "Russia would have things all her own way in Europe after the war." To which Churchill replied:

> Oh, I don't think so. When this fellow [Stalin] goes you don't know what will happen. There may be a lot of trouble.[58]

At about the same time, Churchill drew up a memorandum, which he later published as "an authentic account of his thought" about

---

[56] Churchill, *Triumph and Tragedy*, p. 155. These words occurred in a message to London, September 13, 1944. Churchill sent an even more questionable message to the British commanders in the Mediterranean: "The Americans talk without any hesitation of our pushing on to Vienna, if the war lasts long enough" (p. 156). The official British military history more accurately says that "the Americans had not opposed such a move" at Quebec and were willing to consider it "provided Italy had been cleared" (Ehrman, *Grand Strategy*, Vol. 6, p. 86).

There is a myth in the literature of World War II that the Americans went along with the proposed operation across the Adriatic into Istria. Ronald Lewin among others says that the Americans and even Admiral King "were prepared to accept an advance into the Po Valley and amphibious operations in Istria" (*Churchill as Warlord* [Stein and Day, 1973], p. 256). King merely accepted the drawing up of a plan of an amphibious operation in the Istrian Peninsula, and Admiral Leahy stipulated that the operation had not been approved and might never be carried out. David Eisenhower apparently trusts Churchill's version and writes that the American Joint Chiefs of Staff "urged" Churchill to take "Vienna so as to block the Russian advance into central Europe" (p. 452). As the official record shows, no such urging was ever made.

[57] Bryant, *Triumph in the West*, p. 204, note 6.

[58] Lord Moran, *Churchill Taken from the Diaries of Lord Moran* (Houghton Mifflin, 1966), p. 218. Hereafter *Moran Diaries*.

future relations with Soviet Russia. It contained a clear anticipation of what came to be known as the "convergence theory":

> We have the feeling that, viewed from afar and on a grand scale, the differences between our systems will tend to get smaller, and the great common ground which we share of making life richer and happier for the mass of people is growing every year. Probably if there were peace for fifty years the differences which now might cause such grave troubles to the world would become matters for academic discussion.[59]

As late as February 6, 1945, Moran recorded Churchill as saying: "I do not think that Russia will do anything while Stalin is alive. I don't believe he is unfriendly to us."[60]

We are now approaching the fifty years that Churchill foresaw with such hope and comfort. It is easy for some to scoff at such prophecies, which were not very different from some remarks attributed to Roosevelt. Life during the war would have been far harder to endure without hoping against hope for a better world and a more stable peace. Like some others, Churchill wavered between fearing the Soviet Union when it came too close for comfort and taking a far more relaxed view from a longer perspective. Meanwhile, his fears came to dominate.

As a result, he could not shake off his concentration on Austria, as if that country were the key to saving the West from Russian clutches. He brought the subject up again, even more urgently, at the Malta Conference in early February 1945. The record reads:

> The Prime Minister said that he attached great importance to a rapid follow-up of any withdrawal or of any surrender of the German forces in Italy. He felt it was essential that we should occupy as much of Austria as possible as it was undesirable that more of Western Europe than necessary should be occupied by the Russians.[61]

It should be noted that this exhortation was again predicated on a German collapse in Italy, which would have opened the way across the Adriatic with a minimum of risk. Actually, there was no such

---

[59] Churchill, *Triumph and Tragedy*, p. 233.

[60] *Moran Diaries*, p. 241. Historians have used these diaries extensively, though there is some question about how much they can be trusted. It is most unlikely, however, that all the words attributed to Churchill are open to doubt, especially since some ideas are expressed repeatedly.

[61] *Foreign Relations of the United States: The Conferences at Malta and Yalta* (Government Printing Office, 1955), p. 543.

collapse for another two months; fighting in Italy went on until the end of April. Churchill was still speaking largely for himself; whenever he returned to his *idée fixe*, he reduced Brooke "almost to despair."[62] The official British military history blames the difficulties of fighting on the Italian front, not on the Americans, for frustrating Churchill.[63] There was never any expectation that the British and Americans could fight their way into Vienna ahead of the Russians. American as well as British opposition to the venture was far more military than political.

The most recent study of the Italian campaign, by two British historians, has this to say on the prospect of advancing from Italy to Vienna:

> The military side of this option, put up in outline by [General] Alexander, to be immediately rejected by the Combined Chiefs of Staff, was to gain the head of the Adriatic by a combination of land and amphibious thrusts and then advance on Vienna via the so called "Ljubljana Gap." The plan ignored the fact that the Allies had taken over a year to battle their way up the length of Italy where the natural defensive lines, though strong, at least were long enough to offer some room for manoeuvre and surprise. Yet it envisaged an advance in winter along a narrow mountain route 250 miles long, first over the Julian Alps, then through the high pass or "gap" near Ljubljana, no more than thirty miles wide and offering many good defensive positions, along the valley of the Save and then over the great Alpine massif. Central Europe as a goal was political and military moonshine.[64]

February 1945 was in any case very late in the day to raise such an alarm. In February, the Russians had gone on the offensive all along the eastern front. They had crossed the Austrian border on March 30, but the Germans still fought back and Vienna was not entered until April 7.[65] A Western push across the Adriatic, with only a single mountain road through the Ljubljana Gap, on to Vienna with a handful or two of available divisions would not have been much competition.

Even if the Western Allies had beaten the Russians to Vienna, with a heavy Russian tide of whole armies flowing all around them,

[62] Bryant, *Triumph in the West*, p. 294.

[63] Ehrman, *Grand Strategy*, Vol. 6, p. 336.

[64] Dominick Graham and Shelford Bidwell, *Tug of War: The Battle for Italy, 1943–1945* (St. Martin's, 1986), p. 400.

[65] Earl F. Ziemke, *Stalingrad to Berlin: The German Defeat in the East* (Center of Military History, U.S. Army, 1968), pp. 440, 445–46.

the zones of occupation already proposed by the British would have complicated any effort to take advantage of Churchill's advice. Austria had been, quixotically, declared a "liberated" state back in 1943, so that the return of Austria to full sovereignty was foreordained. The British had taken the initiative in August 1944 in proposing temporary zones of occupation, with Vienna to be administered by all three powers. Satisfying everyone was so difficult that full agreement was not reached until July 1945. In any event, the British and Americans—the latter at first did not even want a zone—would have gained little in occupying "as much of Austria as possible" so long as they were bound to end up with three roughly equivalent zones of occupation.[66]

In the case of Vienna, then, it is hard to see what reality there was to Churchill's call in February 1945 to occupy as much of Austria as possible in order to keep the Russians out of as much of Western Europe as possible. Yet the failure of the Western Allies to get to Vienna first has been taken as one of the three capital exhibits to show their abdication in the face of the Soviet advance into Western Europe.

David Eisenhower deals with the issue of Vienna whenever it directly concerns General Eisenhower. When the subject had first arisen, in June 1944, while Eisenhower was still hard-pressed in Normandy and was counting on assistance from the Anvil landings in southern France, he had responded that the whole idea of "wandering overland via Trieste to Ljubljana" was to "indulge in conjecture to an unwarrantable degree at the present time" and to entail "dispersion of our effort and resources."[67] David Eisenhower comments that General Eisenhower "needed reinforcements, and assurances of close Russian cooperation in the coming weeks and months." The general undoubtedly needed and wanted reinforcements in Normandy as well as close Russian cooperation, but both appeared to be mandatory for military reasons. It was not necessary for him to act and think politically to oppose investing scarce resources in a diversionary campaign to Vienna.

Many years later, David Eisenhower talked with General Lucius Clay, who had joined Eisenhower's headquarters in Normandy as

---

[66] Ehrman, *Grand Strategy*, Vol. 6, pp. 106–7.
[67] *Eisenhower Papers*, Vol. 3, p. 1958.

deputy for administration and civil government in the summer of 1944 and who later served as Eisenhower's intimate adviser. Clay

> readily acknowledged the implications for Eisenhower's political future of likely postwar charges that high officials had treasonably accepted Soviet influence over Allied military strategy, charges that originated in Eisenhower's arguments with the British beginning in late June 1944. I asked Clay if Eisenhower perceived these political implications at the time, and whether he was in fact aware that he was being marked as a future political figure. Clay replied, "Of course."

It is interesting to learn that Clay thought that Eisenhower was aware as early as late June 1944 that "he was being marked as a future political figure." Presumably Clay knew because he had heard Eisenhower say something about it, which would have been quite out of order in the military service for someone of Eisenhower's rank, or else Clay had read Eisenhower's mind. But David Eisenhower also makes Clay appear to say that Eisenhower at that very time had perceived that his arguments with the British—apparently over Anvil and Vienna—were likely to engender "postwar charges that high officials had treasonably accepted Soviet influence over Allied military strategy."

If Clay had actually meant to say this, many years after the event, one wonders how trustworthy it can be. It clearly suggests that Eisenhower was so prescient that in 1944 he had anticipated that treason charges would be made after the war, something that no one else had foreseen or could have foreseen so far in advance.[68] Even if Eisenhower was so farsighted that he was aware of such future charges while he was desperately embattled in Normandy, such awareness had no necessary connection with "Soviet influence over Allied military strategy." Close Soviet cooperation in June 1944 was a military imperative for Eisenhower by virtue of the German ability to move forces from east to west and vice versa. Brooke was equally opposed to the Vienna proposal for purely military reasons. Clay's remarks are uncritically dropped on the page, apparently to bolster the thesis of Eisenhower's overriding political concerns during the

---

[68] Curiously, much later, David Eisenhower says that "it is doubtful that Eisenhower, in March 1945, foresaw the intensity of the debates ahead or realized how misunderstood Allied restraint on Berlin would be" (p. 731). If he did not anticipate the charges over Berlin in 1945, it is hardly likely that in 1944 he was aware of future charges over Anvil and Vienna, as Clay implied.

war. The use of this interview long after the event raises more questions than it answers.

8

Berlin was a much harder case. Eisenhower was a central figure in it, and the military and political aspects were far more serious.

In August 1944, Montgomery had presented his plan to commandeer all available resources for a strike toward Antwerp, seizure of the Ruhr, and the capture of Berlin in one "pencil-like" drive. At that time, Eisenhower had appeared to be more opposed to Montgomery's method than to his objectives. Eisenhower had assured Montgomery: "Clearly, Berlin is the main prize, and the prize in defense of which the enemy is likely to concentrate the bulk of his forces. There is no doubt whatsoever, in my mind, that we should concentrate all our energies and resources on a rapid thrust to Berlin."[69] At the same time Eisenhower had given himself plenty of leeway to deflect Montgomery from Berlin in an order that could be read in more than one way. Nothing more than the capture of Antwerp had come immediately from this move, and it had left Montgomery permanently embittered because he thought he had not been given enough forces to do the whole job.

In any case, Eisenhower continued to agree on the importance of Berlin. In October he repeated his understanding that Montgomery would be in a position for a "direct thrust upon Berlin" after capturing the Ruhr. In January 1945, he foresaw "a thrust northeast towards Berlin or a thrust eastward towards Leipzig," whichever proved to be the most promising. Marshall seems to have agreed at this time that the principal objective was still Berlin. The real difference over Berlin came later.[70]

The dispute over Berlin, then, was not a simple one. The nature of the question changed over time. Eisenhower seems to have backed away gradually from the commitment to make Berlin the objective

---

[69] *Eisenhower Papers*, Vol. 4, p. 1957. Eisenhower's memoirs are less than candid at this point. He merely says that Montgomery mistakenly wanted to "rush right into Berlin" (*Crusade in Europe*, p. 305). He wholly neglects to mention his own commitment to "a rapid thrust to Berlin," an omission hard to explain except that he was embarrassed by it. Montgomery's memoirs do not fail to mention it (*Montgomery Memoirs*, p. 248).

[70] *Eisenhower Papers*, Vol. 4, pp. 2223, 2451; Forrest C. Pogue, *George C. Marshall: Organizer of Victory, 1943–1945* (Viking, 1973), p. 513. Eisenhower's memoirs do not mention any of these later references to Berlin.

of a "rapid thrust" or a "direct thrust." The main obstacle, as Eisenhower first saw it, was how to satisfy the preconditions for a successful "thrust," not the goal itself. In mid-January 1945, the Russians were still about three hundred miles from Berlin; they were not so close that an equal race for the city from the east and west was inconceivable.

But in mid-January the Russians carried out a great offensive, which brought them by the end of the month all the way to the Oder River, only about thirty to forty miles from Berlin. The British-American forces had not yet crossed the Rhine and were just recovering from the Ardennes setback. A lucky break enabled Hodges's 9th Armored Division to find a Rhine bridge intact at Remagen on March 7, after which the Western forces were drawn up along the river, still about three hundred miles from Berlin. It was in these circumstances that Eisenhower had to reconsider Berlin as a prime objective or, for that matter, any objective at all.

By mid-March, Eisenhower was worried about the coming encounter between the British-American and Russian armies somewhere in Germany. How to prevent the onrushing armies from colliding if no agreements had been reached on where they were to stop demanded his immediate attention. On March 28, Eisenhower sent a message to Stalin outlining his plan in the west. In effect, it proposed a junction on the Erfurt–Leipzig–Dresden line along the Elbe River. This message set off the last great controversy between the British and Americans; the old struggle over Berlin broke out anew and with an intensity that shocked Eisenhower.

The British were infuriated by the message for two reasons. They charged that Eisenhower had no business communicating with Stalin directly, without the approval of his military and political superiors—a complaint they later withdrew. But, more important, they immediately realized that Eisenhower had written Berlin off as a Western objective, inasmuch as it was about sixty miles east of the Elbe at the closest point.

The internecine struggle that broke out between March 29 and April 18 in the very last days of the war is a study in how the closest allies can misunderstand each other on an issue that had been actively before them for months. The argument still rages over whether Eisenhower did the right thing or cravenly surrendered a key Western citadel to the Russians without resistance. Some even try to make it appear that all of Western history to our day would have been different if only the Americans had beaten the Russians to Berlin.[71]

There has been so much bitter controversy over the Berlin decision that it is well to follow the argument as it developed in the words of the principals:

Eisenhower to Marshall, March 30, 1945: "May I point out that Berlin itself is no longer a particularly important objective."

Eisenhower to Montgomery, March 31, 1945: "That place [Berlin] has become, so far as I am concerned, nothing but a geographical location."

Eisenhower to Combined Chiefs of Staff, March 31, 1945: "Berlin as a strategic area is discounted as it is now largely destroyed and we have information that the ministries are moving to the Erfurt-Leipzig region. Moreover, it is so near to the Russian front that once they start moving again they will reach it in a matter of days."

Churchill to Eisenhower, March 31, 1945: "I do not consider that Berlin has yet lost its military and certainly not its political importance. The fall of Berlin would have a profound psychological effect on German resistance in every part of the Reich . . . But while Berlin remains under the German flag it cannot, in my opinion, fail to be the most decisive point in Germany."

Churchill to Roosevelt, April 1, 1945: "The Russian armies will no doubt overrun all Austria and enter Vienna. If they also take Berlin will not their impression that they have been the overwhelming contributor to our common victory be unduly imprinted on their minds, and may this not lead into a mood which will raise grave and formidable difficulties in the future? I therefore consider that from a political standpoint we should march as far east into Germany as possible, and that should Berlin be in our grasp we should certainly take it. This also appears sound on military grounds."

Eisenhower to Churchill, April 1, 1945: "Quite naturally if at any moment 'ECLIPSE' conditions [the collapse of Germany] should suddenly come about everywhere along the front we would rush forward and Lübeck and Berlin would be included in our important targets."

---

[71] An effort was made almost two decades ago by Stephen E. Ambrose to dispel some of the "myths" in his *Eisenhower and Berlin, 1945* (Norton, 1967). It does not seem to have done much good. The Berlin mythology was most recently resurrected by Sir John Colville, Churchill's wartime private secretary, in his article "How the West Lost the Peace in 1945" in *Commentary* (September 1985). One would never know from this article that Eisenhower had to take into account (1) the huge Russian army bearing down on Berlin from the east; (2) General Bradley's estimate of about one hundred thousand American casualties to take Berlin from the west; (3) the risks of a Soviet-American collision; (4) the dubious residual importance of Berlin in ruins, with the German commanders only days away from surrender; and (5) the agreement on a four-power administration of Berlin far behind the Soviet zone of occupation, first proposed by the British themselves.

Churchill to Eisenhower, April 2, 1945: "I deem it highly important that we should shake hands with the Russians as far to the east as possible."

Eisenhower to Churchill, April 3, 1945: "If Berlin can be brought into the orbit of our success the [British-American] honors will be equitably shared."

Montgomery to Eisenhower, April 6, 1945: "I would personally not agree with this [that Berlin was not any longer an important objective]; I consider that Berlin has definite value as an objective, and I have no doubt whatever that the Russians think the same; but they may well pretend that this is not the case!"

Eisenhower to Marshall, April 7, 1945: "At any time that we could seize Berlin at little cost we should, of course, do so. But I regard it as militarily unsound at this stage of the proceedings to make Berlin a major objective, particularly in view of the fact that it is only thirty-five miles from the Russian lines. I am the first to admit that a war is waged in pursuance of political aims, and if the Combined Chiefs of Staff should decide that the Allied effort to take Berlin outweighs purely military considerations in the theater, I would cheerfully readjust my plans and my thinking so as to carry out such an operation. I urgently believe, however, that the capture of Berlin should be left as something we would do if feasible and practicable."

Eisenhower to Montgomery, April 8, 1945: "As regards Berlin, I am quite ready to admit that it has political and psychological significance but of far greater importance will be the location of the remaining German forces in relation to Berlin. It is on them that I am going to concentrate my attention. Naturally, if I get an opportunity to capture Berlin cheaply, I will take it."

Eisenhower to Combined Chiefs of Staff, April 14, 1945: "The essence of my plan is to stop on the Elbe and clean up my flanks."

April 18, 1945: British Chiefs of Staff reluctantly agree to Eisenhower's final plan.[72]

The bare words of this exchange hardly begin to convey the anger and anguish with which it was conducted. Eisenhower had his way because he was supported by Marshall and the American Joint Chiefs of Staff. When he challenged the Combined Chiefs of Staff to order him to take Berlin, they made no move to do so. Eisenhower had taken the precaution of consulting Bradley on the probable casualties resulting from an effort to take Berlin from the west; the answer,

[72] These citations are derived from: *Eisenhower Papers*, Vol. 4, pp. 2551–2610; Churchill, *Triumph and Tragedy*, pp. 463–67; Ehrman, *Grand Strategy*, Vol. 6, pp. 148–49.

one hundred thousand, undoubtedly helped to persuade him that the price was too high.

Meanwhile, the Russians were prepared to pay a higher price for Berlin. After reaching the Oder early in February, the armies of Marshal Zhukov found that they still had to fight every step of the way. The Russians prepared the attack on Berlin, south, center, and north of the city, with over 190 divisions containing at least 2.5 million men in arms. The Russian offensive opened from the Oder to Berlin on April 15; the defense, however futile, was still so tenacious that the first Russian forces did not enter the German capital until April 24, and the city's encirclement was not complete until the following day. The Russians had to fight for virtually every street and every story of the Reichstag. Hitler did not give up all hope until April 30, when he committed suicide in his bunker. The end came with the military surrender on May 2. Even then German units continued to fight in the suburbs. From April 16 to May 8, the Russian casualties amounted to 304,887 men killed, wounded, and missing. The total cost of Berlin to both sides is estimated at half a million men.[73]

By chance, the American division of which I was the historian would have been given the assignment to Berlin if it had been ordered. The 84th Infantry Division reached the Elbe on April 16, just as the Russian offensive across the Oder was starting off. Six Russian divisions came up to the river on May 2. We did not know when they were going to arrive, because liaison was nonexistent; the only indication came from the hordes—literally thousands—of German soldiers and civilians fleeing ahead of them as the Russians came closer.[74]

According to one account, the week before the 84th's arrival at the Elbe, Eisenhower asked the division commander, General Alexander R. Bolling, where he was going next. "Berlin," Bolling replied, "we're going to push on ahead, we have a clear go to Berlin and nothing can stop us." Bolling later recalled Eisenhower's reply: "Alex, keep going. I wish you all the luck in the world and don't let

[73] John Erickson, *The Road to Berlin* (Westview Press, 1983), pp. 539–622.

[74] Lieutenant Theodore Draper, *The 84th Infantry Division in the Battle of Germany* (Viking Press, 1946; reprinted Nashville: Battery Press, 1985), pp. 237, 247. Two veterans of the division have recently put out a remarkably vivid and unsparing history of a single company in combat: Harold P. Leinbaugh and John D. Campbell, *The Men of Company K: The Autobiography of a World War II Rifle Company* (Morrow, 1985; Bantam, 1986).

anybody stop you."[75] If we can believe this story, Bolling let some-one—Eisenhower—stop him a few days later. Either Eisenhower had changed his mind or else he was trying to break the news gently. In any case, it seems that the 2nd Armored Division and the 84th Infantry Division were all set to head for Berlin as if it was going to be a joyride—when they were told the trip was off.[76]

Such was the dim view from the bottom of the Army's ladder. From the top, the factors that went into Eisenhower's decision were vastly more complex. Who was right—Bradley with his probable one hundred thousand casualties or the Ninth Army generals with their nonexistent German resistance? What was likely to happen if the Americans did make it into Berlin unopposed just as the Russians were fighting their way in or around the city? Was Berlin just a "geographical location," as Eisenhower claimed, or had it retained its major military and political importance, as Churchill maintained? What might be the repercussions on British-American relations of rejecting Churchill's urgent advice? Was it going to matter so much whether the Russians went into the city first so long as a four-power administration was supposed to be set up according to the zonal agreement?

After Berlin came Prague with some of the same contentious is-sues. Beyond the affair of the three capitals were the suspicions and anxieties which they engendered. None of them would have gone so far if the alliance with the Soviet Union had been similar to the alliance between Great Britain and the United States.

---

[75] Ryan, *The Last Battle*, p. 292.

[76] Twenty years later, Lieutenant General W. H. Simpson, commander of the Ninth Army, to which the 84th belonged, declared: "My plan was to have the 2nd Armored Division accompanied by an infantry division in trucks take off at night and push down the autobahn toward Berlin. With only 60 miles or less to go they could have reached Berlin by daylight the next morning. The remainder of the army would have followed of course." Major General A. C. Gillem, Jr., commander of the XIII Corps of the Ninth Army, said that "I had very aggressive commanders . . . and specifically General Bolling I thought was a most able commander . . . and he had one of the leading divisions . . . It is my judgment that we could have been in Berlin ahead of the Russians because the distance was relatively nothing; that is, maybe a day and a half march the rates we were making, and the German resistance was nonexistent" (Weigley, *Eisenhower's Lieutenants*, pp. 699, 771). I, of course, was not told of this higher-up imbroglio at the time and learned about it almost four decades later from Weigley's book. This expected truck ride through no resistance was described as "the momentous drive to Berlin" that Eisenhower allegedly frustrated for purely political reasons, according to Paul Seabury in *Commentary* (August 1986, p. 49). Seabury must have mistaken the Russians for Americans.

9

The decision to let the Russians take Berlin and Prague created a more acute military-political crisis in the British-American alliance than anything else in World War II. It came at the very end of the war when the Supreme Commander, General Dwight D. Eisenhower, had finally begun to live up to his lofty title. The decision was essentially his, and he has been blamed the most for it.

David Eisenhower raises the question: "Did Eisenhower oppose Berlin?" In the end, there is no doubt that he did, and the question might well be rephrased: "When and why did Eisenhower oppose Berlin?"

The subject again gives David Eisenhower the opportunity to stress the Russian aspect of Eisenhower's problems and policies, because Berlin was a potential prize for both the Russians and the Americans. The American generals waited anxiously to see how soon the Russians would strike out for Berlin after they had reached the Oder River, only about thirty-five miles from the German capital at the end of January 1945. The long Russian delay of over two months enabled the Americans to reach the Elbe River about sixty miles away but still without any assurance that they could get there first if the Russians suddenly decided to go all out for the city.

At one point, David Eisenhower leans toward the view that Eisenhower for months past "had long since ruled out Berlin but even the firmest plans rested on one major contingency: that the Russians act in timely fashion to take Berlin." In effect, the Russians could have taken Berlin without stirring up any Western ambition to beat them to it if they had not stopped for so long at the Oder to resupply their forces for their stupendously massive assault. David Eisenhower also traces Eisenhower's decision on Berlin to his "broad-front strategy decision in August 1944, which had all but ensured that Russian forces would be at the German frontier when the Allies invaded." Some historians go all the way back to the British holdup of the Normandy invasion in 1943 as the root reason for the Western predicament over Berlin.

David Eisenhower's view that Berlin had long been ruled out does not seem to do justice to the abundant evidence of Eisenhower's wavering on the issue. He had after all, committed himself, at least in principle, in August 1944 to a "rapid thrust to Berlin," and in October 1944 to a "direct thrust upon Berlin." By the first week of

April 1945, he was taking the position that the cost of taking Berlin was uppermost in his mind—it was worth doing but only "at little cost" or "cheaply." According to General Omar N. Bradley, his leading field commander, "the capture of Berlin was still under active consideration by us as late as April 15, the day before the Russians jumped off."[77] Eisenhower did not make the decision on the probable cost by himself; he had consulted with Bradley, who had estimated the probable casualties at one hundred thousand and had concurred in the verdict. In the end, Eisenhower had to decide how much Berlin was worth for how many American lives. When he decided that "Berlin itself is no longer a particularly important objective," the cost in lives to take it had, in his mind, become exorbitant.

Thus the issue hinges on a judgment that depended on conditions in March–April 1945 that were very different from those in August–October 1944. If so, it would seem dubious that Eisenhower had "long since ruled out Berlin," except for the Russian contingency, unless he had been dissembling in 1944. Yet if the British were genuinely shocked at the end of March 1945 by the revelation that he was ready to forgo Berlin, something had gone wrong. Either he had failed to open his changing mind to his allies or he had kept his intentions to himself because he was still not sure of them. Either way, the British seem to have had a real grievance.

What Eisenhower cannot be accused of is having made his decision merely to please the Russians. It is clearly possible to disagree with him, but it is not right to do so as if he had deliberately capitulated to the Russians. When he came to give the grounds for his action, they were perfectly reasonable and tenable. One of his explanations was given in a published interview with Alistair Cooke. It is worth recalling because it is not so well known and seems to reflect most accurately what was uppermost in his mind:

> My own feeling was this: Political decisions had already divided Germany for occupational purposes. Remember that. There was no possibility of the Western Allies capturing Berlin and staying there. If we'd captured it, the agreements were made and approved. And, in fact, after the fighting stopped, we had to retreat from Leipzig 125 miles to get back into our own zone.
>
> Now, this brings up two things. One, was it tactically possible, under the situation we then had, to capture Berlin? and, second, what did we hope to gain? Because, as I said, we had to retreat back to our

[77] Bradley and Blair, *A General's Life*, p. 432.

own place as quickly as the fighting was over. Just remember this, when my final plans were issued, we were about two hundred miles to the westward of Berlin. The Russians, ready to attack, were thirty miles off Berlin, eastward, but with a bridgehead already west of the Oder River. It didn't seem to be good sense to try, both of us, to throw in forces toward Berlin and get mixed up—two armies that couldn't talk the same language, couldn't even communicate with each other. It would have been a terrible mess. What would be the gain? Today people have said, well, we'd have gotten prestige. I just want to know whether this matter of prestige was worth, let's say, ten thousand American and British lives, and possibly thirty thousand. [General Bradley] put it much higher.[78]

From this it appears that the division of Germany into occupation zones was a crucial factor in Eisenhower's thinking. It made no sense to him to sacrifice lives for a city for which a four-power administration had already been agreed upon and which was located far inside the Russian zone. The American generals who were hell-bent on getting into Berlin assumed that they were going to ride into it as if on a holiday. On the front of my own 84th Infantry Division, which would have been assigned the mission to Berlin, an estimated two hundred Germans with their backs to the river fought bitterly on April 21, five days after our leading elements had reached the Elbe, and three companies had to be used to deal with them.

Bradley may well have been right about the casualties that would have resulted from sending a spearhead into Berlin. There is no precedent in modern history for the kind of resistance put up by the Germans in what had clearly been a lost cause for months. The proposed operation really assumed that the Germans around Berlin would resist the Russians but not the British and Americans; it was a highly dubious assumption so long as Hitler was alive and the German forces still took their orders from him. Very likely it was Hitler's death and not the loss of Berlin itself that liberated the German generals to surrender: alive and out of Berlin he probably could have spilled a good deal more blood.

Eisenhower's second critical reason was that Russians attacking in overwhelming force from the east and Americans riding, carefree, from the west could easily have got "mixed up" and have brought about "a terrible mess." This fear was not imaginary. Russian and American aircraft had already fired on each other. No damage had

---

[78] *General Eisenhower on the Military Churchill* (Norton, 1970), pp. 55–56. The explanation given in Eisenhower's memoirs is not much longer and is much less explicit.

been done, but Eisenhower considered that "some serious incident" was inevitable unless precautions were taken.[79] Trucks hurtling along at night without lights on strange roads in a foreign land would have had to be recognized immediately as American by both Russians and Germans, assuming the drivers knew how to get to Berlin and did not lose their way, as some were not unknown to do in the best of circumstances.

None of the reasons offered by Eisenhower in his talk with Alistair Cooke or in his memoirs gives any reason to believe that Eisenhower was thinking and acting as a politician "by such actions as his decisions to cede Berlin and Prague to the Russians," as David Eisenhower alleges in his introduction. If the major factor that made the American commanders draw back was the risk of "running headlong into Russian forces," that factor was military and not "political" in any relevant sense.[80]

Eisenhower had decided on the Elbe as the best available dividing line precisely in order to avoid just such a nightmare as an unintended Russian-American collision by armies accustomed to shoot first at the least sign of unexpected movements. Even if a few American divisions had succeeded in winning a race to Berlin, the Russians were not likely to call off their prodigiously prepared offensive; they were still going to smash their way around and beyond the city, leaving the Americans with, at best, the rubble of Berlin and with their lines of supply and communication possibly at the mercy of surrounding Russian forces. No American or British plans had ever been made for such an eventuality; it would have had to be done on the spur of the moment—for which these armies were not particularly well suited. Montgomery, who was famous for his meticulous preparation, was the last man to urge such an extemporaneous junket.

There has been much speculation about Stalin's moves and motives

---

[79] *Eisenhower Papers*, Vol. 4, pp. 2602–3.

[80] David Eisenhower writes in his introduction: "My grandfather's reticence, which was typical of the American and British military leaders, about any aspect of his job that could be considered 'political,' as distinguished from 'military,' makes it perilous at times to generalize. But the loyalty he felt toward his civilian superiors cannot alter the nature of his job, that in Eisenhower, as [Bruce] Catton wrote of Lincoln, 'war and politics walked together . . . not merely hand in hand but in one body.' " Eisenhower was not merely "reticent" about any "political" aspect of his job; he insisted repeatedly that he would have no part of it. The analogy with Lincoln shows how perilous the political generalization about Eisenhower is. Lincoln was a politician; he was President and as a consequence bore the highest constitutional political responsibilities. The analogy with Grant, who was a political cipher, would have been more convincing.

after receiving Eisenhower's message of March 28, 1945, that the Americans were going to stop at the Elbe and not try to go on to Berlin. One thing to remember is that the interpretations are always speculative. In his authoritative work *The Road to Berlin*, John Erickson points out that on April 1, Stalin ordered "the gigantic Soviet offensive" aimed directly at Berlin on the same day that he had replied to Eisenhower agreeing that Berlin was not a major objective. The timing seems to be suspicious; it has been interpreted to mean that Eisenhower's message was somehow responsible for Stalin's decision to move on Berlin before the Americans could get there. But just what Stalin had in mind is not so clear. Stalin ordered the offensive to be launched no later than April 16 and to be carried through in the span of twelve to fifteen days. He was apparently not so much in a hurry that he could not wait sixteen days for the offensive to start and a month for it to be completed. Moreover, Erickson also notes that Marshal Zhukov was already making plans for a direct assault on Berlin on the very day that Stalin received Eisenhower's message (pp. 528–29).

The question arises: Since Stalin had been assured by Eisenhower that there was not going to be any Allied race for Berlin, why did Stalin have to rush to get there first? What difference could it have made, if Stalin had not ordered the Soviet offensive on April 1, as long as he knew that the Americans were going to stop at the Elbe? All the more strangely, Stalin is supposed to have "exploded" at a meeting with his generals on April 1, "Well, now, who is going to take Berlin, will we or the Allies?" (p. 531). Does this mean that he did not trust Eisenhower's disclaimer and thought that a race was on? If so, why postpone the assault for sixteen days? Erickson has no answer to these questions, and none is likely to be forthcoming in the present state of our knowledge of Stalin's mind.

Eisenhower justly asked: What did we hope to gain? Churchill's answer had been that the fall of Berlin was bound to be decisive militarily; that the Russians should not be permitted to take it, because it would give them the sense of having done most for the common victory and would make them too headstrong in future relations; and that "from a political standpoint we should march as far east into Germany as possible." Each of these considerations was highly dubious.

It was too late to prevent the Russians from thinking they had done most for the common victory; they had faced and overcome about three quarters of the German armed forces; snatching a ruined Berlin out of their grasp would hardly have been likely to do more than infuriate them. The fall of Berlin itself was never in doubt; the only question was whether the Russians or British-Americans would claim credit for it. The Russians expected to fight bloodily for it; the British-Americans expected to enter the city unopposed. Some American generals would, temporarily, have won the battle for headlines (no negligible factor in those days) but hardly the glory they also craved. If they had reached the city, they would have put themselves in the position of defending the German survivors from the Russians. The city itself was scarcely worth fighting for. It was largely destroyed; ministries had already left for the south, aiming at a last-stand National Redoubt the Germans did not have time to set up. Even if Berlin represented something of psychological value, whatever that was worth, its political and military significance at this stage was being exaggerated in the interests of something else.

10

The deeper reason for wanting to beat the Russians to Berlin and go as far east as possible was the desire to register a largely symbolic change in the British-American relationship with Soviet Russia. Churchill had come back from the Yalta Conference in February 1945 publicly satisfied with the results. After Yalta, everything seemed to fall apart. Churchill himself had made a quick turn in his estimation of coming events and soon regarded Soviet intentions with the greatest pessimism. Just what he had hoped to achieve by going as far east as possible is not altogether clear, most likely because it was not yet clear in his own mind. He seems at most to have wished to use the territories gained by the Western Allies in Germany in order to reach a new "settlement" with the Soviets.[81]

What Churchill most probably meant has been given an authoritative interpretation by the official British military history.

This interpretation is important enough to give at some length:

> For the British attitude at this stage should not be misunderstood. It is perhaps easy, in view of developments in the following decade, to see in it the emergence of a policy which later became orthodox throughout the Western world. But attitudes and policy should not be

[81] Churchill, *Triumph and Tragedy*, pp. 456–57.

confused. In the first place, even if the Prime Minister and the Foreign Secretary—the authorities principally concerned at this stage—had decided in the spring of 1945 that action should be taken on the assumption that Russia might be a potential enemy, there was no likelihood of such action being adopted by their country or in the United States. But secondly, they did not so decide. Disappointed, distrustful, and sometimes deeply alarmed as they were, their hopes, and British policy, rested on a continuing partnership of the three powers expressed in and operating through the instrument of the United Nations to which it was complementary.

The strategy they wished to adopt in Germany was designed, not for reasons of defence or attack against Russia—which should then have taken high priority in the campaign—but with the object, which they recognized must remain subsidiary to the immediate military task, of negotiating from strength. In the atmosphere of the time, this seemed to them a useful—possibly an essential—contribution to the tripartite alliance, guarding it from that threat of excessive Soviet ambition which Soviet conquests appeared to foster. The British in fact had not abandoned the objects, or even entirely the hopes, of the Yalta Conference. Rather, they had returned to the attitude they first adopted in the late summer of 1944. They did not despair of a solution with the Russians: indeed they expected it. But they expected it as a result of firm and timely measures which would remind their ally of his obligations, and whose inception depended on the movements of the Western armies in the few weeks that remained.[82]

It is admitted here that Churchill at that time could not have put across a policy based on the assumption that Russia might be a potential enemy—even in Great Britain, let alone the United States—and that he had had no intention of doing so. At most, he wanted to negotiate from strength to achieve the objects, or even the hopes, of the Yalta Conference. The British and Americans at the Elbe, it should be recalled, were already deep inside the Russian zone of Germany. Eisenhower had not interpreted the zones to be a boundary of military action but had considered that the zones made military occupation a temporary expedient. In his memoirs, Churchill never mentions what would have happened to the zonal agreement, largely British in inspiration, if the British and Americans had held on to their German territory until some sort of "settlement" had been reached.

Paradoxically, the State Department feared a British proposal that "our respective armies will stand fast until they receive orders from

[82] Ehrman, *Grand Strategy*, Vol. 6, pp. 150–51.

their governments" on the ground that it might inspire the Russians to race for remaining German areas in order to get as much territory as possible before the war ended.[83] Two could play at that game; it was doubtful that a hundred or so more miles of German territory in British and American hands would have forced the Russians to back away or produced a better standoff than the zonal arrangement already agreed on. Churchill's approach suffered from trying to do too much with too little—and prematurely.[84]

Churchill's talent for phrasemaking sometimes obscured his strategic limitations. "Soft underbelly" and "stab in the armpit" had little to do with the physical reality on the ground in southeastern Europe. He sometimes drove his military advisers to despair by demanding that something should be done and then being utterly uninterested in whether it could be done.[85] He blew up the importance of Berlin out of all proportion to its real merit as a political or strategic objective, as if his country or the United States were ready to begin the postwar struggle with Soviet Russia as the war with Germany was just coming to an end.

It is dangerous to isolate a single event, such as Berlin, from all that went before and pass judgment on it. The balance of forces at Berlin in March–April 1945 was the result of the way the entire war had been fought. If Churchill was right about the portentous importance of Berlin at that late date, open military competition on the ground with Soviet Russia over the future of Europe would have had to start long before. Churchill should not have tried to delay the "second front" even beyond mid-1944; nor should he have wanted to peck away at the periphery of southern Europe while the Russians were moving at frightful cost into the European heartland; nor should he have agreed to zones of occupation that were sure to bring the Russians into central Europe.

In the controversy over Berlin, Eisenhower repeatedly insisted that his decisions had been based on strictly military rather than political grounds. He said that he regarded it "as militarily unsound

---

[83] *Eisenhower Papers*, Vol. 4, p. 2584, note 1.

[84] Even a Churchillian admirer such as Ronald Lewin agrees that Churchill's determination to take Berlin was "unrealistic" and that "the stakes for which Churchill was playing were visionary" (*Churchill as Warlord*, p. 261).

[85] Churchill "kept aloof from all details, drew magnificent plans, and left others to find magnificent means"—as Horace Walpole said of another great war leader, William Pitt (*Memoirs of the Reign of King George II* [London, 1846], Vol. 3, p. 173).

at this stage of the proceedings to make Berlin a major objective," and he had challenged the Combined Chiefs of Staff to order him to put political ahead of military considerations.[86] It is one thing to assert that his military decisions had political implications, even if he did not take them into account; it is another to make Eisenhower "think and act as a politician" in making those decisions, as David Eisenhower alleged. Curiously, David Eisenhower succeeds in arriving at an original interpretation of this issue only by making his grandfather seem to have been guilty of dissimulation.

The supreme irony was that Eisenhower as Supreme Commander earned derision and contempt from his British and American subordinates when he compromised with them. In the Berlin case, he actually came forth boldly as Supreme Commander; he knew his own mind and refused to give way to pressure from the British or from the American generals in the Ninth Army. He was scorned when he did not play the part, and he was no better off when he did.

11

Prague and Berlin presented the same kind of problem to Eisenhower but not in exactly the same way.

By the time the Prague decision came up in late April 1945, Eisenhower was working harmoniously with the Russians to determine where the respective armies should meet in order to avoid "unfortunate incidents." They were exchanging messages and reaching common decisions. Again the Russians were moving ponderously from the east, the Americans and British, against minimal resistance, from the west. The German forces east of Prague were either still fighting the Russians desperately or trying desperately to escape from the Russians into the arms of the waiting Americans. This turn of events, here and elsewhere, put the Western forces in the awkward position of being used by the Germans as their saviors from the wrath of the Russians. It also opened up the old question between the British and Americans about who should get there first.

At the end of April, when both Russian and American forces were approximately equidistant from the Czechoslovak capital, Churchill and the British Chiefs wanted the Americans to do in Prague what they had failed to do in Berlin. Churchill urged the new President,

[86] Eisenhower to Marshall, April 7, 1945, *Eisenhower Papers*, Vol. 4, p. 2592.

Harry S. Truman, to make General Eisenhower aware of "the highly important political considerations" involved in "the liberation of Prague and as much as possible of the territory of western Czechoslovakia." A similar message went to General Marshall from the British Chiefs of Staff.

Eisenhower again decided to resist pursuing a "political prize" that was "militarily unwise," unless specifically ordered to do so by the Combined Chiefs of Staff. Marshall backed him up with the comment that he "would be loath to hazard American lives for purely political purposes."[87] By implication, the British wanted to use Prague as a bargaining chip, and the Americans did not think the objective was worth any more American lives and did not wish to risk any contretemps with the Russians over a city that was about to fall to one of them one way or another.

At first the decision was less difficult, because Eisenhower expected the Russian forces to get there first anyway. If that had happened, Prague and Berlin would have been very much alike. But the Russian steamroller was delayed by German resistance to such an extent that Patton's Third Army was able to move into position to win the race to Prague. Patton's advance toward the Czech border while Marshal Konev's forces were held back almost made Eisenhower change his mind. On May 4, Eisenhower was disposed to let Patton go into Prague instead of stopping him, as he had planned, on the line of Pilsen–Karlsbad, within Czechoslovakia, about forty miles west of Prague. If Eisenhower had done so, Patton was almost sure to have made it into Prague before the Russians could get there—a circumstance that made Prague different from Berlin, where the odds had been different.

But Eisenhower in a gesture of cooperation took the precaution of advising Marshal Alexei Antonov, the Russian Chief of Staff, of his change of plans. Antonov quickly protested, with an argument that put Eisenhower in a corner. It turned out that Eisenhower had previously asked Antonov to stop the Russian advance short of Lübeck, at the entrance to Denmark, in order to leave the way open for Montgomery. The sequence of events at this point is confusing because both Montgomery's forces and the Russians under Marshal Rokossovsky seem to have proceeded as if there had been no understanding between Antonov and Eisenhower. Montgomery trium-

---

[87] Ibid., p. 2662.

phantly reported to Brooke on May 2 that "we only just beat the Russians by about twelve hours" to Lübeck.[88]

The connection between Berlin and Lübeck is raised by David Eisenhower in such a way as to cast doubt that Churchill ever really wanted the Western Allies to take Berlin. In the body of his book, David Eisenhower cites a message from Churchill to Eden on April 19, 1945, to the effect that superior force was bound to favor the Russians on Berlin: "The Russians have two-and-a-half million troops on the sector of the front opposite that city. The Americans have only their spearhead, say twenty-five divisions, which are covering an immense front and are at many points engaged with the Germans." It is true, as David Eisenhower says, that once Churchill had given up hope of taking Berlin, he was primarily interested in preventing the Russians from getting into Denmark through Lübeck. But this does not mean, as David Eisenhower claims in his introduction, that the British aimed at occupying "northwest Germany and Denmark, rather [than] to challenge the Russians for control of east Germany." It would be truer to say that Churchill would have preferred to challenge the Russians for both east and west Germany but as usual he put the best face on things and settled for Lübeck when he knew that he could not get Berlin.

David Eisenhower suggests that Eisenhower had tried to arrange a trade of Prague for Denmark. If there was such a trade between Eisenhower and Antonov, Montgomery and Rokossovsky do not seem to have done much about it. In any case, Eisenhower changed his mind again after Antonov's protest and ordered Patton to hold up at Pilsen, which he occupied on May 5. Since the Germans, after Hitler's death on April 30, had been ordered to resist the Russians but not the Americans, Patton could have "captured" Prague on May 6 or 7 in time to avert the bloodletting following the rising of the Czech resistance movement on May 6. The Russians did not get into the city until May 9. Prague would have been different by two or three days.

Nevertheless, the Western Allies betrayed some embarrassment that the Germans were still doing most of the fighting against the Russians. On May 8, the Combined Chiefs of Staff informed their Soviet counterparts: "We do not accept that any German forces may continue to fight the Red Army without, in effect, fighting our forces

---

[88] Hamilton, *Monty the Field-Marshal, 1944–1976*, p. 499.

also." When the German commander, Field Marshal Schörner, was captured by the Americans, he was handed over to the Russians.[89] Even Montgomery had acted in the same way. On May 3, when the German northern commanders tried to surrender their forces to him, he had replied: "Certainly not! The armies concerned are fighting the Russians. If they surrender to anybody it must be to the Russians. Nothing to do with me."[90] It was an indication of how strong the wartime bonds still were in the field, even as other forces were pulling them apart.

The same question that Eisenhower asked about Berlin may be asked about Prague: What did we hope to gain?

To answer that question, a glance at the map helps. Prague happens to be in the westernmost part of Czechoslovakia. At best, it meant that the Americans would hold the capital and about one sixth of the country, the Russians five sixths, without the capital.[91] At worst, the Russians might have flowed past Prague to avoid contact with the Americans and moved around the city north and south to make it a virtual hostage. At the very worst, the two advancing forces might have found themselves firing at the wrong side.

Much depends, then, on how one reckons the mystique of a capital city. Both sides were committed to eventual withdrawal from all of Czechoslovakia. Capitals can be made just as helpless as any other big city. They do not function in a vacuum; they play their leading roles only so long as they have viable, united countries in which to play them. Prague torn from the rest of Czechoslovakia was not the

[89] A recent British biographer of Eisenhower confuses Prague with Czechoslovakia as a whole: "In fact, he [Eisenhower] was willing to sacrifice Czechoslovakia to secure good relations with the Russians, who were pathologically suspicious about Western intentions" (Piers Brendon, *Ike: His Life and Times* [Harper & Row, 1986], p. 184). The most that Eisenhower could have "sacrificed" at the time was Prague; the rest of Czechoslovakia was not his to sacrifice. If there was a trade, it was brought about by Eisenhower's prior request for the Soviet forces to stop short of Lübeck, which Brendon never mentions. In fact, the disposition of Czechoslovakia was subsequently arranged to the satisfaction of both sides. The same fatuity—among many others—is committed by Nigel Hamilton in *U.S. News & World Report*, September 1, 1986, p. 30. Typically, in this piece, two successive sentences get everything wrong: ". . . Montgomery was denuded of the forces he needed to secure the Danish peninsula . . . Czechoslovakia also was surrendered to Stalin's forces." That Montgomery had the forces he needed to secure the Danish peninsula before the Russians got there is reported in Hamilton's own book (*Monty the Field-Marshal, 1944–1976*, p. 499). Czechoslovakia was largely occupied by Stalin's forces by the time the question of Prague had arisen; Prague, not Czechoslovakia, was the only issue.

[90] Pogue, *The Supreme Command*, p. 505.

[91] Hamilton, *Monty the Field-Marshal, 1944–1976*, p. 503.

same as Prague the capital of a unified Czechoslovakia—as was equally true of Berlin torn from the rest of Germany. Moreover, the political fate of Czechoslovakia differed from that of Poland. The country was occupied by both American and Russian forces. The Communist takeover of Czechoslovakia took place in 1948 long after the Americans and Russians had left the country.

Just what Churchill thought he could achieve by holding on to Prague is still hard to fathom. His foreign secretary, Anthony Eden, once thought that "it might do the Russians much good if the Americans were to occupy the Czech capital, when no doubt they would be willing to invite the Soviet ambassador to join the United States and ourselves in contrast to the behavior the Russians have shown to us."[92] If the political point of the exercise was to teach the Russians better etiquette, Eisenhower and Marshall were probably right that it was not worth doing.

The deeper question in the spring of 1945 was whether an isolated capital such as Prague offered the right time and place for a showdown with the Russians. Public opinion in both Great Britain and the United States was wholly unprepared for it. The two countries' immediate interests were not synchronous. Great Britain knew that it could not break away from its European connection; the United States, at that moment absorbed in the changeover from Roosevelt to Truman, still thought that it had to fight a savage war in the Far East and had not even made up its mind that it wanted to stay in Europe. In the end, the similarities between Berlin and Prague proved to be stronger than the differences.

12

The two main themes I have been pursuing in this reconsideration of the Second World War in Europe are the nature of its coalition warfare and the relationship with the Soviet Union. There was a British-American alliance and a British-American-Soviet "alliance." Each was troubled to such an extent that it sometimes seems improbable that the coalition survived to the end of the war. The first managed to work itself out successfully, while the other virtually broke apart.

During the war, the British-American struggle over strategy and

[92] Churchill, *Triumph and Tragedy*, p. 516.

policy overshadowed the struggle with the Soviets, simply because the British-American relationship was so much more intimate. For the most part, two wars against Germany went on separately and simultaneously in the east and west, with a measure of coordination coming only toward the end. Marshall and Eisenhower, Brooke and Montgomery were far more preoccupied with themselves than with their Soviet counterparts, whom they hardly knew and whom they dealt with, if at all, at arm's length. A study of Eisenhower as Supreme Commander inevitably deals more with his embroilments with the British than with the Soviets. One almost feels that he was fighting two wars at once—a war against the Germans and a "war" with the British—and that the latter took up most of his time and energy.

Some British war memoirs and other war literature have been very rough on Eisenhower. Montgomery's memoirs and Brooke's diary were particularly wounding. Many of the complaints against Eisenhower seemed to be based on alleged personality faults in his makeup, unfitting him to play the role that had been assigned to him. Thus the question arises whether another general might have done better, or at least avoided the interminable British-American wrangling.

Though Montgomery contributed more than anyone else to the denigration of Eisenhower's military reputation, he must be given credit for seeing starkly and coldly what the real British-American differences were about. "It was always very clear to me," he wrote, "that Ike and I were poles apart when it came to the conduct of the war."[93] That was the real trouble. They were poles apart, because they differed on basic concepts of how to conduct the war; those differences were British and American as much as Montgomery's and Eisenhower's. Back of those differences was not only a clash of ideas but a struggle for power within the coalition. Personalities exacerbated the disputes; they did not beget them. In the matters that really counted, Eisenhower did not follow an Eisenhower plan; it was an American plan, behind which stood the awesome figure of Marshall, who could always have overridden him.

Any other American general would have been put in the same position. Sir Alan Brooke, Chief of the Imperial General Staff, once tried to use Bradley to get rid of Eisenhower as ground commander. The only other American candidate might have been Patton—a

[93] *Montgomery Memoirs*, p. 235.

frightful possibility. Either of them would have given the British far more trouble; they would not have made so many concessions to British demands; they could hardly bear to stay in the same room with Montgomery. If Marshall had had Eisenhower's job, it is unthinkable that he would have been as conciliatory. For months Eisenhower had gone so far to appease Montgomery that Air Chief Marshal Sir Arthur Tedder, the deputy supreme commander, had had to warn him that "his own people would be thinking that he had sold them to the British if he continued to support Montgomery without protest."[94] Tedder was right; Bradley and Patton virtually accused Eisenhower of having sold out to the British. Eisenhower *was* the best American general the British had, but he could only give them half a loaf, and they wanted or needed the whole thing.

Churchill, the old master, knew better than his chief generals and tried to call off their relentless vendetta against Eisenhower. When Brooke tried to force Eisenhower out as ground commander, Churchill demurred. He told Brooke that "he did not want anybody between Ike and the Army Groups, since Ike was a good fellow who was amenable and whom he could influence. Bradley, on the other hand, might not listen to what he said!" Brooke replied resentfully that "I could see little use in having an 'amenable' Commander if he was unfit to win the war for him."[95]

It is hard to know what would have happened if Eisenhower had not been so amenable and Churchill had not been so canny. If personalities had mattered the most in holding the coalition together, these two, in their different ways, mattered the most. The great merit of Eisenhower was that he really believed in making coalition warfare work, even to the point of worrying Secretary of War Henry L. Stimson that he might "lose sight of the necessity of supporting sufficiently our national views where they were at variance with the British."[96] When Eisenhower said that in a coalition it was necessary "to forget nationality," it rings true.[97] It is not so easy to imagine any other American general sending an officer home because he had shouted that someone was "a *British* so-and-so."

As a Supreme Commander who was never supreme and could

[94] Tedder, *With Prejudice*, p. 566.
[95] Bryant, *Triumph in the West*, p. 346.
[96] Pogue, *George C. Marshall: Organizer of Victory, 1943–1945*, p. 509.
[97] *General Eisenhower on the Military Churchill*, p. 65.

rarely command, Eisenhower's weaknesses were almost indistinguishable from his strengths. He behaved as a dedicated civil servant in an international organization should behave and seldom does. According to General Francis de Guingand, Montgomery's chief of staff, Eisenhower "had a magic touch when dealing with conflicting issues or clashes of personalities; and he knew how to find a solution along the lines of compromise, without surrendering a principle."[98] This was no ritualistic tribute; it alone can explain why Eisenhower succeeded in winning over the high British officers attached to his headquarters, so that no solid British front was ever ranged against him. His British deputy, Tedder, stepped in more than once to defend him against the anti-Eisenhower cabal in London, and suffered for it. Eisenhower was not brilliant; he compromised; he backed and filled; but the job needed something other than brilliance, unwillingness to compromise, and inability to see some merit in opposing arguments.

Churchill's great merit in the controversies of the coalition was that he knew when to stop. He goaded Eisenhower and his own generals mercilessly with ideas that were often logistical or strategic pipe dreams. He created many of Eisenhower's problems, but he also put the worst of them to rest, as Brooke and Montgomery would not do. Once he saw that he could not have his way, he relented gracefully—until the next time. His generals knew how to handle him, how to cajole him out of the most extreme fancies or wait him out until he had forgotten what he was after. He recognized, however much it hurt, that the balance of power in the alliance and in the world had turned against Great Britain—and Churchill knew that power was the ultimate arbiter. This saving realism permitted him to indulge his most unrealistic extravagances without ultimate harm to the common cause. The official British military history notes that Churchill seldom had his way in the last two years of the war.[99] He certainly did not fail for lack of trying. Yet he managed to keep everyone's affection and respect, primarily because he never pushed a disagreement beyond the limits of compromise or retreat.

It would be naïve to imagine that the British-American alliance survived its incessant crises at the top only because these two men prevented it from falling apart. The factors that held Great Britain

---

[98] De Guingand, *Generals at War*, p. 193.
[99] Ehrman, *Grand Strategy*, Vol. 6, p. 335.

and the United States together throughout the war were deeply rooted in self-interest, cultural affinity, historic connections, and common abhorrence of a world dominated by such an enemy as Hitler. But in the matters that have been discussed here, again and again one is driven to wonder what might have happened for the worse if someone else had been Supreme Commander and someone else had been Prime Minister. In this story of coalition warfare, we can safely say that they prevented the worst.

13

Why was there no more than an "alliance" with the Soviet Union?

The same reason was given by both Stalin and Churchill. It is the best and shortest answer we are likely to get. Stalin told Tedder, when the latter visited Moscow in December 1944: "It would be foolish for me to stand aside and let the Germans annihilate you; they would only turn back on me when you were dispensed with. Similarly it is to your interest to do everything possible to keep the Germans from annihilating me."[100] Churchill needed only a single sentence: "They [Communist Russia and the Western democracies] had lost their common enemy, which was almost their sole bond of union."[101]

The wartime alliance and "alliance" betrayed themselves in their origins. There was no compelling threat to the United States in 1940 when President Roosevelt set a quasi-military alliance going with the transfer of fifty destroyers to Great Britain. The Roosevelt-Churchill relationship during the war was unique in the history of such partnerships. They agreed far more than they disagreed; and they agreed to disagree even when they disagreed. When Germany attacked Soviet Russia in June 1941, Churchill immediately said: "I have only one purpose, the destruction of Hitler, and my life is much simplified thereby. If Hitler invaded Hell I would make at least a favorable reference to the Devil in the House of Commons."[102] In his remarks in the House of Commons on the day Russia was attacked, Churchill did not say anything favorable about the Communist Devil; he said that "we shall give whatever help we can to Russia and the Russian

[100] Tedder, *With Prejudice*, pp. 649–50.
[101] Churchill, *Triumph and Tragedy*, p. 456.
[102] Ibid., p. 370.

people." With those words he initiated the "alliance." His motive had nothing to do with mutual economic interests, political sympathies, or cultural consanguinity. He was forced to embrace the Communist Devil by virtue of Britain's desperate state in 1941. To the extent that there was collaboration with the Soviet Union during the war, it was almost wholly military, and even that was gratingly frustrating.

In military terms, the differences within the British-American alliance were tactical; those within the British-American-Soviet "alliance" were strategic. The first held because it was based on far more than temporary military calculations; the second came apart because it had little more in common than a common enemy.

The way the "alliance" came to an end in 1945, with the defeat of Germany, portended that it was going to turn into its opposite. This aspect of the origins of the "cold war" is still something of a skeleton in the historical closet. Historians have generally traced those origins back to the early Truman period, where its earliest symptoms have probably been exaggerated. The implications of Churchill's desire to get to Vienna, Berlin, and Prague before the Russians and to push as far east as possible went far beyond what he himself was willing openly to recognize or admit.

On the surface, Churchill's intentions seemed to be vague and confusing. He wanted to get a satisfactory "settlement" with the Russians on all outstanding postwar questions before giving up any Western-occupied territory. How he thought he could get so much with so little is hard to understand, and he did not try to explain how it could be done. In the shadows, however, there was more to it than that.

As early as July 27, 1944, not long after the landings in Normandy, Brooke had had an intriguing conversation with the Secretary of State for War, Sir James Grigg. His diary reads:

Back to War Office to have an hour with Secretary of State discussing post-war policy in Europe. Should Germany be dismembered or gradually converted to an ally to meet the Russian threat of twenty years hence? I suggested the latter and feel certain that we must from now onwards regard Germany in a very different light. Germany is no longer the dominating power in Europe—Russia is. Unfortunately Russia is not entirely European. She has, however, vast resources and cannot fail to become the main threat in fifteen years from now. Therefore, foster Germany, gradually build her up and bring her into a Federation of Western Europe. Unfortunately this must all be done under the cloak of a holy alliance between England, Russia and America. Not an easy policy, and one requiring a super Foreign Secretary.[103]

Churchill himself, if we may trust General de Guingand, later had much the same thought. In March 1945, as the decision over Berlin was coming up, he told de Guingand that "the danger to the Allies was in future going to be more from the Russians than from Germany."[104] In his memoirs, Churchill claimed that he had already known and felt that "henceforward Russian imperialism and the Communist creed saw and set no bounds to their progress and ultimate dominion."[105]

On May 24, 1945, after the German surrender, Brooke returned to the theme in his diary:

> This evening I went carefully through the Planners' report on the possibility of taking on Russia should trouble arise in our future discussions with her. We were instructed to carry out this investigation. The idea is, of course, fantastic and the chances of success quite impossible. There is no doubt that from now onwards Russia is all-powerful in Europe.[106]

On the American side, there is to my knowledge only one such statement by anyone in a high official position. It was made by General Patton, whose ranting could not have been taken seriously and who died in a road accident later the same year. On May 7, 1945, the day that General Alfred Jodl signed the declaration of unconditional surrender at Reims, Patton had a conversation with Under Secretary of War Robert P. Patterson. Patton recorded in his diary that he had told Patterson to

> present a picture of force and strength to these people [the Russians] . . . If you fail to do this, then I would like to say to you that we have had a victory over the Germans and have disarmed them, but have lost the war . . . I would have your State Department or the people in charge, tell the people concerned [Russians] where their border is, and give them a limited time to get back across. Warn them that if they fail to do so, we will push them back across it . . . They could probably maintain themselves in the type of fighting I could give them for five days. After that it would make no difference how many million men they have, and if you wanted Moscow, I could give it to you.

[103] Bryant, *Triumph in the West*, p. 180.
[104] De Guingand, *Generals at War*, p. 158.
[105] Churchill, *Triumph and Tragedy*, p. 456.
[106] Bryant, *Triumph in the West*, pp. 357–58.

Patterson protested: "You don't realize the strength of these people." Three days later, according to the editor of Patton's diary, the general wanted to rehabilitate the Germans to fight the Russians.[107] A full investigation into American official and public opinion might turn up other such cases, but my impression is that nothing similar to the views expressed by Brooke and Churchill is likely to be found in comparable American circles.[108]

Some of the alarm and pessimism in this late-war and early postwar period proved to be excessive. The Russians were not "all-powerful in Europe" and could not exploit all of their power in all of Europe. It was bad enough that they were able to impose their own political and social system wherever they had wrested military supremacy from Germany in Eastern Europe. But Stalin was not ready to try to swallow all of Europe in one gulp. He indicated the kind of deal he was willing to make by permitting the Western powers to take the lead in Italy without protest, a plain signal that he expected them to do the same for him in Poland.

The power-sharing arrangement Stalin was willing to settle for in 1945 was no longer in Eastern Europe, as Churchill had contemplated the year before, but rather in an exchange of Eastern Europe for Western Europe. The division of Europe into a Soviet-dominated East and a non-Soviet West was more than anything else reflected in the agreement on the zones of occupation, which could have been dispensed with only by keeping the armies in place indefinitely or risking a confrontation between them. Whether an armed stalemate between the Soviet Union and the Western powers for an indefinite period would have resulted in anything better than the withdrawal to the agreed-on zones of occupation is at least doubtful.

The Second World War was, like all wars, full of might-have-beens. It is futile to take one moment in the war and lament that if only it had been handled differently the entire future would have been infinitely better. It was not handled differently, because the entire past conspired to make it what it was. Yet if there is to be an inquest

---

[107] Blumenson, *The Patton Papers 1940–1945*, Vol. 2, pp. 698, 709.

[108] The only other American general who ever avowed pro-German sentiments, as far as I know, was Albert C. Wedemeyer, and he apparently held them in the earliest stage of the war. As he himself told the story, he had been exposed "to constant propaganda about the Bolshevik menace" during his two years at the German War College in 1936–38; it had convinced him that the "world-wide Communist conspiracy" was a greater menace than "the German search for *Lebensraum*." He does not say how he felt at the end of the war (Albert C. Wedemeyer, *Wedemeyer Reports* [Henry Holt, 1958], p. 10).

into the way the war ended, it is unrealistic to think that the choice was between the present division of Europe and beating the Russians to Vienna, Berlin, or Prague, or grabbing a few more miles to the east. The real choice was between the halfway house of the present and a complete, classical, instantaneous *renversement des alliances*, risking some form of immediate conflict with the Soviet Union. No one in a responsible position was prepared for that in the spring and summer of 1945. It came to seem, at least to some, to have been the right thing to do, because it had in it the seeds of the future. But like all seeds these needed to mature. The unripe fruit of such a policy was not digestible in 1945, even if we have had to live with the regret that things did not work out otherwise.

(*The New York Review of Books*, September 25, 1986,
October 9, 1986, and October 23, 1986)

American Hubris

1

THE DEADLY INCIDENT on May 17, 1987, in the Persian Gulf in which thirty-seven American sailors were killed and the Navy frigate *Stark* was disabled by an Iraqi missile has again raised the question: What is happening to American foreign policy? Is it merely that we have suffered a series of unlucky mishaps—in Korea, Cuba, Vietnam, Lebanon, and now the Persian Gulf? Or is something seriously at fault with the doctrine that has governed our actions ever since the end of the Second World War?

A series of costly misadventures over several decades cannot be considered a string of aberrations. Something deeper and more troublesome must be at work to account for them. They cannot be blamed on one party or the other; they have afflicted Democratic as well as Republican administrations. Former UN Ambassador Jeane Kirkpatrick is not wrong to call herself a Truman Republican; the so-called Reagan Doctrine is a variant of the Truman Doctrine—if there is any real difference between them.

This doctrine has been the source of American hubris for forty years and shows no sign of being retired. It is time to reexamine it and to assess what its consequences have been. How did the Truman Doctrine come about in the first place? Where has it led us?

To understand the origin and influence of the Truman Doctrine, it is necessary to go back to what the United States was like in world affairs before 1947.

The United States had begun to consider itself a "world power" only a half century earlier. The term itself apparently appeared in its original German version, *Weltmacht*, where it seems to be more at home, in the 1880s. It was first applied to the United States in 1898 as a result of the so-called Spanish-American War, primarily through the acquisition of the Philippine Islands, which was an unintended by-product of that war. The first American book with the title *World Politics* came out in 1900.[1] The first book with the title *America As a World Power* appeared in 1907, and another one, *The United States As a World Power*, the following year.[2]

The change from a hemispheric to a world power was reflected in the various editions of James Bryce's celebrated *The American Commonwealth*. In the first edition published in 1888, Bryce thought that he had to say "but little" about American foreign relations. In the revised edition of 1920, he noted: "Americans have latterly been wont to speak of themselves as having become, through the events of 1898, a World Power." Mr. Dooley sighed at the time for the good old days before we became "a wurruld power" and "now, be Hivins, we have no peace iv mind."

The United States may have awakened one day in 1898 to find itself a "world power," but it was only a beginning. Theodore Roosevelt tried in the next decade to play a role befitting such a status, without much success. Woodrow Wilson backed into the First World War at a late stage and died disappointed that he could not make the country live up to what he considered to be its international responsibility. The 1920s were two-faced—political isolationism went along with economic and financial internationalism. Franklin D. Roosevelt found in 1937 as a result of the hostile reaction to his "quarantine speech" against the Japanese aggression in China that the United States was still unwilling to assert itself in international conflicts.

In effect, the United States may have been a world power at the outbreak of the Second World War, but it was not equipped like one and it did not act like one. Militarily, according to the Chief of Staff, General George C. Marshall, it was "not even a third-rate" power. He commanded "the bare skeletons of three and one-half divisions scattered in small pieces over the entire United States" with no facilities and funds even to train them. The Air Force could

---

[1] Paul S. Reinsch, *World Politics* (Macmillan, 1900).

[2] John Holiday Latané, *America As a World Power, 1897–1907* (Harper, 1907); Archibald Cary Coolidge, *The United States As a World Power* (Macmillan, 1908).

"hardly have survived a single day of modern aerial combat."[3] Diplomatically, the United States was not much more impressive. Secretary of State Cordell Hull's staff numbered twenty-one. I doubt whether there is any country in the world today, no matter how small, whose foreign minister does not have a larger staff.

So pessimistic was Roosevelt at the beginning of World War II that the most the United States could do, he said, was to maintain itself as a "citadel" in which Western civilization "may be kept alive."[4] Yet, only two years later, Roosevelt conceived of the United States as a "world policeman."[5] During the war he increased the number of policemen from two (with Great Britain) to three and finally to four—the United States, Great Britain, Soviet Russia, and France. The transition from besieged "citadel" to "world policeman" took place in Roosevelt's mind within two years—from 1939 to 1941.

As a world power, then, the United States matured, as it were, overnight. There was no time to prepare for the new role, to slide into it gracefully. Doctrines, principles, theories, and, above all, experience of what it meant for the United States to behave as a preeminent world power were lacking. Other imperial powers had learned over centuries; the United States was given a few short years.

2

By the end of World War II, less than six years from the beginning, a sense of absolute power captured the political imagination of Allied leaders. The period did not last long—only about six months—from April to September 1945. That it happened at all, however, shows how far the idea of world power had briefly gone.

This sense of absolute power came with the atomic bomb. The Americans were not the only ones to be temporary victims of the atomic illusion. As early as August 1943, in the midst of the war, when the bomb was still an unknown quantity, Sir John Anderson, then in charge of the British atomic effort, confided to Prime Minister

---

[3] *Biennial Report of the Chief of Staff of the U.S. Army, General George C. Marshall* (July 1, 1943–June 30, 1945).

[4] *The Public Papers and Addresses of Franklin D. Roosevelt* (Macmillan, 1941), p. 150 (September 21, 1939).

[5] He seems to have expressed the idea in so many words for the first time to Churchill on August 11, 1941, at the Atlantic Conference, which also gave birth to the Atlantic Charter (*Foreign Relations of the United States*, Vol. 1, 1941, p. 366).

Mackenzie King of Canada that the first country to possess atomic bombs would gain "absolute control of the world."[6] When Secretary of State James F. Byrnes briefed the new President, Harry S. Truman, on the bomb in April 1945, Byrnes said that it "might well put us in a position to dictate our own terms at the end of the war."[7] Soon afterward, Secretary of War Henry L. Stimson told Truman that the atomic bomb "would be certain to have a decisive influence on our relations with other countries."[8] On May 13, Stimson referred in his diary to the bomb as a "master card."[9]

All this soothsaying took place before the bomb was tested on July 16 and before anyone could be sure that there was a bomb. After the test, heads were again turned. The Chief of the Imperial General Staff, Field Marshal Lord Alanbrooke, has probably left an exaggerated account of Winston Churchill's megalomania: "He [Churchill] had at once painted a wonderful picture of himself as the sole possessor of these bombs and capable of dumping them where he wished, thus all-powerful and capable of dictating to Stalin!"[10] Alanbrooke went equally far in the opposite direction; he thought that the Russians, who had not yet built a bomb, would try to use it as "a means of obtaining complete control of the Western Hemisphere, if not the whole world."[11] Churchill himself told the House of Commons in August that those who had the bomb possessed "powers which were irresistible."[12] There seems to be enough evidence from different quarters to indicate that the first effect of the bomb was intoxicating.

In any case, the bomb should have had its maximum psychological effect on the Soviets soon after it was dropped in August 1945. By chance, the Soviet reaction was tested only a month later when the newly formed Council of Foreign Ministers met in London in September. The Americans apparently expected the Soviets to capitulate to the bomb. According to Stimson's diary, Byrnes went to London "very much against any attempt to cooperate with the Russians"

---

[6] J. W. Pickersgill, *The Mackenzie King Record*, Vol. 1 (University of Toronto Press, 1960), p. 532.

[7] Harry S. Truman, *Memoirs*, Vol. 1: *Years of Decision* (Doubleday, 1955), p. 87.

[8] Ibid.

[9] Stimson diary, May 13, 1945 (Yale University Library).

[10] Arthur Bryant, *Triumph in the West* (London: Collins, 1959), p. 477.

[11] Ibid., p. 488.

[12] *Parliamentary Debates* (Hansard), August 16, 1945, col. 78.

because he was counting on "the presence of the bomb in his pocket, so to speak."[13]

But the Soviet Foreign Minister, V. M. Molotov, behaved as if the atomic bomb did not exist. In London, he was more demanding and disagreeable than ever. Anyone reading the record of that conference might easily imagine that Molotov had come with the bomb in his pocket. Byrnes returned to Washington sadly disillusioned. He told one person that he was "almost ashamed" of himself because of the treatment he had suffered from Molotov; he confided to another that the Russians had adopted an indefensibly "aggressive attitude" on political and territorial matters.[14] Byrnes seemed to have forgotten that he was supposed to have been the aggressive one. He lost the confidence of the President, and his career was finished.

A great deal of historical mischief was caused by the "revisionist" thesis that the atomic fantasy of Secretary Byrnes and others toward the end of the war was the basis of what was called cold-war "atomic diplomacy." It was at best a half-truth. The half-truth was that the bomb did dominate the thinking of some American leaders until August 1945. But the Americans soon learned that there was no such thing as "atomic diplomacy," or, to put it another way, that the atom bomb was not a useful diplomatic instrument. In the next decade, John Foster Dulles was no more successful than Byrnes had been in using the new strategic weapons for diplomatic purposes.

Whatever the bomb or the rhetoric, the United States was effectively forced to share world power with the Soviet Union—and knew it from at least the last quarter of 1945. Yet a popular phrase, "Pax Americana," took hold. There was no such "Pax," or at best it was a "Half-Pax." A Pax Sovietica-Americana would have been closer to the truth, and even that would have been an oversimplification for some parts of the world.

Nevertheless, the illusion of a Pax Americana produced a sense of frustration in American leaders. It was never given up and it was never achieved. Every effort to make good on it has produced disappointment that the rest of the world persistently refuses to play its assigned role in the American scheme of things.

---

[13] Stimson diary, September 4, 1945.
[14] John Lewis Gaddis, *The United States and the Origins of the Cold War, 1941–1947* (Columbia University Press, 1972), pp. 266–67.

3

The Truman Doctrine was the original codification of the Pax Americana illusion. The policy was enunciated in reaction to a specific, local situation and took shape in response to a vision of universal ascendancy.

Greece had traditionally been a British client state. As a result of the black winter of 1946, the British in February 1947 decided that they could no longer afford to subsidize Greece. To make matters worse, Communist-led guerrillas were threatening to come down from the north. The imminent British withdrawal from the country set the stage for the Truman Doctrine.

In March and April 1947, Under Secretary of State Dean Acheson testified before the Senate Committee on Foreign Relations on the need for the United States to replace Great Britain in Greece. Unfortunately, this testimony was not made public for twenty-six years and was then virtually ignored. The inner history of the Truman Doctrine cannot be understood without it.

Acheson made clear that by 1947 the Truman Administration had effectively given up all hope of "liberating" Eastern Europe. "It is true that there are parts of the world to which we have no access," he said. "It would be silly to believe that we can do anything effective in Romania, Bulgaria, or Poland. You cannot do that. That is within the Russian area of physical force. We are excluded from that."[15] None of the senators present, headed by the Republican chairman, Arthur H. Vandenberg, demurred at this stark presentation of the facts of life in Eastern Europe.

Acheson also explained that Americans were going to take the place of the British in Greece but on a far larger scale. To the Americans at the time, it made no sense to put money, matériel, and manpower into a country that they knew was run by a chaotic and corrupt government and administration. It made sense to see that the money was well spent—which meant to them that Americans had to oversee the spending. So Acheson told the senators that it would be necessary to put Americans "into the essential key [Greek]

---

[15] "Legislative Origins of the Truman Doctrine," *Hearings Held in Executive Session Before the Committee on Foreign Relations, U.S. Senate, 80th Congress, 1st Session* (Historical Series), made public January 12, 1973, p. 22.

Ministries which are necessary to control the basic factors." At another point, Acheson declared: "You have to have people in these places I talked about [Greek ministries and administrative bureaus], who have the authority to say to Greece, 'Stop doing this! You are draining off your resources.' "[16]

We need not go into the rights and wrongs of this policy; it seemed necessary at the time. Whatever the rationale, several things are striking about it.

There was no precedent outside the Western Hemisphere for putting Americans directly or indirectly in charge of a foreign administration. If the British had been able to maintain their position in Greece, the occasion for making such a leap in American policy would not have arisen and would not have forced a sudden, improvised escalation of American responsibilities. It was another example of how little time the Americans had to prepare for and think through their new responsibilities.

They succeeded, as Acheson testified and events proved, in arriving at a workable postwar foreign policy only after separating the problems of Eastern and Western Europe. If the Truman Administration had actively tried to re-create both halves of Europe, the attempt would almost surely have been doomed to failure—or war. The Marshall Plan the following year settled for less and accomplished what is still the greatest postwar success of American policy.

But something else haunted and continues to haunt American policy. The practical policy was limited to a region where it could work successfully—Western Europe. Yet the terms used by President Truman to justify that policy were universal. The limitations of the policy could not or in any case would not be admitted publicly. The mixture of a universal doctrine with limited means of action created a dangerous mixture of illusion and reality which we have yet to rid ourselves of.

Byrnes could not bring the two together; he was sacrificed to keep the illusion alive. Acheson could do nothing about the Chinese Communist victory; he was pilloried for it. Dulles and the Republicans were right when they charged that Truman and Acheson had effectively written off Eastern Europe—and they were just as helpless as the Democrats had been.

[16] Ibid., p. 82.

4

It has long been puzzling why the Truman Doctrine was cast in universal terms.

The immediate problem for Truman was to get Congress to appropriate $250 million for Greece and $150 million for Turkey, which was also considered to be endangered. He might have been content to explain why the two countries needed the money desperately and why they could get it only from the United States. The State Department drafted a message from him to Congress in this vein, which he later contemptuously described as sounding like "an investment prospectus." Truman returned it with instructions that he wanted more emphasis on "a declaration of general policy."[17] In effect, he wanted to universalize a local, particular condition.

The metamorphosis of Greece into the universe was accomplished by the "domino," or, as it might have been called, the "rotten-apple," principle. Its author was Acheson. The scene of the transformation was the closed meeting of the Senate committee at which the request for aid was presented. According to his own account, Acheson was dissatisfied with the presentation made by Secretary of State Marshall. He injected himself into the discussion to say the following:

> In the past eighteen months, Soviet pressure on the Straits, on Iran, and on northern Greece had brought the Balkans to the point where a highly possible Soviet breakthrough might open three continents to Soviet penetration. Like apples in a barrel infected by one rotten one, the corruption of Greece would infect Iran and all to the east. It would also carry infection to Africa through Asia Minor and Egypt, and to Europe through Italy and France, already threatened by the strongest domestic Communist parties in Western Europe.[18]

Acheson says that this argument persuaded the senators to go along. He swayed them by extending the crisis from Greece—which Stalin had previously awarded to the British sphere of influence in return for British acquiescence in Soviet domination of most of Eastern Europe—to three continents, to all of the Middle East and much of the West. Iran was then as now one of the endangered species.

[17] Harry S. Truman, *Memoirs*, Vol. 2: *Years of Trial and Hope* (Doubleday, 1956), p. 105.

[18] Dean Acheson, *Present at the Creation: My Years in the State Department* (Norton, 1969), p. 219.

President Eisenhower later substituted dominoes for rotten apples, but the reasoning was the same. The universalization of American policy needed the universalization of the Communist threat.

By the time Acheson's reasoning was echoed by Senator Vandenberg, the process had taken on the character of a fatality. To a correspondent Vandenberg soon wrote: "Greece must be helped or Greece sinks permanently into the communist order. Turkey inevitably follows. Then comes the chain reaction which might sweep from the Dardanelles to the China sea."[19]

That something genuinely new had entered American policy was recognized at that time by the sponsors of this legislation. The new element was not so much aid to another country as the enunciation of a general doctrine that could be applied automatically everywhere.[20] It was on this ground that the language of the President's message to Congress was criticized by George F. Kennan, its most thoughtful critic from within the State Department. Kennan accepted the necessity "to stiffen the backs of the non-Communist elements in Greece," though he saw no reason to treat Turkey the same way. As he later explained, he objected to the passage in the speech that gave it the character of an indeterminate doctrine—that "it must be the policy of the United States to support free peoples who are resisting subjugation by armed minorities or by outside pressures."

Kennan's criticism was just as basic as the doctrine itself:

> This passage, and others as well, placed our aid to Greece in the framework of a universal policy rather than in that of a specific decision addressed to a specific set of circumstances . . . It seemed to me highly uncertain that we would invariably find it in our interest or within our means to extend assistance to countries that found themselves in this extremity. The mere fact of their being in such a plight was only one of the criteria that had to be taken into account in determining our action.[21]

A doctrine of this sort could easily become a substitute for thought. It gave the United States a license to intervene anywhere and everywhere at any time in any way, if only the right formula was used to justify the move.

[19] *The Private Papers of Senator Vandenberg* (Houghton Mifflin, 1952), p. 342.

[20] In his memoirs, President Truman interpreted his new doctrine to mean that American foreign policy had "now declared that wherever aggression, direct or indirect, threatened the peace, the security of the United States was involved" (*Memoirs*, Vol. 2, p. 106).

[21] George F. Kennan, *Memoirs: 1925–1950* (Little, Brown, 1967), p. 320.

All this began in 1947, only about two years after the evanescent fantasy of absolute power induced by the bomb. The Soviet Union did not even have the bomb at this time and did not have one for two more years, though everyone knew that it was making every effort to get one. The highs and lows of American hopes and fears are among the most peculiar aspects of this period—an oscillation that still afflicts us.

5

The doctrine of universal responsibility led to another deformation of policy. The United States is almost never prepared for a particular application of the doctrine. One reason is that no country can plan for everything that is likely to happen all over the world. Planning presupposes that there is some sense of specific, definable self-interest or some other form of limitation that guides the planners to what they need to plan for.

Unlimited commitments require unlimited power. Not even the United States has that kind of power, and its relative power has steadily decreased as the rest of the world has recovered and the Soviet Union has caught up in nuclear and conventional weaponry.

In 1950, Acheson, then Secretary of State, tried to delimit American commitments, despite his previous role in making them wide open. He publicly defined the "defensible perimeter" of the United States in such a way as to exclude the Asiatic mainland, including Korea. He was even strengthened in this conviction by a similar statement a year earlier by General Douglas MacArthur, before the latter's fall from grace.

Nevertheless, President Truman did not hesitate to intervene in the Korean War, for which no American plans or preparations had ever been made. He could not in good conscience claim that Korea itself was an American responsibility. Instead, he resorted once more to the rotten-apple or domino principle, and so imaginatively that he made Western Europe stand or fall in Korea.[22]

Somewhat the same thing happened in the case of the Vietnam War. At first no responsible American leader could imagine that we

[22] "But if we had not persuaded the United States to back up the free Republic of Korea, Western Europe would have gone into the hands of the communists" (*The Autobiography of Harry S. Truman*, edited by Robert H. Ferrell, Colorado Associated University Press, 1980, p. 102).

would get into that war at all. In 1954, President Eisenhower declared that "no one could be more bitterly opposed to ever getting the United States involved now in a hot war in that region [Vietnam] than I am" and that he could not "conceive of a greater tragedy for America than to get heavily involved now in an all-out war in any of these regions, particularly with large units." In 1963, President Kennedy said: "In the final analysis, it is their war. They are the ones to win or lose it." In 1964, President Johnson said: "We are not about to send American boys nine or ten thousand miles away from home to do what Asian boys ought to be doing for themselves."

But then, when Johnson decided to get the United States involved in a hot war, take over their war, and send American boys to do what Asian boys ought to be doing, he abruptly decided that it was better to fight in Vietnam than in Honolulu, as if one followed from the other. The Republican spokesman at the time, Richard Nixon, goaded Johnson to get in there and fight, with a pathological exhibition of the rotten-apple or domino theory. The fate of Vietnam, he said, was the fate of all of Southeast Asia as far as Burma and Indonesia, the United States would have to fight a major war to save the Philippines, Japan would inevitably go neutralist, the Pacific would become a "Red sea," and Australia was going to be attacked in only four or five years by Communist China.[23]

What had happened in these and other cases of American intervention was that the Truman Doctrine was being substituted for any rational calculus of means and ends. The doctrine had begun to live a life of its own, undisturbed by specific, practical, complex circumstances, such as those that had called it forth.

As a result, the pattern has been action first, thought afterward. The decisions to fight in Korea and Vietnam were made before any serious attention was given to the nature of the wars and how to cope with them. The nature of the Vietnam War was so unclear to the American military that a serious student of the war, Colonel Harry G. Summers, Jr., has stated that its nature was still in question almost a decade after American involvement.[24]

Colonel Summers also remarks: "Neither our civilian nor our military leaders dreamed that a tenth-rate undeveloped country like

---

[23] Speech of March 15, 1965, in the *Congressional Record*, Senate, September 2, 1965, pp. 21928–30.

[24] Harry G. Summers, Jr., *On Strategy: A Critical Analysis of the Vietnam War* (Presidio Press, 1982; Dell paperback, 1984), p. 122.

North Vietnam could possibly defeat the United States, the world's dominant military and industrial power."[25] This fallacy has plagued the United States in one of these far-flung wars after another. The mistake arises from the notion that the war is going to be decided by general, overall military and industrial power rather than by the power that can be brought to bear locally at the point of combat. The United States could undoubtedly have defeated North Vietnam if it had been willing to fight no matter what the cost or duration of the struggle. But when a country as strong as the United States undertakes to fight everywhere under all conditions, it cannot afford to use more than a fraction of its military and industrial power, especially against a tenth-rate undeveloped country. If the conditions are not suitable for its men, machines, and tactics, it is quite capable of being outfought and outstayed.

Yet Vietnam did not teach us enough about how not to apply the Truman Doctrine. When U.S. Marines were attacked at the Beirut airport, the tired old words were trotted out once again. After 241 Marines were killed in the truck bombing in October 1983, Secretary of State Shultz intoned that the Marines would stay because "it is a region of vital strategic and economic importance for the free world, because it is an area of competition between the U.S.A. and the Soviet Union [and] because we have a deep and abiding commitment to Israel."[26] President Reagan justified the slaughter on the ground that "the area is key to the economic and political life of the West" and if "that key should fall into the hands of a power or powers hostile to the free world, there would be a direct threat to the United States and to our allies." Incredibly, he claimed that the Marines were attacked for the very reason that they were "accomplishing" their mission.[27]

In December of that year, President Reagan told Congress that the Marines had to stay in Lebanon because "the international credibility of the U.S.A. and its partners" was at stake. A report prepared by both Secretary Shultz and Secretary of Defense Weinberger warned that any "premature withdrawal" of the Marines would "call into question the resolve of the West to help the Free World defend itself."

[25] Ibid., p. 167.
[26] October 24, 1983.
[27] October 27, 1983.

On February 7, 1984, however, the President announced that most of the Marines were going to be "redeployed" to ships offshore. He revealed a week later that the "restationing of our forces" had been planned "for quite some time," evidently while he and other high officials were telling the American people how great the stakes were and how vital it was to keep the Marines in place. Most amazingly of all, the President maintained that moving the Marines to ships offshore represented an "improvement" over the airport for the fulfillment of their mission. He even said that he expected the Marines to stay offshore for another eighteen months, though he hoped that it would not be necessary.

All this was deception or self-deception or something of both on a prodigious scale. The main criticism of the disaster was tactical—that the Marines should never have been confined passively in the airport waiting for terrorists to strike. But there was also a preposterous disparity between the doctrinal rationale and the practical action. If the stakes were really as great as President Reagan and Secretary Shultz said they were—"vital strategic and economic importance for the free world," "the international credibility of the U.S.A. and its partners," "the resolve of the West to help the Free World defend itself"—the means employed were derisory and the denouement was incongruous.

Did the President and his men really believe what they had been saying? More likely, the words were hostages of a doctrine that has bewitched Administration after Administration. The doctrine is so compelling because it gives the United States and its leaders a rationale for showing how powerful they are, even if they prove in action to be less powerful than the rationale says they are. The action in Lebanon was relatively small-scale; the reasoning behind it was monumentally inflated. When the Marines were withdrawn from Beirut, the vital interests and credibility and resolve of the United States and the free world were just about what they had been before.

I have gone into the background of American "world power" and the Truman Doctrine because they still have a bearing on American policy-making. The doctrine has been treated as if it were a sacred text that cannot be questioned. We are again on the verge of allowing it to take us down the slippery slope to disillusionment. As if nothing had been learned from the past, we have returned to rotten apples, dominoes, and the doctrine.

6

A sure sign that the doctrine is being applied mechanically, with a minimum of discrimination, is the language used to put it into effect. It is always necessary to use the words "vital interest," "national security," "free world," "peace is at stake," and, above all, some version of the "Soviet threat." If these phrases were not employed, it might be necessary to do some thinking and explain the policy in less simplistic and apocalyptic terms. In that case, it is hard to know whose intelligence would be strained the most—our policymakers' or the general public's.

When President Reagan undertook to explain his policy of sending U.S. ships into the Persian Gulf, he repeated or played variations on all of these themes. Five days after the *Stark* was struck on May 17, he said: "Peace is at stake here; and so too is our own nation's security, and our freedom." Peace in the Gulf, surely; our own security, dubiously; and our freedom, absurdly. Twelve days later, he played at full blast the whole doctrinal organ music—"national security," "economic disaster," "freedom of navigation," "commitment" to the "peace and welfare" of "our friends and allies," preservation of "peace."

A perfectly mindless expression of the doctrine was contributed by Secretary of Defense Weinberger on June 9. "The fundamental issue is leadership," he told the House Armed Services Committee, "the leadership of the free world to resist the forces of anarchy and tyranny." One would imagine from this hyperbolic verbiage that we were about to get into a war of epic proportions, worth any cost or sacrifice. These incantations have become so routine that the words will not be meaningful if they are really needed.

One wonders whether the policy could have been put over on the American people if the President had told them how Iraq and Kuwait had manipulated the United States with the aim of getting us into the middle of the Iran-Iraq war.

Kuwait is little more than a gigantic oil well. It has been independent only since 1961, before which time it was a British protectorate. It has the population of Houston and an area two-thirds that of Vermont.[28] Only 23 percent of its population is native Kuwaiti and only about 40 percent are citizens, forcing it to depend largely on

[28] Area: 6,880 square miles; population: 1,710,000 (1985).

an alien labor force, many of them Palestinians. Thanks to its oil, which provides over 94 percent of its revenue, its per capita income is close to a phenomenal $11,500 a year, with no need for anyone to pay taxes. This cornucopia of oil is ruled by the hereditary al-Sabah dynasty, with close ties to a similar ruling caste in Saudi Arabia.

Kuwait and Iraq, its northern neighbor, were not always so friendly. As soon as the British protectorate in Kuwait came to an end in 1961, Iraq's ruler at the time, General 'Abd al-Karim Kassem, announced that Kuwait was really Iraqi territory; British troops had to come back hastily to prevent him from taking possession. Kuwait was not recognized by Iraq until after General Kassem was overthrown in 1963, but frontier fighting between the two went on for years. Iraq, in fact, temporarily seized adjoining Kuwaiti territory in 1973 and has long used threats of territorial aggression to extort vast sums from the overflowing Kuwaiti exchequer. This is not a region of fastidious diplomatic relationships.

Kuwait's relations with the United States have also been checkered. For years its press was one of the most anti-American in the region, largely because of Kuwait's fiercely anti-Israel policy. Kuwait cut off oil shipments to the United States after the Six-Day War in 1967, an action suggesting that we can hardly depend on Kuwait in all circumstances. In 1983, Kuwait refused to accept as ambassador a veteran U.S. diplomat, Brandon H. Grove, Jr., because he had served as U.S. consul general in East Jerusalem. The *Washington Post* correspondent in Kuwait, David B. Ottaway, observed as late as June 24, 1984, that Kuwait was "accustomed to blaming the United States for all the ills afflicting the Arab world, and the gulf in particular." Kuwait modulated its anti-American line in that year because Iran had begun attacking Kuwaiti tankers and had taken the place of the United States as the main enemy.

In 1980, President Carter's State of the Union message pledged that the United States would go to war, if necessary, to prevent "any outside force" from gaining control of the Gulf region. At that time, ironically, the Kuwaiti minister of foreign affairs objected to the U.S. commitment on the ground that "the people of this region are perfectly capable of preserving their own security and stability."[29]

---

[29] *Political Handbook of the World: 1986*, edited by Arthur S. Banks (CSA Publications, 1986), p. 314.

The predicament of Kuwait in 1987 arose from its increasingly close ties with its former bugaboo, Iraq, dating from the reckless attack on Iran by the present Iraqi dictator, Saddam Hussein, in 1980. Kuwait mortgaged its fate to Iraq by supporting it to the tune of billions of dollars and by acting as its receiving and transshipment point for war matériel, much of it from the Soviet Union. The pretense that Kuwait was neutral was sheer humbug; Kuwait was Iraq's foremost ally.[30]

The Iran-Iraq war has been one of the most savage in modern times. Iraq's Saddam Hussein has resorted to chemical weapons, Iran's Khomeini to the mass sacrifice of children on the battlefield. In 1984, since the fighting was stalemated on the ground, a war against tankers, in which Iran was most vulnerable, broke out. The tanker war was started by Iraq, just as it had started the entire war. Iraq uses a pipeline through Turkey and Saudi Arabia; Iran must transport its oil by sea in tankers from many foreign countries and companies. More than three hundred tankers and freighters had been hit by both sides, with the loss of about two hundred lives, but only one tanker had been sunk. In 1985, three quarters of the attacks were Iraqi; in 1986, 60 percent. More recently, Iran has concentrated its fire on Kuwaiti tankers, though no Kuwaiti ship has been hit since October 22, 1986. There were no Kuwaiti losses for eight months before the Reagan Administration decided to get agitated about the threat to Kuwaiti shipping.

Yet the October incident was soon followed by a change in Kuwaiti policy. A decision was made to entangle the great powers instead of keeping them out. But Kuwait did not appeal first to the United States. That distinction was reserved for the Soviet Union.

Despite the evident political disparities between Kuwait and the Soviet Union, their relations had been remarkably close for some years. In 1979, Kuwait made known that it was receiving Soviet arms,

[30] Since the United States gave a pledge of neutrality in the Iran-Iraq war, it seems to be essential to the U.S. case that Kuwait should also be considered to be "neutral." When Assistant Secretary of Defense for Public Affairs Robert B. Sims was asked whether the United States would be living up to its neutrality pledge if it escorted Kuwaiti tankers, he answered, "Absolutely," and explained: "The fact is, Kuwait is not a belligerent in the war. The war is between Iran and Iraq" (*The Washington Post*, June 5, 1987). National Security Adviser Frank C. Carlucci has also pretended that Kuwait is "a neutral state" (*The Washington Post*, June 16, 1987). The fact also is that Kuwait is an active ally of a belligerent and doing everything in its power for one side against the other. The dictionary says that neutral means "not engaged on either side." Kuwait is not technically a belligerent, but neither is it neutral.

including ground-to-air missiles. Deputy Prime Minister Sabah al-Ahmad al-Jabir Al-Sabah of the ruling family visited the Soviet Union in April 1981 and the Eastern-bloc countries of Bulgaria, Hungary, and Romania the following September. The East German head of state, Erich Honecker, came to Kuwait in October 1982. Then, in August 1984, Kuwait signed a far-reaching agreement for the purchase of more arms from the Soviet Union. This deal is of particular interest because it was virtually a dress rehearsal for the present tanker operation.

First, Kuwait wanted "Stinger" anti-aircraft missile weapons and F-16 jet fighters from the United States, but these requests were turned down. Instead, Washington offered a different $82 million air defense package. Then Kuwait went to the Soviet Union and arranged for the purchase of arms reported to be worth $327 million. With the arms came Soviet technicians and advisers. After this, the Reagan Administration relented and sold more military equipment to Kuwait, the total officially reported to be worth $1.5 billion by 1985.

Kuwait, in short, had some practice playing the United States off against the Soviet Union. Its foreign policy had long been one of nonalignment, which it still professes. Its problem has been that it is too rich to be left alone and too weak to defend itself. The West may adopt Kuwait, but Kuwait does not choose the West.

Iraq had also managed to achieve exceptionally close relations with the Soviet Union. Increased Soviet support for Iraq seems to have come in 1983 when Iran cracked down on the Tudeh (Communist) Party of Iran. The Soviet Union has been Iraq's main arms supplier, at least since 1983,[31] with Kuwait the intermediary between the two countries. Saddam Hussein succeeded in getting the backing of a most peculiar combination, including the Soviet Union, France, Saudi Arabia, and the United States. Communist China had become one of Iran's major arms merchants.

7

How tiny Kuwait managed to enlist the support of both the United States and the Soviet Union is one of the most extraordinary feats of modern diplomacy.

[31] *Military Review* (an official Defense Department publication), December 1983, p. 10.

According to the best available information, the government-owned Kuwait Oil Tanker Company informed the U.S. Coast Guard on December 10, 1986, that it wished to put the U.S. flag on its ships to gain them U.S. protection. During that same month, Kuwaiti officials went to Moscow and worked out an agreement with the Soviet Union. It provided for Kuwait to charter three Soviet tankers on a renewable one-year lease, with the additional stipulation that two more might be added on "short notice." It also permitted Kuwait to lease to the Soviet Union an unspecified number of additional tankers "to be rechartered to the Kuwait side thereafter whenever the government of Kuwait so requests."

These provisions were worked out to enable Kuwait to increase its Soviet-protected tankers if the United States did not come across. When the United States did not quickly grab at the bait, Kuwait's oil minister, Ali al-Khalifa al-Athbi Al-Sabah, formally requested that the United States agree to the "reflagging" of some Kuwaiti ships on January 13, 1987. Still, no American reply was forthcoming until a report was received in Washington on March 2 that a deal had been struck between Kuwait and the Soviet Union for the protection of Kuwaiti tankers. Five days later, the United States decided to outbid the Soviets by offering to put the U.S. flag on eleven Kuwaiti tankers. Kuwait now had both powers on its string; the agreement with the Soviet Union was signed on April 1. All this attracted very little attention until the *Stark* was hit on May 17.[32] Kuwait is so ecumenical politically that it subsequently invited Communist China to join in protecting Kuwait's capitalistic oil trade. In effect, Kuwait did not wish to be beholden to any one of the great powers and preferred to have them compete for the privilege of serving its interests.

It thus appears that Kuwait hooked our guardians in Washington by confronting the United States with a Soviet-Kuwaiti deal. However, the Senate Foreign Relations Committee was also told on May 9 by Assistant Secretary of State for Near Eastern and South Asian Affairs Richard W. Murphy that the Kuwaiti decision to seek Soviet protection had come in November 1986, a month before the Kuwaiti oil company had first turned to the United States and the Soviet Union. Murphy interpreted this Kuwaiti overture to the Soviets as

---

[32] This chronology is based on the articles by Don Oberdorfer and Jonathan C. Randal in *The Washington Post*, May 31 and June 5, 1987.

having been inspired by the news that same month that the Reagan Administration had secretly sold missiles to Iran. If so, Kuwait took the initiative to bring in the Soviets in order to punish the United States for arming Iran.[33]

Let us recall: the "tanker war" had been going on, more and more ferociously, for over three years. In all these years, only seven Kuwaiti-owned tankers had been hit by Iran.[34] Well over 95 percent of the Gulf's oil had been reaching customers around the world. No U.S. ship had been touched before the attack on the *Stark*. Secretary of State Shultz affirmed that Iran had "respected" the "American presence." All this time no one in Washington had thought that the shipment of oil from Kuwait was so endangered that it was necessary to do anything to protect our "vital interests" or "national security," or to save us from the "Soviet threat."

The rest is hallucinatory. On May 17 the U.S. frigate *Stark* was hit by an Iraqi missile in the Persian Gulf. But this shot was heard in Washington as if it had come from an Iranian missile. Not so long ago the Reagan Administration had sold missiles to Iran for use against Iraq. Now it was Iraq's turn to be protected against Iran. By some political prestidigitation, an Iraqi missile provided the occasion for a hasty decision to plunge the United States into the midst of the conflict on the side of Iraq—in fact if not in name.

That the decision was precipitous there can be no doubt. First it was decided to put the American flag on eleven tankers of Iraq's ally, Kuwait—originally a Kuwaiti idea, not an American one. This step led to the next one—protection of the tankers by a much stronger U.S. military "presence" in the region. Only after these decisions were made was any thought given to what the risks were, what methods should be employed, and whether the whole enterprise was practicable at all.

8

Without any practical policy in sight, we were fed dubious statistical propaganda about the indispensability of Gulf oil. Senator Daniel Patrick Moynihan wrote luridly that "the West risks losing control

---

[33] The source of this information is Senator Daniel Patrick Moynihan, *The New York Times*, June 7, 1987.

[34] *The Washington Post*, June 5, 1987.

of two-thirds of the world's oil reserves. The great geo-political prize of the twentieth century is now in their [the Soviets'] grasp."[35] Another Persian Gulf warrior, former National Security Adviser Zbigniew Brzezinski, obviously used a similar source: "Access to Persian Gulf oil reserves, which contain two-thirds of the free world's proven reserves, is the principal stake in southwest Asia."[36]

The emphasis on "reserves" implied that we were supposed to be worrying about the distant future, as if we could do anything about it by putting the American flag on eleven Kuwaiti tankers. If there was an immediate risk, we were meeting it with ridiculously picayune means. Our leaders were, in effect, playing the old game of dominoes to scare us half to death in order to put across a policy that did not begin to face the horrendous crisis that allegedly awaits us.

Gulf oil is useful but hardly a matter of life or death now. It is least vital to the United States, which gets only 4 percent of its oil through the Strait of Hormuz at the entrance to the Persian Gulf. But even if the Strait of Hormuz were closed, the cutback in oil shipments could be readily compensated for by another of our friends in the area—none other than Saudi Arabia. A recent study of the Gulf states pointed out:

> A cut-off of Gulf oil that did not include Saudi production would be ineffective, because, due to the enormous Saudi production capacity, that country alone could match most current Gulf petroleum exports. More important, Saudi Arabia is the one Arab Gulf producer that has alternative routes (i.e., non-Gulf routes) for the export of petroleum. (Saudi Arabia has opened one pipeline on the Red Sea, and will soon have a second ready for operation.) Indeed, one of the Saudi pipelines also carries Iraqi crude.[37]

Another authority on the world supply of oil, Professor S. Fred Singer, pointed out:

> With about one-eighth of Free World oil in gulf tanker traffic, as much as one-half of that traffic would have to be interrupted on a steady basis to make a strong impact on the price. That translates to about twenty supertanker sinkings a week! Any lesser interruption can be made up by existing pipelines and from the excess production capacity of other suppliers—and they'll be glad to do it.

[35] *The New York Times*, June 7, 1987.

[36] *The Washington Post*, June 7, 1987.

[37] Mazher A. Hamseed, *Arabia Imperilled: The Security Imperatives of the Arab Gulf States* (Middle East Assessments Group, 1986), p. xv.

Professor Singer went on:

> The bottom line on the benefits of avoiding modest oil-supply dislo-cations: hardly any for the U.S. or its allies. The question then be-comes: Is it worth risking American lives in order to lower insurance premiums for Kuwait and other gulf producers?[38]

If there is an acute long-term problem of oil reserves, it will have to be met in a long-term way. Much can change in the use of oil before the problem becomes acute. In any case, that is no present problem, even with the Iran-Iraq war; the long-term problem was not going to be met by reflagging eleven Kuwaiti tankers or by getting en-meshed in the war. The alarm about oil reserves in the distant future was a cover for taking some immediate action that had little or no bearing on the long-term problem.

The technique of the scaremongers is to suggest that something awful is about to happen and to use veiled language that stops short of saying what they really mean—that the Persian Gulf must be made an American monopoly by any means including that of force. Senator Moynihan put it this way:

> All the more reason, then, that Congress should be seen to support the policy of every American President back to Harry S. Truman. We have no choice. The Persian Gulf is vital to American interests. It is not vital to Soviet interests. We cannot accept their intrusion.[39]

What must we do if "we cannot accept their intrusion"? Clearly, we must expel them. And how, if we are not going to use force? Leaving aside the determination of what a "vital interest" is in these circum-stances, countries have a right to use an international waterway even if they have no "vital interest" there. Incidentally, it is interesting to note how the ghost of Harry S. Truman hovers over this entire affair.

Brzezinski also used the same semantic cover-up:

> Consequently, the United States has no choice but to stand firm against any challenges in the defense of Western interests in the Persian Gulf . . .
> The major beneficiary of a U.S. retreat would be the Soviet Union . . .
> The United States must do whatever is necessary to assert Western interests in the Persian Gulf—alone, if necessary. If Iran strikes Amer-

[38] *The Wall Street Journal*, June 9, 1987.
[39] *The New York Times*, June 7, 1987.

ican forces engaged in protecting third-party shipping in the Gulf, the United States should retaliate against Iranian military facilities and do it in a way that will be militarily decisive.[40]

These are weasel words for the forcible control by the United States of the Persian Gulf. The chosen enemies are both the Soviet Union and Iran. Just what "standing firm" against the Soviet Union means is left to the imagination of the reader. Since the Soviet Union has shown no signs of threatening the United States militarily in the Gulf, Brzezinski must mean that the very presence of three Soviet naval vessels in the Gulf is threatening. How he thinks it is possible to get rid of them without the use of force defies understanding. He is clearer on Iran, but only if it strikes American forces protecting third-party shipping. If non-American shipping should be struck, he fails to enlighten us on what to do about it. By the very nature of the Iranian regime and its popular support, a "militarily decisive" retaliation is not easy to envisage. It would certainly entail more than taking out missile batteries.

But oil was covering up the real issue. Kuwait, acting for Iraq and Saudi Arabia, was really interested in something else. All three had in mind luring the Soviet Union and the United States into intervening in the Iran-Iraq war in order to get the great powers to stop it. Iraq and its allies needed Soviet-American collaboration for their intrigue to have any chance of succeeding. Ironically, the anti-Soviet twist that the Reagan Administration and its fellow travelers gave the Kuwait–Iraq–Saudi Arabia scenario was not according to their script.

9

If the free passage of tankers had been the real issue, it would have had to be faced long ago. It was not faced when the "tanker war" was raging, because the Iran-Iraq war was still considered to be a local quagmire that could only get worse if the great powers got into it with their own military forces. The important thing was to isolate it, until both sides dropped out from exhaustion, not to transform it into a contest between world powers. Such exhaustion was what actually brought Khomeini around by 1988, not the maneuvers of the superpowers.

[40] *The Washington Post*, June 7, 1987.

But a number of other things had injected themselves. One was the U.S. withdrawal from Lebanon, which alarmed the Arab states because it indicated to them that the staying power of the United States in the region was limited.[41] The revelations of the Reagan Administration's secret sale of missiles to Iran were even more demoralizing, because the Arab regimes under Sunni leadership were terrified by the threatened conflagration from Iran's militant Shi'ite fanaticism. There was also the inability of the UN's Security Council to pass a resolution calling for a cease-fire and arms embargo owing to the resistance of Iran's ally, Communist China. Iraq, now chastened by its losses and the recognition that it could not possibly win the war, was entirely willing to accept such a resolution, leaving Iran as the real object of the arms embargo.

In these circumstances, the obvious way out for Iraq and its paymasters, Kuwait and Saudi Arabia, was through the intervention of the great powers. The hopeless war, together with the oil glut, had caused a dangerous drain on their resources. From trying to keep the great powers out, Iraq–Kuwait–Saudi Arabia policy had shifted to dragging them in. The Kuwaitis have made no secret of their strategy. The *New York Times* correspondent in Kuwait, John Kifner, was told by Under Secretary Suleiman Majid Al-Shaheen of the Kuwaiti Foreign Ministry:

> We have approached all our friends. We don't want any country to have an upper hand with Kuwait. The Soviet Union is ready to cooperate, and it is the right of any country to increase its economic activities.

Kifner added: "Mr. Shaheen, a key strategist in the Foreign Ministry, which is headed by Sheik Sabah al-Ahmed al-Sabah, a member of the ruling family, confirmed that a main goal of the Kuwaiti strategy was to seek an end to the war between Iran and Iraq by involving the superpowers."[42]

The same Kuwaiti strategy was reported by *The Washington Post*'s Jonathan C. Randal on June 14, 1987. The tanker war, he noted, was "a manageable side-show" of far less significance than "Kuwait's gamble that its ingenuity in seeking superpower protection for per-

---

[41] If a Fatuity Prize were given, it would certainly have been won in 1987 by Norman Podhoretz, who attributed our fiasco in Lebanon to "squeamishness" (*New York Post*, May 26, 1987).

[42] *The New York Times*, June 8, 1987.

haps a third of its oil exports will force Moscow and Washington to impose an end to the nearly seven-year-old war."

Most opportunely, an Iraqi attack on a U.S. naval vessel gave the Reagan Administration the occasion for doing what Iraq and Kuwait had long wanted it to do. The President's major statement of May 29, 1987, did not even mention Iraq, as if it were the innocent party in the war in the Persian Gulf. Instead, the only two countries mentioned with hostility were Iran and the Soviet Union, on the assumption that they had to be prevented from imposing "their will upon the friendly Arab states of the Persian Gulf" and Iran had to be deterred from blocking "the free passage of neutral shipping."[43]

Here was Iraq, which had not only been at least as guilty as Iran in blocking the free passage of shipping in the Gulf, but had declared a "free-fire" or "exclusion" zone on the Iranian side of the Persian Gulf in which it felt free to attack any vessel, even a U.S. warship. The Iraqi pilot who had attacked the frigate *Stark* was proudly said to be a veteran who had to his credit fifteen successful missile attacks on Iranian tankers. Kuwait, the most active ally of Iraq, was now, however, reclassified by the United States as "neutral." In effect, President Reagan implicitly put the United States on the side of Iraq and its Kuwait–Saudi Arabia allies.

One of the typically doctrinal aspects of this whole affair was the buildup of the Soviet threat. There surely have been Soviet threats, but this one was not like any other. When Secretary Shultz said, "We don't have any desire to see the Soviets assume a role in the Persian Gulf," he was apparently oblivious to or willing to ignore the fact that the Soviets had assumed a role at the behest of our present associates. After all, our latest ward, Kuwait, had brought in the Soviets by getting them to lease it tankers. Iraq had brought in the Soviets by making them one of its major arms suppliers. The entire game played by Iraq and Kuwait had depended on getting Soviet aid in order to inveigle the United States to do the same things for them—or more.

---

[43] Yet it should be noted that President Reagan later appeared to cut the ground from under his own anti-Soviet assumptions. On June 11, 1987, he granted that the Soviets "have a stake, too, in peaceful shipping and the openness of the international waters," and were as a result eligible to be asked to take part in a peaceful settlement of the Gulf war. On June 15, 1987, he reverted to his previous anti-Soviet line with the words: "If we don't do the job, the Soviets will," to the jeopardy of "our own national security and that of our allies." This gyration is typical of a policy that has not been thought through and veers crazily from one side to the other.

It was absurd to link Iran and the Soviet Union, as if they were confederates in a plot to block free passage of the Gulf. Iran showed its displeasure with the Soviet Union in September 1986 when an Iranian naval vessel boarded a Soviet arms ship and impounded it temporarily in an Iranian port. Two Soviet merchant ships had been attacked, one by Iranian forces with antitank rocket-propelled grenades from a speedboat, and another hit by a mine. Iran was backed by Communist China, which was hardly the Soviets' favorite. It was the suppression of the Iranian Communists in 1983 that turned the Soviet Union against Iran. The Muslim fanaticism across the Soviet border in Iran is an infection that the Soviet Union would gladly keep out. Even more absurdly, the United States and the Soviet Union had been holding discussions for months at the United Nations on ways to bring the Iran-Iraq war to a close. If there was to be any UN resolution or action, Soviet cooperation was indispensable, and denouncing the Soviets for trying to impose their will on the Gulf states was no way to get it.

These discussions at the UN would be incomprehensible if the United States and the Soviet Union did not have a common interest in restoring peace in the Persian Gulf. Yet Assistant Secretary of State Murphy could not see that the Soviet Union has a vital interest in the area. When it was pointed out to him that the Persian Gulf was only eight hundred miles from the Soviet Union and about seven thousand miles from the United States, he maintained that "it is our vital interest, not their vital interest," because of Western dependence on the oil that passes through it.[44] It did not seem to occur to Secretary Murphy that there is more than one kind of vital interest and that oil is not the be-all and end-all of international relations.

We should not be too hard on Secretary Murphy, however, because he has on other occasions blurted out more of the truth than other officials have done. He told the Senate Foreign Relations Committee on May 29, 1987, that "what is driving our policy at this point" is that "we don't want the Soviets to get a handle on a vital lifeline" of the world's oil supply. Whatever "handle" may mean here, we should be grateful for being told that what had been driving our policy was anti-Soviet in motivation.

Murphy was also the one who got into trouble for saying that there was some risk of "war" with Iran in the present U.S. policy. He was

<hr>

[44] *The Washington Post*, May 31, 1987.

immediately repudiated by the White House spokesman Marlin Fitzwater, who was followed by President Reagan with an assurance that "I don't see the danger of war. I don't see how one could possibly start." As if this were not confusing enough, Assistant Secretary of Defense Richard L. Armitage told the Senate Foreign Relations Committee on May 29 that "there is a risk, a very real risk," in giving U.S. naval protection to "reflagged" Kuwaiti vessels.[45] Meanwhile the Chairman of the Joint Chiefs of Staff, Admiral William J. Crowe, Jr., insisted that the United States should not escort Kuwaiti tankers without a commitment to retaliate for any attacks on U.S. ships.

There was something about the commitment in the Persian Gulf that brought out the worst in our highest officials. Secretary Shultz, usually a sensible person, was responsible for this non sequitur: "If our ships get attacked anywhere, including the Persian Gulf, we will defend ourselves. That's not going to war with somebody. That's defending ourselves."[46] Such attacks and counterattacks are just what acts of war are, whether they are called defensive or offensive. There would be few wars in history if all those who claimed to be fighting "defensive wars" were absolved from fighting wars.

10

The question for policymakers is not merely "what" but "how." It is a good rule, especially in international affairs, not to decide on what needs to be done until it is clear how it is going to be done and whether it can be done successfully. It is especially important to decide for ourselves and not because others have drawn us in by putting out bait for us to snap at. The Kuwaiti ruse of first going to the Soviet Union for assistance and then getting the Reagan Administration to bid up for Kuwait's favor was a ludicrous example of rising to the bait.

It has not always been so.

We were once saved from getting embroiled in Vietnam for the very reason that the "what" did not come before and without the "how." The time was 1954 after the French disaster at Dienbienphu. The crisis then in Vietnam was far more advanced than it was in the

[45] Ibid., May 31, 1987.
[46] The New York Times, May 29, 1987.

Persian Gulf. President Eisenhower did not want the Viet Minh, as the Vietnamese Communists were called, to prevail. But he was up against domino thinking, including his own, which, as a recent study has put it, "demanded that victory be denied the Viet Minh."[47] Though Eisenhower had made up his mind against putting U.S. ground forces into Vietnam, he was equivocal about other forms of military aid to the French. His method of operation was to commission studies and encourage his top aides to debate the issues. Eisenhower let this process of pondering the means and consequences go on for months.

The main military advocate of all-out U.S. intervention was the Chairman of the Joint Chiefs of Staff, Admiral Arthur Radford. The main military objector was Army Chief of Staff Matthew B. Ridgway. The latter sent an army team of experts in every field to study the problem on the ground. Ridgway concluded that "we could have fought in Indo-China. We could have won, if we had been willing to pay the tremendous cost in men and money that such intervention would have required."[48] Ridgway claims that Eisenhower quickly decided against intervention when he saw the report—a version that has been challenged.[49] Eisenhower was still wavering; it was at this time that he publicly spoke of the "domino principle." Yet he was determined to take no action that both the Republican and Democratic leadership would not endorse and that did not have both French and British support. After Dienbienphu fell, Secretary of State John Foster Dulles made a little-known retreat from domino thinking: "We do not want to operate on what has been referred to as the domino theory, where the loss of one area will topple another and another." Still, after all the hesitation and uncertainty, the United States was saved for a decade from the gratuitous bloodletting and humiliation of the Vietnam War.

In the case of the Persian Gulf, there was no prior attempt to consult or get agreement with the Republican and Democratic lead-

---

[47] Richard H. Immerman, "Between the Unattainable and the Unacceptable: Eisenhower and Dienbienphu," in *Reevaluating Eisenhower: American Foreign Policy in the 1950s*, edited by Richard A. Melanson and David Mayer (University of Illinois Press, 1986), p. 123. I have largely based this account on Immerman's study, which has used recently declassified documents and shows that Eisenhower's conduct in this matter was more complex than previously thought.

[48] General Matthew B. Ridgway, *Soldier* (Harper, 1956), pp. 275–77.

[49] Immerman, "Between the Unattainable and the Unacceptable: Eisenhower and Dienbienphu," pp. 136–37.

ership. A policy was announced before the policymakers had any idea of how to carry it out or what the cost would be. After deciding on the policy, they made a pretense of seeking allies in Western Europe to participate in it with us, knowing full well that our closest allies there had no intention of sharing in our folly.

11

The entire U.S. policy in the Persian Gulf was bedeviled by an infernal confusion of motives.

One was that we wished to protect Kuwaiti tankers with the U.S. flag and warships. Another was that we wished to ensure "free navigation" in the Gulf for all ships of all nations because it is an international waterway. A third was that we wished to prevent Soviet domination of the Gulf and, in an even more extreme version of this aim, to exclude the Soviets from the Gulf altogether.

The first aim, to protect Kuwaiti tankers, would be accomplished if we succeeded in the second—to ensure the free passage of all shipping of all nations. Ironically, we would also protect the tankers of Iran, which needed protection the most. These aims were specific and limited, and they depended above all on the cooperation of all interested nations, including the Soviets, for which reason we had been seeking agreement with them at the United Nations. These aims did not involve a struggle for power in the Persian Gulf between the United States and the Soviet Union. The third aim, however, was very different in kind. It implied that only the United States had the right to send warships into the Persian Gulf or play a "role" in it.

The third aim was a sure recipe for disaster. The Soviet Union could not be expelled from the Gulf without the use of force, which had been ruled out by the President and our highest officials. No other nation could support us in an effort to make an international waterway into an American or even Western military lake. Yet by turning an incident brought about by an Iraqi missile into an anti-Soviet crusade, we were heading into the wrong confrontation at the wrong place at the wrong time for the wrong reason.

It will not help to remind us that we are a "world power," as Professor Brzezinski did. To persuade us that the United States should "assert Western interests in the Persian Gulf—alone, if necessary," he instructed us: "We must recognize that the United States holds the status of a world power, and our allies are simply regional powers."[50] This distinction is not original with Brzezinski; it should have been copyrighted by his predecessor, Henry Kissinger.[51]

The term "world power" is a snare and a delusion if it is taken to mean that the United States has the power to decide matters all over the world. We are obviously stronger in some places than in others, and in some places we are not strong at all. North Vietnam was a tenth-rate "regional power," but it was in the right place with the right strength at the right time. Our European allies are much closer to the Persian Gulf; they have a much greater stake in Middle East oil. They refused to get embroiled with us not because they are "regional powers" and do not have sufficient military strength to act but because it makes no sense to them to intervene in the Iran-Iraq war or seek a showdown with the Soviet Union in the Persian Gulf. What separated us from them was policy, not power.

The words "Truman Doctrine" and "world power" seem to have a hypnotic effect. They resemble the slogan about "standing tall," which made voters for Reagan feel better, stronger, and more patriotic, no matter that the words are almost empty of political content and no guide to what the country's real problems and capabilities are.

Until the *Stark* was hit, our policy was based on ensuring free passage of the waterway with the cooperation of the Soviet Union. We were not interested in taking sides in the Iran-Iraq war or using force to gain our ends. We did not whip up a storm of anxiety about the threat to our security, our peace, and our freedom. We understood that the war was between two regimes that had nothing in common with us and were almost equally detestable. We did not expect that it would be easy or quick to achieve our ends in these unpleasant circumstances, but there was no reason to believe that Western civilization hung in the balance in this struggle to the death between Saddam Hussein and Khomeini.

As soon as the *Stark* was hit, this policy gave way to one virtually its opposite. We began to take the side of Iraq against Iran—without, of course, admitting it. Our very security, peace, and freedom were said to be endangered. We cast about for a quick fix for a nasty little

---

[50] *The Washington Post*, June 7, 1987.

[51] "The United States has global interests and responsibilities. Our European allies have regional interests" (*Department of State Bulletin*, May 14, 1973, p. 594). This statement in his "Year of Europe" speech created an angry furor in Europe at the time.

war. We suddenly made the Soviet Union the enemy—or at least the obstacle—in the Persian Gulf. Our Secretary of State permitted himself to rule out any Soviet "role" in the Gulf. Supporters of the new line took to accusing the Soviets of unacceptable "intrusion" in an international waterway, as if it were necessary to expel them. Suddenly, acts of war such as preemptive strikes—defensive or otherwise—were on front pages.

There was no need to make this bewildering flip-flop. If we are a "world power," we should have enough staying power to outlast the temporary damage that these unpleasant belligerents may inflict.

(*The New York Review of Books*, July 16, 1987)

Reagan's Junta

1

THIS IS SUPPOSED to have been the era of the imperial Presidency. It has turned out to be the era of Presidencies that have tried to make themselves imperial—and failed. The attempt in the Iran-Contra affairs by the Reagan Presidency is only the latest of this kind. The basic elements that went into the Reagan effort were also not new. Other Presidents had used and misused the National Security Adviser; other Presidents had deliberately kept their Secretaries of State in ignorance of Presidential policy; other Presidents had found ways to keep Congress in the dark about what they were doing.

Yet there was something new about the Reaganite phenomenon. The elements might be familiar, but they had taken a different and more ominous form. A would-be imperial President prepared the way for a would-be Presidential junta.

The transition has been a very long one. In his study of the imperial Presidency, Arthur M. Schlesinger, Jr., began the story with the disputes over Presidential power in George Washington's Administration. But the present crisis of Presidential power has a different dimension; it is a crisis not only about what a President has the power to do; it is also about the power of those around or behind him to do in his name.

The roots of the present predicament go back to the efforts of at least the last seven Presidents to extricate themselves from the constitutional limitations of their office. Schlesinger places the "presidential breakaway" after the Second World War. "The postwar

Presidents," he asserts, "though Eisenhower and Kennedy markedly less than Truman, Johnson, and Nixon, almost came to see the sharing of power with Congress in foreign policy as a derogation of the Presidency."[1] This version lets Franklin D. Roosevelt off on the ground that though his "destroyer deal" with Great Britain in 1940 was arranged without congressional authorization, it was done for good and sufficient reasons. Schlesinger exonerates Roosevelt because the prospect of a British collapse represented a genuine national emergency, and because Roosevelt privately consulted with the Republican and Democratic leadership. But Roosevelt knew that his action was constitutionally dubious and at first did not want to send the destroyers to Great Britain without legislative approval. As Schlesinger notes, the leading authority on the Presidency, Professor Edward S. Corwin, regarded the deal as an "endorsement of unrestrained autocracy in the field of our foreign relations." The road to Reagan was paved with good intentions.

The imperial Presidency, then, is one that acts autocratically. It does so far more in foreign than in domestic affairs. Yet it was not always so. As long as the isolationist tradition was still strong, Presidents had less incentive or opportunity to act alone. Once the so-called Truman Doctrine of 1947 seemed to provide a license to intervene everywhere in the world, Presidents were far less inclined to restrain themselves, especially in periods of congressional complaisance.

Before the end of the Second World War, Presidents did not have the bureaucratic means to carry out policy by themselves. They might insist on making decisions unilaterally, but they could not bypass the existing bureaucracy in order to carry them out. Roosevelt did not have a Central Intelligence Agency or a National Security Adviser with his own staff; the "destroyer deal" was no secret from the State Department, Congress, or anyone else. The CIA and the National Security Council were set up in 1947, the latter headed by an assistant for national security affairs, better known as National Security Adviser. From a handful, the NSC professional staff has grown to about fifty, enough to divide up the entire world among its own specialists. With these two new agencies, Presidents were able to do things that had not been feasible for them to do before.

Again, the change came by stages. The CIA was originally charged

---

[1] Arthur M. Schlesinger, Jr., *The Imperial Presidency* (Houghton Mifflin, 1973), p. 206.

with coordinating, correlating, evaluating, and disseminating foreign intelligence information; the National Security Adviser was given the task of coordinating the policy options open to the President and the recommendations to him. A decision was made at an early stage that foreshadowed the end of the State Department's traditionally predominant role in the making and execution of American foreign policy. Truman's Secretary of State, James F. Byrnes, wanted the new intelligence organization to be responsible to the State Department.[2] When he was turned down, the CIA went on to live a life of its own, increasingly at the expense of the State Department. In 1948, another new agency, loosely linked with the CIA, was set up, disarmingly called the Office of Policy Coordination, to engage in covert activities; in 1951, it was fully integrated into the CIA, which henceforth carried out both covert intelligence and covert operations.

The Truman Administration was basically responsible for these innovations; yet Truman himself did not realize where they were going to lead. Eleven years after he had left office, Truman confessed: "I never had any thought when I set up the CIA that it would be injected into peacetime cloak-and-dagger operations." He no longer liked what he had wrought: "For some time I have been disturbed by the way CIA has been diverted from its original assignment. It has become an operational and at times a policy-making arm of the government." After watching what had resulted, he wanted no more of it: "I, therefore, would like to see the CIA be restored to its original assignment as the intelligence arm of the President, and whatever else it can properly perform in that special field—and that its operational duties be terminated or properly used elsewhere."

Finally, he reflected: "We have grown up as a nation, respected for our ability to maintain a free and open society. There is something about the way the CIA has been functioning that is casting a shadow over our historic position and I feel that we need to correct it."[3] To a correspondent he wrote: "The CIA was set up by me for the sole purpose of getting all the available information to the President. It was not intended to operate as an international agency engaged in strange activities."[4]

---

[2] Harry S. Truman, *Memoirs*, Vol. 2: *Years of Trial and Hope* (Doubleday, 1956), p. 57.

[3] *The Washington Post*, December 22, 1963.

[4] *Off the Record: The Private Papers of Harry S. Truman*, edited by Robert H. Ferrell (Harper and Row, 1980), p. 408.

These activities have grown stranger and stranger, until under Reagan the President himself claimed that he did not know how they happened. Yet there is one thing that he could not fail to know— that he used his National Security Adviser instead of the Secretary of State as his chosen instrument in the conduct of American foreign policy. If this displacement had happened for the first time, it would be serious enough. But it has happened frequently before, though not in the extreme Reaganite form.

Too much attention has been paid to the minutiae of the Iran-Contra affairs and not enough to the implications it has for the institutions and structure of our government. Long after the exact details of the diversion of funds to the Contras have been forgotten, the institutional cost will still have to be paid. For a full appreciation of how deep and acute the problem is, it is necessary to look back and see how it has developed over the past quarter of a century. This institutional crisis mainly concerns the President, Secretary of State, and National Security Adviser, the first two offices as old as the Republic, the third a comparative newcomer in the American scheme of governance.

2

The post of National Security Adviser did not take off until early in the Kennedy Administration in 1961. The post was held by Mc-George Bundy, who with his deputy, Walt W. Rostow, according to Arthur M. Schlesinger, gave the White House "an infusion of energy on foreign affairs with which the State Department would never in the next three years . . . quite catch up." At first, it is said, Kennedy wanted the State Department to be the "central point" in all aspects of foreign affairs. But he was soon "disappointed" in its makeup and performance, with the result that he came to depend on Bundy and his staff or on Theodore Sorensen, his special counsel. The Secretary of State, Dean Rusk, and Kennedy's entourage were so different from each other in outlook and manner that they hardly spoke the same language. To Kennedy himself, Rusk's views "remained a mystery."[5] Sorensen says that Rusk "deferred almost too amiably to White House initiatives and interference." If Kennedy had lived to

[5] Arthur M. Schlesinger, Jr., *A Thousand Days* (Houghton Mifflin, 1965), pp. 150, 407, 420–21, 435.

have a second term, Bundy would have been a "logical candidate for Secretary of State."⁶

Kennedy was not the first President to make foreign policy in the White House rather than in the State Department. The pattern had been set by Franklin D. Roosevelt, who made his Secretary of State, Cordell Hull, almost a figurehead. But Roosevelt had not built up a substitute or shadow foreign-policy agency; he had preferred to work through other cabinet officers, at first Under Secretary of State Sumner Welles, and then through other members of the Cabinet or his personal emissary Harry Hopkins. Yet Roosevelt and the proliferation of quasi-foreign-affairs agencies during World War II were responsible for starting the State Department on its downward path. Presidents who wanted to be their own foreign ministers followed his example by choosing weak Secretaries of State and depending on others to carry out their wishes.

The President who gave this system a pathological twist was Richard Nixon. We know just how pathological it was because his National Security Adviser, Henry Kissinger, has told us all about it. Nixon hardly knew Kissinger when he took him on; his choice as Secretary of State, William Rogers, was one of Nixon's closest friends and a former law partner. When Nixon chose Rogers, Nixon knew him to be unfamiliar with foreign affairs. According to Kissinger, Nixon immediately told Kissinger to build up a "national security apparatus" in the White House. The only region that Nixon entrusted to Rogers was the Middle East—for one reason because Nixon believed at the time that any active policy there was doomed to failure. The "back channel" that Nixon and Kissinger set up with Soviet Ambassador Anatoly Dobrynin cut the State Department out of the most important field of Soviet-American affairs. According to Kissinger, Nixon repeatedly lied to Rogers, especially about Kissinger's trips to China in 1971 and to Moscow in 1972.

Why did Nixon humiliate his old friend? Kissinger's explanation clearly suggests a pathological motive. In the past, it seems, Rogers had been the "psychologically dominant partner" in the relationship. Now Nixon "wanted to reverse roles and establish a relationship in which both hierarchically and substantially he, Nixon, called the tune for once." Kissinger was only too willing to collaborate in the diseased machination, of which he was the chief beneficiary. "I do not

⁶ Theodore C. Sorensen, *Kennedy* (Harper and Row, 1965), pp. 263, 270.

mean to suggest that I resisted Nixon's conduct toward his senior Cabinet officer," Kissinger confessed bashfully. "From the first my presence made it technically possible and after a time I undoubtedly encouraged it."

One precedent set by Kissinger came back to haunt Reagan's Secretary of State George Shultz. Kissinger used the U.S. ambassador in Pakistan to prepare for his China trip without either of them informing Secretary of State Rogers. The hostages-for-arms deals with Iran were managed by Lieutenant Colonel Oliver L. North on the National Security Council staff, against the better judgment of Secretary Shultz, who professed to be "shocked" when he learned about them. Shultz found it necessary to protest against the use of Kissinger's precedent as a justification for treating him as Rogers had been treated, with the argument that Kissinger was unique— "They broke the mold when they made him." Unfortunately, they did not break the mold of what he did, which was far more important in the long run than what he was. If Kissinger had been National Security Adviser vis-à-vis Shultz, it would seem, Shultz would have made no complaint.

In retrospect, Kissinger knew that there was something wrong with his theatrical China coup. In his memoirs, he admitted:

> The State Department should be the visible focus of our foreign policy; if the President has no confidence in his Secretary of State he should replace him, not substitute the security adviser for him. If he does not trust the State Department, the President should enforce compliance with his directives, not circumvent it with the NSC machinery. Yet, while these postulates are beyond argument as a matter of theory, they are not easy to carry out. To achieve the essential coherence of policy there is need for a strong Secretary of State who is at the same time quite prepared to carry out Presidential wishes not only formally but in all nuances.[7]

So it was Secretary of State Rogers's fault for having been too weak to carry out the Presidential wishes. But Nixon had deliberately chosen a weak Secretary of State and then had made him all the weaker by treating him with open contempt and cutting him out of his own constitutional responsibilities. As for the conspiratorial secrecy that enveloped Kissinger's first trip to China in 1971, it was not anything the Chinese had wanted or demanded. They were, in

---

[7] Henry Kissinger, *White House Years* (Little, Brown, 1979), p. 728. All the evidence of the dealings by Nixon and Kissinger comes from this book.

fact, "extremely suspicious of our desire for secrecy." It was wholly contrived for American consumption, to confront the American public with an accomplished fact.

Nixon fancied himself a great expert in foreign affairs; Carter had no such illusions. But Carter also wanted to be seen as his own master in foreign policy and, therefore, chose a Secretary of State, Cyrus Vance, who would not be too obtrusive. His National Security Adviser, Zbigniew Brzezinski, was from the first determined to be the President's prime agent in foreign policy. Brzezinski quickly contrived to freeze out the CIA in the daily intelligence of the President, which he insisted on giving every morning without anyone else present. He saw himself as Carter's mentor and in the first months gave him lessons in "conceptual or strategic issues." Brzezinski's National Security Council staff controlled "the policy-making output of both State and the Defense Department," as well as the activities of the CIA. Brzezinski and Secretary Vance increasingly disagreed on major issues, with Vance unable or unwilling to assert himself. Vance's "reluctance to speak up publicly, to provide a broad conceptual explanation for what our Administration was trying to do, and Carter's lack of preparation for doing it himself, pushed me to the forefront," Brzezinski later explained, adding in parenthesis, "I will not claim I resisted strongly." Finally Vance could stand no more and resigned as a result of his disagreement over the ill-fated mission to rescue the hostages from the Tehran embassy. Another Secretary of State had spent almost four miserable, humiliating years in office, at least as the National Security Adviser later described them.[8]

Reagan's first Secretary of State, Alexander M. Haig, Jr., was another casualty. Having been Kissinger's deputy on the staff of the National Security Council, Haig well knew about the rivalry and threat from that quarter to the Secretary of State. When he took the office, he says, the President told him that he would be "*the* spokesman" in foreign affairs and "I won't have a repeat of the Kissinger-Rogers situation." Reagan also assured him that the new National Security Adviser, Richard Allen, "would act exclusively as a staff coordinator." Haig does not seem to have had much trouble with Allen. They were both deprived of direct, regular access to the President, the factor that Haig later thought had brought both of them

[8] Zbigniew Brzezinski, *Power and Principle* (Farrar, Straus and Giroux, 1983), pp. 37, 65–66, 72.

down. For most of his tenure, Haig attributed his woes to the White House staff, especially James A. Baker and Michael K. Deaver, or, as Haig put it, "Baker, Deaver, and their apparat." Without access to the President and subject to their control of what went to the President, Haig was mortally handicapped by "not knowing his methods, not understanding his system of thought, not having the opportunity of discussing policy in detail with him." The same might be said of some of his predecessors and their knowledge and understanding of the Presidents who had chosen them.

After Allen's inglorious departure as National Security Adviser in January 1982, a real rival and threat confronted Haig in his successor, William Clark, whose deputy was Robert C. McFarlane. As Haig tells the story, he began to be bypassed by Clark during the Lebanon crisis of that year. Soon Haig was worried by a situation "in which a presidential assistant [Clark], especially one of limited experience and limited understanding of the volatile nature of an international conflict [at that time the Falklands crisis], should assume powers of the Presidency." Clark would draft a message to Israel for the President to sign without showing it to Haig. Yet in the end, Haig himself came to denigrate the constitutional position of the Secretary of State to such an extent that he offered the view that "it does not really matter whether the Secretary of State or the National Security Adviser, or some other official carries out the President's foreign policy and speaks for the Administration on these questions." The would-be imperial President, it seems, was permitted to use anyone to make the Secretary of State a figurehead instead of a "vicar."[9]

The imperial Presidency has not materialized. Kennedy's Presidency was cut short. Johnson came to grief over Vietnam. Nixon was disgraced and dethroned. Carter was not successful enough to win a second term. Now Reagan has been exposed as a hollow idol—the great delegator who gave away much of his power to those to whom it had been delegated.

But though the imperial Presidency has failed to come about, Presidents have distorted the institution they have inherited by seeking to get rid of checks and balances in the conduct of foreign affairs. The expansion of Presidential ambitions in foreign policy has been concurrent with the expansion of the country's global power. This

---

[9] Alexander M. Haig, Jr., *Caveat: Realism, Reagan, and Foreign Policy* (Macmillan, 1984), pp. 12, 53, 84, 306–7, 339, 341, 356.

expansion, on a scale never envisioned by pre–World War II Presidents, has made foreign affairs the main test of Presidential greatness. Presidents have deliberately appointed weak Secretaries of State or rid themselves of those who did not bend to their will in order to free themselves from traditional or constitutional constraints. The last strong Secretaries of State were Truman's George C. Marshall and Dean Acheson and Eisenhower's John Foster Dulles a quarter of a century ago. It is unthinkable that any President would have treated them the way Rusk, Rogers, Vance, Haig, and Shultz have been treated, or that Marshall and Dulles would have submitted to such treatment.

3

While much is murky about the Iran-Contra imbroglio, the main thing is indisputable. The essentials can now be reconstructed without the aid of a congressional inquiry or pleading with Rear Admiral John M. Poindexter and Lieutenant Colonel Oliver L. North to come clean.

On January 17, 1986, President Reagan signed a secret intelligence "finding" authorizing the sale of weapons and spare parts to Iran. This directive also enjoined that it should not be made known to Congress, and, even more remarkably, it was not imparted to four members of the National Security Council. The four left out were Secretary of State Shultz; Secretary of Defense Caspar Weinberger; the Chairman of the Joint Chiefs of Staff, Admiral William J. Crowe, Jr., and Secretary of the Treasury James A. Baker III. The four in the know were Vice President George Bush, CIA director William J. Casey, Attorney General Edwin Meese, and Presidential chief of staff Donald T. Regan. The "finding" attributed the need to exclude Congress to "extreme sensitivity" and "security risks." So secretive was the order that only one copy was made of it and it was deposited in the safe of National Security Adviser Poindexter.

This "finding" was not made by President Reagan in a fit of absentmindedness. It can be understood only by going back to two previous meetings of the National Security Council. On December 6, 1985, a "full-scale" discussion had been held on the subject of arms sales to Iran. It was not a new subject for Secretary Shultz; he said that he and the then National Security Adviser Robert C. McFarlane had been considering it ever since June of that year.

Whatever Shultz knew or did not know, one shipment of American arms was sent from Israel in August 1985 with the approval of the President, according to McFarlane, and a second in September. At the meeting of December 6, both Shultz and McFarlane came out against the proposal—Shultz evidently on principle, McFarlane because he had been disappointed in his previous dealings with the Iranians. The decision at that time went in favor of engaging "in a dialogue [with the Iranians] if they release our hostages but that we would not sell them arms," as Shultz put it in his testimony of December 8, 1986.

But the President was somehow prevailed on to reopen the subject. Another "full-scale discussion" was held on January 7, 1986. This time both Shultz and Weinberger openly opposed changing the policy of not selling arms to Iran. Nevertheless, as Shultz disclosed, he could see that he was now on the losing side. Thus the January 7 meeting led to the secret decision of January 17. Shultz and Weinberger were "cut out" of the subsequent dealings, because they were opposed to the arms sales. In any case, the critical decision of January 17 had been made after about six weeks of intensive discussion and conflicting views.

Whatever the vagaries of President Reagan's decision-making process may have been, he made this decision fully aware of what it entailed. No one else can be held responsible for it.

Ordinarily, the CIA would have been given the task of carrying out the January 17 directive; it had all the means to do so and in any case the plan could not be fully implemented without it. But past misbehavior had made the CIA suspect and dictated that a less exposed agency should be put out in front. The National Security Adviser and his staff served the purpose because they were considered to be responsible to the President alone and not even to the National Security Council as such, let alone to Congress. Yet Poindexter and his main aide in the operation, Lieutenant Colonel North, had no physical means to carry out an arms deal with Iran. They were helpless without the cooperation of the CIA and the arms, which could be obtained only from the Defense Department.

Thus, as Casey explained, the CIA put itself in a "support mode" to Poindexter.[10] The CIA requested the arms from the Secretary of Defense, who ordered the Army to release them from its stocks and

---

[10] Interview with Casey, *Time*, December 22, 1986, p. 31.

transfer them to the CIA. Secretary Weinberger, who did not approve of the deal but was aware that it was the President's wish, did nothing to hinder it. A stickler for form, he knew that he was bound by the Economy Act, which regulated the transfer of property between government agencies. Weinberger insisted that the Defense Department should be paid $12 million for the arms, a price obviously far less than they were worth but with the inestimable advantage that it was $2 million less than arms sales that had to be reported to Congress. The arms were then transported to Israel and elsewhere in chartered planes of a company controlled by the CIA. The money obtained from the Iranian intermediaries was put into secret bank accounts in Switzerland. The transaction could not have been carried out without the CIA, while at the same time director Casey was able to shift the responsibility to the NSC, which, he later claimed, "was operating this thing."

Thus was set up what amounted to a Presidential junta. It was not led by a single, outstanding personality of the Kissinger type. Its main figures were relatively obscure military characters—a rear admiral and a lieutenant colonel on active service. They could get things done only by acting in the President's name. Even Secretary Weinberger, who must have suspected that something untoward was afoot when he was told to "sell" arms to the CIA, apparently entrusted the transaction to only two of his closest aides. Extraordinary measures were taken to keep the affair a secret—and it was kept a secret for months.

The diversion of funds to the Contras, whatever it amounted to, was only a minor by-product of the deal with Iran. It was made possible by the junta-like operation, which was so self-contained and so far removed from the rest of the government that it could be managed by a single insider. The worst that North could be charged with was having done something illegally—providing the Contras with funds that Congress had refused to approve—that Reagan wanted done unobtrusively, in a way that would not technically violate the Boland Amendment prohibiting the government from supplying such funds.

Far more important than the diversion of funds to the Contras was the damage done to the conduct of a credible, responsible American foreign policy. For years, official American spokesmen had fulminated against making deals with terrorists or terrorist nations, and especially against selling arms to Iran. On October 1, 1986, Secretary of State Shultz met in New York with the six Persian Gulf foreign ministers, organized in the Gulf Cooperation Council. He assured them that the United States was intensifying its efforts to discourage the sale of arms to Iran, feared by all of them. By that time, the United States had been secretly, for months, intensifying its efforts to sell arms to Iran, directly and indirectly.

No doubt Secretary Shultz did not mean to deceive. But he was not a member of President Reagan's junta, which was pursuing an altogether different foreign policy. Thus arose the curious phenomenon of two conflicting American foreign policies—the junta's and the Secretary of State's. Both in a sense emanated from the President, but only one was credible and genuine on October 1, 1986, when Shultz conferred with the Gulf ministers.

Yet government by junta cannot operate without the voluntary ignorance and complaisance of those who are in a position to resist it. Shultz, Weinberger, and others were aware of "bits and pieces of evidence," as Shultz put it, that arms were going to Iran. They knew as much as they wanted to know, which was just enough to permit them to protest that they did not know enough. So long as it was the President's policy, they looked the other way, despite a conviction that it was indefensible. Secretary Weinberger permitted himself to say that the President had received "very bad" advice and that "there aren't any moderate elements in Iran with whom we can deal." But he had authorized the transfer of arms to the CIA for Iran and, like Shultz, had put loyalty to the President ahead of faithfulness to his own view of the best interests of the country.

4

The implications of government by secret Presidential junta strike at the very roots of the American system of government. One way to think about them is to note how the Iran-Contra affairs were defended or rationalized by those politically or ideologically closest to the President.

A most striking motif was the line drawn between the President himself and rank-and-file conservatives or Republicans. This distinction came out most crudely in the tirade by Patrick J. Buchanan, at that time the President's communications director, or propaganda minister, in *The Washington Post* of December 8, 1986. Buchanan raged against "the Republican Party establishment," which had "headed for the tall grass" instead of showing its gratitude and loyalty to a President to whom it owed "all it has and all it is." For Buchanan, the President was truly an imperial ruler whose party was merely a retinue to whom self-interest ought to dictate unquestioning service and obedience.

A variant of this theme was put forward by Irving Kristol, the neoconservative ideologue. The trouble, according to Kristol, was that Reagan's major appointments in the foreign-policy area, both in the State Department and the Pentagon, "have been from the traditional-conservative wing of the Republican Party," rather than the "populist conservative and American nationalist" wing—the latter a neoconservative formula. Since most of the Republicans in Congress also come from the traditional-conservative wing, "Mr. Reagan has not only found his hands tied by Congress—he has managed to tie his own hands as well." Thus the State and Defense departments were most responsible for what went wrong in Reagan's foreign policy because they refused to go along with it in Iran, Syria, and Nicaragua. It is a curious sophistry—they were in fact least responsible because they opposed it, but precisely this, according to Kristol, made them most responsible. Kristol suggested that the President had to "cut out" both his State and Defense departments from the Iran intrigue—"this is no way to conduct a foreign policy"— because they were filled with traditional conservatives.[11]

Buchanan's mindless loyalism is as far from traditional Republicanism as Kristol's casuistic neoconservatism is from traditional conservatism. In both cases, the blame can be shifted from Reagan only by invoking a political or ideological ethos alien to American institutions and practices.

Still another neoconservative version came from Norman Podhoretz. Unlike Buchanan, who ranted against the Republicans, and Kristol, who blamed the State and Defense departments, Podhoretz's villains were in Congress, especially its Democrats. Podhoretz wrote:

> And in foreign affairs, we now had not an Imperial Presidency but an Imperial Congress attempting to make policy instead of consenting to or opposing presidential initiatives.

[11] *The Wall Street Journal*, December 17, 1986.

It seemed to have escaped him that the "Imperial Congress" could not oppose the Presidential initiative in "the Iran-*contra* scandal" (as he himself called it), because it was not permitted to know anything about it until it was too late. Congress's alleged "imperial position" was also made inexplicable; he asserted that "Reagan, drawing on his great popularity, finally succeeded in persuading a narrow and reluctant Congressional majority to authorize military aid to the [Nicaraguan] resistance" and "prevailed" over the congressional opposition. This would seem to be an odd way for Congress to demonstrate its "imperial position" and "make policy." Congress's chief fault, according to Podhoretz, is that it is "too large and diverse" to "run an activist foreign policy," as if that were what Congress had been trying to do in the Iran-Contra affairs and as if the size and diversity of America as a nation were not integral to the conduct of any democratically conceived and executed foreign policy.[12]

And then there was the view of our former UN ambassador, Jeane J. Kirkpatrick. She was in Tel Aviv after the diversion of funds was revealed, but that did not stop her from bitterly assailing Secretary of State Shultz, Attorney General Meese, and Chief of Staff Regan. Like Buchanan's, her main theme was that of unconditional loyalty to President Reagan. "At critical points," she complained, "the President was pushed to center stage and his chief advisers faded into the background, whereas it should have been the other way around." She did not explain how Secretary Shultz, who had been cut out, or Regan, to whom Poindexter and North did not report, could have pushed themselves to center stage to explain what had gone on—and in the case of Shultz without lying about his original opposition. Kirkpatrick also did not think there was anything wrong with the diversion of funds to the Contras, and she described it as "very imaginative."[13]

[12] *New York Post*, December 16, 1986. This column represented Podhoretz's second thoughts on Reagan's Iran policy. In his first, in the *New York Post* of November 18, 1986, he had savagely attacked "this latest and most devastating of Reagan's blows to the anti-terrorist cause," as a "worthy successor to Kennedy's Bay of Pigs and Carter's Desert One." Between November 18 and December 16, the fault had mysteriously shifted from Reagan to the Congress. It may be noted that Podhoretz's second thoughts came after Attorney General Meese's revelation on November 25, 1986, that money from Iranian arms sales had been diverted to the Contras.

[13] I have used the account in *The Jerusalem Post*, December 9, 1986. Kirkpatrick had previously taken the line that it was neither prudent nor useful "to trade or seem to trade arms for kidnapped Americans" (*The Washington Post*, November 24, 1986). Since she had at that time agreed with Secretary Shultz, it is hard to understand how he could have pushed himself to center stage to defend Reagan's Iran policy—or how she could have done so in his place without changing her mind or pretending to do so.

These reactions to President Reagan's predicament tell us something about its implications. The Iran-Contra affairs evoked demands for absolute loyalty to the President, outcries against traditional Republicans or conservatives in general, charges against Congress as the main enemy, and justifications of an admittedly illegal diversion of funds.

Another response was put forward by Charles Krauthammer of *The New Republic*, which touches a deeper level of the problem. "This affair," he held, "is not a Reagan crisis nor a presidential crisis, but a recurring American crisis, rooted ultimately in the tension between America's need to act like a great power and its unwillingness to do so." He further explained: "The problem is not democracy. Democracy is instrumental. Its role is faithfully to transmit the popular will. The problem is American popular will, which is deeply divided on whether to accept the responsibilities of a great power."

Krauthammer finally presented his case in the form of a dilemma. The Presidency

> finds itself in a permanent bind: to fulfill its obligations as leader of a superpower or to fulfill its obligations as leader of a democracy. Confronted with the choice, a president must choose the latter. But it is the choice itself—not the identity of the president or his management style—that is the source of our recurring crisis.[14]

This view conveniently exculpates every President and every "management style" by putting the onus on the "choice." Even as Krauthammer put it, however, the choice should not be so difficult or culpable. We are told that, confronted with the choice, the President "must choose" to fulfill his obligations as leader of a democracy. If that is how he *must* choose, why should the choice itself be responsible for creating the crisis instead of the President who does not make the right and necessary choice?

Yet Krauthammer is clearly of two minds about the primacy of democracy. If democracy is merely "instrumental," then it is not fundamental, as it has long been assumed to be in the American political tradition. Krauthammer himself implied that democracy is something more than "instrumental" if Presidents must choose to be faithful to it and must subordinate superpower status to it. Krauthammer would have much less trouble with Presidents making the choice if he himself had less trouble making it.

---

[14] *The New Republic*, December 22, 1986.

Still, there is something revealing in Krauthammer's dilemma that bears closely on Reagan's "management style" in the Iran-Contra affairs. Reagan's choice of a Presidential junta to carry out his policy was more characteristic of a leader of a runaway superpower than a leader of a healthy democracy. The deliberate decision to exclude Congress for many months from all knowledge, the degrading excommunication of the Secretary of State, the implied edict that disagreement cannot be tolerated and is punishable by exclusion from decision making, the morbid secrecy of the entire enterprise—these are political monstrosities in a democracy such as ours. They are of a piece with those other monstrosities that have recently been advanced—absolute loyalty to the President, repudiation of traditional conservatism in favor of adventurist neoconservatism, the conception of Congress as enemy, and the absolution given to lawlessness on the part of Presidential agents, even military officers.

Despite my reservations about the way Krauthammer dealt with the problem that he posed, it is not a problem that can be easily disposed of. If, as he says, America is unwilling to act like a great power, or the "American popular will" is deeply divided on whether to accept the responsibilities of a great power, what are the further implications of such a "permanent bind"?

The most far-reaching implication of this line of reasoning is that the President and those around him must substitute their will for the "popular will." If a President must choose between being the leader of a superpower or the leader of a democracy, the former must take precedence over the latter or he will be no leader of a superpower. President Reagan made precisely such a choice when he decided to act through a Presidential junta instead of the existing structure of government. The argument that he was forced to rely on his junta because he could not trust Congress, the Secretary of State, the Secretary of Defense, and any others who might disagree with him merely reinforces the ultimate nature of this choice. But there was another way open to him. If he could not trust them, it should have meant that he could not carry through a policy without or against them. At that point, the leader of a democracy would call a halt.

In fact, then, the Krauthammer dilemma is unreal. The reason so many Presidents have failed to make their rule imperial is that they have always, ultimately, come up against the basic institutions of this country, backed by the "popular will." In order for these institutions and will to be overcome, a radical change would have to take place in this country. We are still far from that, but the threat exists so long as the President and his apologists think that he must act like the leader of a superpower instead of the leader of a democracy.

In the end, setting up a Presidential junta as a solution to the problem of being both a superpower and a democracy is self-defeating. Without the support of our democratic structure backed up by popular approval, a President will end up the leader neither of a superpower nor of a democracy. Whenever we act as a superpower at the expense of our democracy, the price is too high. It would be safer and sounder to seek openly to establish a balance between the responsibilities of a superpower and those of a democracy. Whenever the two responsibilities conflict and democracy loses, our system of government becomes unbalanced and finally takes revenge on those who would, in fact, impose an imperial Presidency.

The founders still have something to teach us. "The history of human conduct does not warrant that exalted opinion of human virtue which would make it wise in a nation to commit interests of so delicate and momentous a kind as those which concern its intercourse with the rest of the world to the sole disposal of a magistrate, created and circumstanced, as would be a president of the United States," wrote Alexander Hamilton in No. 75 of *The Federalist*. "The constitution supposes, what the History of all Gov[ernmen]ts demonstrates, that the Ex[ecutive] is the branch of power most interested in war, & most prone to it," wrote James Madison to Jefferson in 1798. "It has accordingly with studied care vested the question of war in the Legisl[ature]."[15]

(*The New York Review of Books*, January 29, 1987)

---

[15] Both of these citations appear in Schlesinger's *The Imperial Presidency*, p. 5.

FROM
AMERICAN
COMMUNISM
TO
GORBACHEV

American Communism
Revisited

1

AMERICAN COMMUNISM has become a minor academic industry. It was not always so. When I worked on the subject a quarter of a century ago, it was mainly of interest to those who had been in or around the Communist and other "left" movements. Now that it has been taken over by a new academic generation, too young to have known what it was like to be for or against the Communist movement in the 1930s or even 1950s, it is inevitably being reconsidered from different political perspectives and personal backgrounds.

By 1982, the subject had attracted enough academic attention to bring about the formation of an organization, Historians of American Communism, with about one hundred dues-paying members of varying political tendencies. Its newsletter indicates that twenty-three dissertations, thirty-five books, and fifty-eight articles have, in one way or another, been devoted to the subject between 1979 and 1984, with an additional eight dissertations in progress. Many more appeared before 1979. When I worked on the subject, there were perhaps two or three books on American Communism worth reading.

Many of these new historians, as they like to call themselves, derive from political and personal backgrounds in the New Left of the 1960s. They were students then and are mainly assistant professors now. "During the last decade," one of them explains, "scholars and former activists have begun to reexplore the history of American communism during the 1930s, 1940s, and 1950s."[1] Another describes the reexploration as the work of "a new generation of historians, influenced by the New Left."[2] The New Left influence is often worn as if it were a badge of honor, immediately thrust on the reader to ensure that the right political credential has been established.

Curiously, the New Left in the 1960s was openly hostile to and contemptuous of the Old Left, which conspicuously included the Communist Party. Yet these post–New Leftists have turned back to the Communist past in their search for a new faith and vision. The change in attitude, according to a leading spokesman, has come about because "the collapse of the apocalyptic expectations of the late 1960s created hunger among this new generation of left-wing activists for a tradition that could serve both as a source of political reference and inspiration in what suddenly looked like it was going to be a long struggle."[3] Those new historians who have concentrated on the Communist Party have done so as if the secret of a new radical rebirth were hidden in it.

I need mention only briefly here a wider setting, within which these more specialized new historians belong. Self-styled Marxist academics are now active in virtually every discipline, especially in the social sciences. They have their own journals and caucuses. Such groups are reported to have more than twelve thousand members, "the largest and most important cohort of left-wing scholars in American history." It is said that "in certain fields, American history for example, Marxism is the mainstream." Two recent presidents of the Organization of American Historians were "Marxists or at least *marxisantes*." The larger Marxist professoriate also "constitute the intellectual legacy of the New Left, the political activists of the 1960s who turned to scholarship in the 1970s in order to make sense of their own experience." With no mass political movement to sustain them any longer, "the temptation to trade the frustrations of politics for the pleasures of scholarship is strong, all the more so when the professional rewards for such a switch are all too obvious."[4]

The new historians of American Communism and the new breed

[1] Kenneth Waltzer, *Reviews in American History*, June 1983, p. 259.

[2] Gary Gerstle, *Reviews in American History*, December 1984, p. 560.

[3] Maurice Isserman, *Radical America*, Vol. 14 (1980), p. 44.

[4] Ellen Schrecker, *Humanities in Society*, Spring–Summer 1983, p. 139.

of academic Marxists constitute a little-noted subdivision of the "Yuppie" social stratum. The assistant professors of today will be the associate and full professors of tomorrow; the new historians are waiting their turn or already have tenure at major institutions— Princeton, Yale, Cornell, Rutgers, Smith, Michigan State, and elsewhere. Most attention has been paid to the recent neoconservative trends, which have been the most fashionable. But while a new generation of intellectuals has gone mainly to the right, a less numerous, though substantial, group has moved to the left, as if a gap had been opening in the center. The two extremes, however, do not enjoy the same opportunities for advancement. The right-wing intellectual Yuppies have far more to gain by gravitating to the corporation-subsidized foundations and institutes or to job openings in Reaganite Washington. The left-wing intellectual Yuppies have few prospects for personal advantage and political gratification other than academic careers.

The post–New Left academics are, of course, far from having taken over the universities. An influx of them into a single specialized field can, however, make a considerable difference. This has happened to the history of American Communism, as many of them have chosen to do their work in it. Moreover, the problems raised by the new historians do not merely concern the history of American Communism. They also call attention to broader questions of historical method and academic fashions. The new history can sometimes be mistaken for the new intellectual couture.

2

For me, the new work on American Communism has been the occasion for a return to a subject that I had given up many years ago. So much has appeared since my last book on American Communism was published in 1960 that I cannot possibly attempt to do justice to all of it. My interest here is in those works that claim to present a new interpretation of American Communist history. Even at that, my focus is necessarily more limited. One such book deals with the autoworkers' unions, another with Harlem in the 1930s, and so on. A number of them are not without solid research, even if they are seasoned with political partisanship. By originating as doctoral dissertations, they were required to satisfy at least minimal academic standards. Thus I will be concerned mainly with the political line and historical bias that have come to be the distinguishing marks of the new historians. They themselves make no secret of their line and bias, and often in the most belligerent and provocative manner.

In order for there to be a new history, there must be an old history to be fought and vanquished. There must be a new generation of historians versus an old. It also helps if there is a new methodology allegedly superior to the old. And to make the struggle between the new and old particularly sharp and heated, historical differences should be treated as political conflicts, preferably among radicals, liberals, and conservatives.

For all these reasons, I have found myself after all these years drawn into a struggle over the historical significance of American Communism.

The time has come for me to declare an interest. I first became aware of the part I had been assigned to play in the political drama staged by the new history in 1981. The editor of the Wesleyan University Press asked me to give an opinion of a manuscript submitted to the press by Maurice Isserman. It was later published as *Which Side Were You On?* and subtitled *The American Communist Party During the Second World War.* I agreed reluctantly; after all, I was expected to spend a week or more away from my own work with a pittance for compensation.

To my astonishment, my name appeared on the very first page of the preface. The author had decided to set me up as the prime example of what had been wrong with the old history. Several themes emerged from the preface. One was that the difference between the old and the new had its roots in a generational conflict. Isserman proudly announced that he "shared a common political and intellectual background with this post–New Left generation of historians as well as family ties to the older Left." The new generation had its "roots in the student movement of the 1960s," which "had initially ignored the CP's bitter and complicated history." Isserman also announced that he was taking a "generational approach" to American Communist history, the generation being those Communists "who joined the CP in the early years of the Depression and remained in it until 1956." Above all, he took issue with something I had written in *The Roots of American Communism*, published in 1957 (Viking).

The fighting ground was provided by the following passage from my book:

A rhythmic rotation from Communist sectarianism to Americanized opportunism was set in motion at the outset and has been going on ever since. The periodic rediscovery of "Americanization" by the American Communists has only superficially represented a more independent policy; it has been in reality merely another type of American response to a Russian stimulus. A Russian initiative has always effectively begun and ended it. For this reason, "Americanized" American Communism has been sporadic, superficial, and short-lived. It has corresponded to the fluctuations of Russian policy; it has not obeyed a compelling need within the American Communists themselves.

The issue of Soviet influence, through the Communist International or Comintern, on American Communism inevitably turns up in other writings by the new historians. For the present, it is enough to note that Isserman had set out to do battle with the idea that the Communist Party responded "blindly to external stimuli," though in the end he conceded so much to this view that his own position was finally far from clear. In any case, the preface promised far more than the book itself delivered. Except for a few general pages at the beginning and end, the work, which had its origin as a dissertation, dealt solely with the war years, 1939 to 1945. In that period, Isserman willy-nilly showed how the American Communists had been "doggedly loyal to the current Soviet line," whatever it was. Following the Nazi-Soviet pact, they described the war in Europe as an imperialist war; following the Nazi attack on Russia, it became an all-out anti-Fascist war; then, after the French Communist leader Jacques Duclos published an article attacking the position of Earl Browder, and Browder was expelled from the Party, they subscribed to the Soviets' version of the cold war. Despite my reservations about the appropriateness of the preface and about claims that went beyond the substance of the book itself, I recommended that it should be published, because I felt that the main body was substantial enough to merit publication. My criticisms of the preface were ignored in the published version of the book.

The publication in 1984 of *The Heyday of American Communism* by Harvey Klehr also brought my name into the controversy stirred up by the new historians. As Klehr noted in his preface, I had made my collection of materials on Communism available to him. That was all; I had nothing to do with his book until it was completed; only then did I read the manuscript, when it was sent to me for an opinion by the publisher. What I thought of the book may be gathered from my recommendation: "It is meticulously documented, politically acute, and remarkably thorough. No one who wishes to be informed about this vexed subject can afford to ignore it." Several published reviews agreed with me.

But the new historians were not pleased. It is difficult to tell whether Klehr suffered more from his connection with me or my connection with him. One typical academic reviewer of the new school took Klehr to task for having tried to write "a Draperian history," though generously conceding that it had "yielded some benefits." The review disparaged the work of both Klehr and myself for being "political" and "institutional." It set forth the new academic marching orders—"social and cultural history of the party." It paid tribute to the Popular Front for having "increased the plausibility" of the "self-perception" of the American Communists in the mid-1930s. According to this "self-perception" they had seen themselves "not only as faithful members of an international Communist movement but also as advocates of an authentic American radicalism." Above all, Klehr had committed the sin of having stressed the theme of American Communism's subservience to Moscow, in which respect his "approach and analysis have been deeply influenced by Draper's work."[5]

Isserman also wrote a review of Klehr's book in which he complained that Klehr's conclusion "echoes Draper." Klehr's treatment of the Popular Front betrays his "myopia." He should have recognized that the young people who joined the Party in the early 1930s "carried with them a style and a set of concerns that marked them off from older Communists." Isserman wondered how it was that the American Communists gained so much influence and membership in the late 1930s, a problem also raised by others. Another count against Klehr is that he used "a traditional method of inquiry" and was not sufficiently impressed by "recent works of oral history and autobiography." Above all, however, it is Klehr's view of what made the American Communists different from members of other radical movements that rankles—the view that "its special relationship to the Soviet Union" set it apart and ultimately determined its fate.[6]

Other reviews by new historians made a number of the same

[5] Gerstle, *Reviews in American History*, pp. 559–66.
[6] *In These Times*, April 4–10, 1984.

points. One criticized Klehr's "fundamentally institutional approach" and wanted him to be concerned with "grass roots organizing." It accused him of "obsessive interest in the heavy hand of the Comintern," which made him go "against the grain of recent scholarship on the CP, which has emphasized its *social* history—the stories of the men and women who passed out leaflets, sold the *Daily Worker* on the corner, and marched in demonstrations" (italics in original). By using oral history, the new scholarship "has generally offered a critical but generally favorable assessment of the party's actions and have [*sic*] emphasized the party's flexibility and responsiveness to local conditions." Again the question is raised, as if it were a mystery never before encountered: "Why did the Communist party appeal to so many committed people and become the dominant force on the American left during the 1930s?" For this reviewer the Party became, despite its close ties with and even subservience to Moscow, "at least for a time, an authentic expression of the American radical tradition."[7]

Another academic reviewer of the same school of thought also connected Klehr's work with my own; the best thing he could say about it was that it is "useful." Unfortunately, however, it is "essentially a political history," unlike the labors of other historians "to reconstruct aspects of the CP's social history." As a result of the difference, "this newer scholarship often presents a more positive view of Communist efforts than Klehr entertains." Better to look forward to studies "which will be less concerned with national party leaders and the Comintern, and more interested in the rank-and-file and other relatively neglected topics."[8]

An openly Communist review of Klehr's book by a tenured professor in a major university was almost apoplectic in its abuse and distortion. It cuttingly put him down as "an intellectual 'relic' of the early 1950s," who identifies with "Theodore Draper, Midge Decter, Sidney Hook, and other aging members of the cold war establishment," all of whom are said to "dream, along with Ronald Reagan," of past glories.[9] Aging, yes, alas, but hardly a harmonious quartet.

---

[7] Roy Rosenzweig, *Political Science Quarterly*, Winter 1984–85, pp. 758–59.

[8] William C. Pratt, *Minnesota History*, Winter 1984, p. 161.

[9] Norman Markowitz, *Political Affairs*, May 1984, pp. 39–40.

I have gone into some detail about these reviews because they show where the battle lines have been drawn. I have brought myself into the story because I have been brought into it. I have thought it worthwhile to revisit the Communist scene, at least historically, because real questions have been raised about the nature of American Communism by a younger generation searching for answers just as my own used to search for them.

The new generation came of age politically in the 1960s and 1970s, yet its interests have little or nothing to do with American Communism during these decades. It appears, rather, to be fascinated by American Communism in the 1930s and particularly during the short-lived Popular Front period. Because I had dealt with the preceding decade, the new historians have found Klehr's book more disturbing than my own, though much of the criticism of his work might just as well have been aimed at mine. The generational aspect of this academic phenomenon is insisted on by the new historians, as if belonging to the right new generation were a condition for doing history the right way.

Still, the questions and problems which have again arisen deserve to be addressed on their own merits. New materials, in the form of ex-Communists' memoirs, oral histories, and specialized studies, have become the stock in trade of the new historians, who seem to think that they can find new revelations in them. I have examined the new material, especially that of greatest interest to the new historians, in search of these revelations. I have mainly found revelations about the new historians.

3

What was the relationship between American Communism and the Soviet Union, the Communist Party of the United States and the Comintern? I have already cited my finding of 1957. Klehr summed it up in 1984 as follows:

> The Party's lurches were not in response to any internal changes in American society or the Party itself, but reflected the pull of an external force. If the needs of Russian policy dictated a revolutionary or sectarian Comintern policy, the American Communists swung over to the left. When those needs changed, they swung back to a more reformist or opportunistic line. Within the limits of their knowledge, American

Communists always strove to provide what the Comintern wanted, no more, no less . . .

In the last analysis, one thing gave every Communist party its specific character among radical movements—its special relationship to the Soviet Union.[10]

One of the ex-Communist memoirs invoked by the new historians is George Charney's *A Long Journey*. Charney was about twenty-seven years old when he joined the Communist Party in 1933, thus making him an exemplar of the 1930s generation. He stayed in for twenty-five years, until 1958, one of the last to leave in that exodus. I knew him slightly; he was a type of sincere, dedicated, hardworking Party organizer. He conforms almost exactly to Isserman's model of the 1930–56 "continuum."

"Not long after I joined the party," Charney tells us, "I came to accept each doctrine promulgated by the party as an 'article of faith,' never to be questioned." One of his first experiences came during the municipal election campaign in New York in 1933 against Mayor Fiorello LaGuardia, then an enemy of the people. "Our policy, of course, originated in Moscow and was determined by the theses of the Sixth World Congress, reiterated only recently at its 13th Plenum, whose main emphasis was the preparation for universal revolutionary struggles."

When the Popular Front was promulgated at the Seventh World Congress of the Comintern in 1935, Charney and those like him were ready for the change. "Overnight we adjusted our evaluation of Roosevelt and the New Deal." The new line "reflected what many of us believed but could not articulate." They would have obeyed the old line, if that had been the will of the Party, but were much happier with the new. Yet, in retrospect, it occurred to him that their immediate adaptation was "one of the tragedies of this history," because "in each case the decision was made elsewhere—by the 'leading party,' the party of the October Revolution." Even in 1935, he "could not but be aware that, just as in 1933, the line originated from abroad." But this time at least, "it coincided with American realities and enabled the party to take on the appearance of an American movement."

The Popular Front lasted only four years. When the Nazi-Soviet pact came in 1939, Charney and the rest were again put to the test.

[10] Harvey Klehr, *The Heyday of American Communism* (Basic Books, 1984), p. 415.

"The pact left us limp and confused." It was a "shock." But shock or no, "such was our attachment to the party that we listened and accepted the explanations."[11]

Earl Browder was ousted as Party leader in 1945. Long after the event, Charney wondered: "How did this happen? How could we accept intervention from an outside source . . . ? Everything was settled in Moscow . . ." The old reflex still operated: "In an amazingly short period of time, the viewpoint we had developed over a decade in the period of democratic unity was virtually washed away . . . Most of us in the ranks and in the middle leadership adjusted to this line without hesitation or caution."

Nikita Khrushchev's "secret speech" in 1956 was something else for Charney's generation. The official recital of Stalin's crimes and atrocities was too much to bear. The Hungarian eruption and Soviet intervention in November of that year added to the turmoil. It took Charney longer than most to react. Finally, he left the Party. In the end, he reflected: "We lived and functioned in good part on the basis of world issues and the direction of the Communist power center, on the basis of our international credentials and the vague expectation that a new radical upsurge would eventually unfold under our leadership." He explained why the shock of 1956 had been so great for his generation: "Moreover, as a product of the 1930's, we had acquired an implicit faith in the Soviet Union as the 'Land of Socialism.' Our illusions about Soviet democracy and justice were greater, and so was the shock of disillusionment."

Yet some new historians have seized on Charney's book as evidence that "in more subtle ways," the Communists "shaped the party to fit their own needs and expectations." Isserman was especially impressed by Charney's story that, in mid-1934, he had put out a leaflet for workers of the Sunshine Biscuit company in New York without ending it with the current Party slogan, "For a Soviet America."[12] The section organizer caught the omission and "crushed" Charney with his criticism. Charney says that the lesson he learned from this little incident, told by him somewhat uncertainly thirty-four years later, was: "The Seventh Congress was still a year away,

---

[11] When I left the Communist movement after the full implications of the Nazi-Soviet pact had become clear, none of my friends from the student movement of the early 1930s left with me. Almost none would have anything to do with me—until 1956.

[12] Maurice Isserman, *Which Side Were You On?* (Wesleyan University Press, 1982), p. xi.

and we found to our dismay that we could be as guilty anticipating a new line as deviating from it after it was adopted. But we were neither prophets nor dissidents."

Charney, still a neophyte with little more than six months in the Party, was hardly in a position to provide any serious evidence of how Communists "shaped the party to fit their needs and expectations." On the contrary, Charney clearly told the story to show how he had gone through "the process of personal transformation, to sublimate myself in the movement, to become a good Communist . . ." The incident cannot be understood in isolation from the rest of Charney's transformation into a "good Communist" for the next quarter of a century. Such scraps of dubious evidence of how the 1930s generation remolded the Communist Party in its own image or had an important part in anticipating the Popular Front tell more about the desperate expedients of some new historians to justify a thesis than they convey any sense of reality about what actually happened to that generation in the Party.[13]

Another memoir by an ex-Communist popular with the new historians is *Steve Nelson: American Radical*, written by two graduate students, James R. Barrett and Rob Ruck, from interviews with Nelson. Nelson was born in Croatia in 1903, came to the United States at the age of seventeen, and was drawn into the Communist movement three years later, formally joining the Party in the mid-1920s. He therefore somewhat antedates the 1930s generation. He became a full-time organizer in 1929; was sent to the Comintern's Lenin School in Moscow in 1931; served as a political commissar in the Abraham Lincoln Battalion during the Spanish Civil War. His disillusionment began to set in with the Khrushchev revelations and Soviet intervention in Hungary in 1956, and he left the following year; nevertheless, his emotional and political break with the Soviet Union did not come until 1968.

His story is that of an authentic Communist middle-level "functionary" or "cadre." It is well worth the effort put into it. Nelson speaks of himself as one who "could not and would not renounce my past" and was "still proud to have been a Communist and still respected many of the people with whom I'd worked over the years." His regret for the years spent in the Party is thus much less acute

---

[13] George Charney, *A Long Journey* (Quadrangle, 1972), pp. 29, 37, 42–44, 59–60, 124, 143–45, 252, 276.

than that of Charney. Nevertheless, they substantially agree on the relationship of American Communism and the Soviet Union. "We treated the Soviet Union as the single pivot in the world around which everything else was centered. Nothing else mattered . . . We had the mentality that the Soviet Union was always right and that its interests were paramount." When the excommunication of Tito came in 1948, "we were still in the habit of tailing the Soviet Party." In one passage he is angry for having been "so blind in our adherence to Soviet policy and so mechanical in our application of Marxism." American Communism "has remained one of the most backward parties in the Western world and one of the most rigid in its adherence to the Soviet line."[14]

Yet the two graduate students who edited the book could not resist distorting it. In their introduction, they made Nelson view the Party as "a foot soldier" and a "rank and file organizer," when he was obviously a well-known leader just below the top rank, entrusted with one important assignment after another. They also softened his own repeated judgment of how much the Soviet Union influenced the American Party by making it seem only half the equation: "While Nelson substantiates the role of the Soviet Union in influencing the American party, he offers a counterpoint—that much of the politics of the American Communist movement came not from Moscow but from its involvement in the social struggles of the times." Nelson knew and says that the Soviet role was more than that of mere "influence"; at one point he decries "our mechanical application of Comintern policies to American problems." Nelson's book, as well as the others, is treated as if it were a department store, where one can buy what one wants and ignore all the rest.

Other memoirs of the 1930s allude to the unequal character of the relationship. A favorite of the new historians is *A Long View from the Left* by Al Richmond. He came into the Communist movement in 1928 at the age of fifteen and stayed in for forty years, most of them spent as editor of the *People's World* in San Francisco. He notes that 1929 and 1945 were turning points in American Communist history—1929 because that was the year Jay Lovestone was ousted from the leadership; 1945, the year Earl Browder was ousted. Both upheavals took place, Richmond recognizes, "with a decisive push

[14] Steve Nelson, James R. Barrett, Rob Ruck, *Steve Nelson: American Radical* (University of Pittsburgh Press, 1981), pp. 249, 250, 290, 387, 393.

from abroad"; both times the problems "were not resolved independently with the inner resources of American communism." In between came the Nazi-Soviet pact—"a megaton shock, stunning, sudden, wrenching." Nevertheless, despite being "unprepared, knocked off balance by this abrupt turn, our reflex defense of the treaty had elements of the frenetic." Khrushchev's secret report also hit with "shattering impact." Richmond again stayed on, still not shattered enough.

What seems to have knocked him over was a trip to Czechoslovakia in 1966 and the subsequent Soviet overthrow of the Dubček regime. He finally unburdened himself in a series of articles which were promptly "castigated" by the present Party leader, Gus Hall. He confides that he should have resigned but did not; he was evidently still a member of the national committee until 1972. His book ends vaguely, as if he could not bring himself to tell how his forty years in the Party came to an end. How tragic the break must have been for him is merely suggested by a remark that he felt like "a solitary old man of fifty-five."[15]

It is noteworthy that in this and in almost all other cases the breaking point came in response to an international crisis brought on by the Soviet Union. Domestic differences could be survived; something that struck at the heart of faith in the Soviet Union could not. As Steve Nelson put it, "As has so often been the case, international events had their inevitable impact on the Party and its domestic relations."[16] The revelations of Stalin's enormities were so shattering because he had for so many years been made sacrosanct. In revolutions as in other faiths, the greater the illusion, the greater the disillusionment.

Two other memoirs have been written by, or written for, black Communists. The most interesting is that of Hosea Hudson, thanks to the remarkable persistence and skill of Nell Irvin Painter. She coaxed a story out of Hudson that belongs with the best of black—or white—autobiographies. It does not have much bearing on the issue of Soviet influence because, as she puts it, he was a "docile Party member who never raised questions prematurely." He joined the Party in Birmingham in 1931 and never suffered disenchantment.

---

[15] Al Richmond, *A Long View from the Left* (Houghton Mifflin, 1972), pp. 144–45, 226, 283, 365, 380, 425, 429.

[16] Nelson et al., *Steve Nelson: American Radical*, p. 290.

It is easy to understand why, when he says: "I found this Party, a party of the working class, gave me rights equal with all others regardless of color, sex, or age or educational standards. I with my uneducation could express myself, without being made fun of by others who could read well and fast." When Browder decided to "liquidate" the Party in 1944 and convert it into an "association," Hudson went along with all the others because "we considered the national leadership knows more about what they were doing than we did." When Browder came under fire from Duclos, "we had a big discussion to see where we made our mistake at. We came out criticizing Browder's position." Hudson's experience is only *one* black Communist's story, representative only in some ways, but of its kind richly worth more attention than it has received.[17]

The other black Communist memoir is something else again. The title chosen by Harry Haywood, *Black Bolshevik* (Lake View Press, 1978), tells how the author conceives of himself. Haywood came into the Communist movement in the early 1920s and was quickly sent to Moscow for political schooling. The main interest of his book is how he was converted under Soviet tutelage to the policy of "self-determination for the Black Belt." Haywood was almost alone at first to embrace this quasi-separatist idea; and it proved to be the cause of his rise and fall in the Party. He rose high in the black leadership as long as the policy was Party doctrine in the early 1930s; he became a misfit when the line changed with the Popular Front in the middle of the decade. Haywood ended up a disappointed, embittered outcast, the last of the red-hot black American Bolsheviks. His political career was completely bound up with the Soviet Union and Soviet-implanted policy.

The new historians make much of these memoirs, as if they provide particularly novel insights into American Communism. They undoubtedly fill out the story with much personal experience and local detail. But on the issue of how much and in what way the American Party was dominated from the Soviet Union, do they really say anything different from what Klehr and I have written? These memoirs virtually shout out the same message, if more in grief than in anger.

---

[17] Nell Irvin Painter, *The Narrative of Hosea Hudson* (Harvard University Press, 1979), pp. 25, 180, 307, 309.

4

The new historians have thus been struggling with an old question to which they think they have found a new answer. The question was implicit in the title of my second book on American Communism, *American Communism and Soviet Russia* (Viking, 1960). As I summed up in the last sentence: "Each generation had to discover for itself in its own way that, even at the price of virtually committing political suicide, American Communism would continue above all to serve the interests of Soviet Russia." This answer has drawn the fire of the new historians.

One of them has tried to use some of the memoirs mentioned previously to reach a different answer. The effort is typical enough to merit closer examination. Professor Roy Rosenzweig starts with a large, general proposition—"if one thread runs through all these accounts it is that we must understand the history of the CPUSA as distinctively American." That is the main challenge of the new to the old history. The challenge is then aimed directly at me—"whether explicitly or not, they seek to refute the concluding line of Theodore Draper's influential study of *American Communism and Soviet Russia*." The evidence for that distinctive Americanism supposedly comes from the memoirs of Nelson and Hudson.

On examination, the most that can be gathered from them, even in Rosenzweig's argument, is that in 1928 and 1929 the new line calling for the organization of "dual" unions—i.e., Communist unions parallel to those in the AFL—was shaped by a combination of Comintern directives and American conditions. Rosenzweig himself says that, while local circumstances contributed to the form of "Party actions," it is still impossible to deny "that the American party carried out Soviet directives with sometimes disastrous results." The directives were basic, the actions dependent on local circumstances. This conjunction hardly bears out the command that "we must understand the history of the CPUSA as distinctively American."

Rosenzweig sums up:

> The problem with Draper's analysis, then, is not with its assertion of the fealty of American Communists to their Russian comrades—that was a connection that American Party members not only never denied but repeatedly affirmed. Rather, it is the suggestion that American

Party members were merely puppets of the Soviet Union with no independent thoughts and actions of their own and that they always put the needs of the Soviet Union above those of American workers. In their detailed depictions of the actions and consciousness of rank and file Communists, these autobiographies clearly refuted such contentions.[18]

This challenge offers an opportunity to get away from generalities and to look more closely at a specific case.

Rosenzweig's original proposition is a basic generalization—that the history of the American Party is "distinctively American." The evidence adduced by him proves to be restricted to a single period, 1928 and 1929, in a single field, trade union policy. Not only does this alleged case prove little by itself about the entire history of the American Party, but it is thoroughly misconstrued. The Communist trade union leader of that period, William Z. Foster, at first opposed Communist dual unions but he did not do so because he expected to be welcomed into the AFL unions from which Communists had been expelled; he opposed dual unions because he saw no future in them and did not wish to give up trying to reach the majority of organized workers in the old unions despite all the obstacles to be faced in them.

It does not matter in this connection whether the Comintern was right to order dual unions or Foster was right to oppose them; what matters is that the order came from Moscow and was reluctantly obeyed. In any event, how could this case history of the American Party show that it was "distinctively American" if it admittedly "carried out Soviet directives" and owed "fealty" to the Russian comrades? "Fealty," indeed, is not a bad word for this relationship; the dictionary says that it means "the fidelity of a vassal or feudal tenant to his lord."

Only exaggeration and distortion make it possible to pick such a quarrel with me. I had never suggested that American Party members were "merely puppets of the Soviet Union with no independent thoughts and actions of their own." In fact, I went to some pains to describe how the American trade union leadership under Foster had opposed the directive to organize new trade unions that had been imposed by Moscow in 1928 and 1929. Foster fell into line only when he recognized that Moscow was bound to prevail, with him or without

[18] Roy Rosenzweig, *International Labor and Working Class History*, Fall 1983, pp. 32–33.

him. My account of this episode was hardly a suggestion of mere puppetry, a word I have never used. It was a suggestion that whatever independent thoughts and actions American Party members had, their fealty to their Russian comrades ultimately prevailed.

The problem of the interaction between the Soviet Union and American Communism haunts the work of the new historians. It seems necessary for them to insist that the two components are equivalent or comparable and come together to make a "blend."

For example, Professor Kenneth Waltzer has complained that earlier historians had written books about the Party "as a monolithic totalitarian organization whose history reflected the shifts and turns in the Comintern line." But now a different presupposition has taken hold. "The reexploration of Communist history proceeds on a shifted assumption: that while affiliated with and obedient to the Comintern, American communism was also shaped by national experience . . . The new view is that Communist behavior was shaped by dictates from Moscow, but also by complicated interaction among national and local factors . . ." Thus he arrives at the rule that "each national communism was a blend of international communism and national experience."[19]

The "blend theory" is one of those half-truths that lead to a greater and more serious untruth. There was a blend, but it was not the kind of blend presented here. The "general line" was always set in Moscow. Its application was left to the various national parties, closely monitored, frequently criticized, and periodically worked over in Moscow. Local leaders tried to apply the general line as best they could, leaving scope for their own initiative—but woe to those who strayed too far for too long. National and local factors "complicated" the application of the "dictates from Moscow"—but the dictates were still dictates, ultimately unchallengeable by those whose task was to apply them.

These so-called complications did not live a life of their own; they were no more than might be expected of human beings trying to put into practice a general line according to their best understanding and in more or less favorable circumstances. The general line and its application were akin to the difference between strategy and tactics,

[19] Waltzer, *Reviews in American History*, June 1983, pp. 259–60, 266. The same general approach is taken by Gerstle, *Reviews in American History*, December 1984, pp. 559–66.

a favorite military analogy in Communist doctrine. Only the tactics, and then not always fully, were left to the initiative of the national parties or to local groups by national leaderships.

This division of power was hardly the "blend" that the new historians have in mind. More often than not, the Comintern dictated the same strategy and tactics to all the parties, and the national parties dictated the same strategy and tactics to all the local units, whatever the national and local "complications." As in all large and far-flung organizations, there were exceptions, lags, and misunderstandings, especially in the case of groups farthest from the center, though usually for relatively brief periods. No broad generalization can be based on them or the exceptions made into the rule, as if they carried equal weight with the main Party line.

Thus the new historians attribute the most inflated significance to the slightest scrap of evidence of local initiative or deviation. George Charney's little leaflet omitting the slogan "For a Soviet America," as I have noted, is made into a demonstration of how most Communists "shaped the party to fit their own needs and expectations." It would have been more persuasive if, at the time, Charney had been in the Party for much more than six months and had been more experienced in following the Party line or had not quickly learned the lesson that it did not pay to anticipate it or deviate from it afterward.

This bad habit of taking isolated and usually abortive individual incidents to make a basic point comes out most sharply and characteristically in the treatment of the Popular Front. More than anything else, it has attracted the favorable attention of the new historians. They have also made themselves the champions of "social history" in order to do battle with the allegedly "political" and "institutional" history of the old historians.

5

The Popular Front phase lasted only about four years, from 1935 to 1939. The American Communist movement was formed in 1919 and has existed in one form or another for sixty-six years. The Popular Front, therefore, occupied less than one sixteenth of the Party's entire history. It may be of peculiar interest as a token of what the Party might have been, if it had been a different kind of party; it cannot be seen as more than a short, aborted interlude. As such, its

significance for any basic generalization about the Communist movement is strictly limited.

One reason the Popular Front holds such charms for the new
historians is that they think it demonstrated an independent American Communist "capacity for independent thinking" and gave
"American Communists the opportunity to act on their genuinely
felt desires to adapt their radicalism to American political traditions
and practice."[20]

Here again it is best to examine how a new historian goes about
making good on these claims.

Professor Gary Gerstle cites two examples of independent thinking. One is that of Sam Darcy, the Party organizer in California, in
1934. Gerstle knows as much about it as he learned from Harvey
Klehr's book *The Heyday of American Communism*. Klehr used, in
part, an interview I had with Darcy. This is Gerstle's version:

> Yet as early as 1934 a number of American Communists had begun
> to experiment with popular fronts of their own. Klehr recounts the
> efforts of Sam Darcy, an important party functionary in California, to
> forge an alliance with Upton Sinclair and his End Poverty in California
> (EPIC) movement. Although Klehr does not explain Darcy's position
> in depth, it seems that Darcy sought an alliance with EPIC in order
> to free the party from the debilitating political isolation that Third
> Period strategies had imposed on it. The party's leadership, however,
> flatly rejected Darcy's proposal, and ordered him to run a full slate of
> Communist candidates against EPIC and to attack Sinclair with
> venom.[21]

This is Klehr's original version:

> Sam Darcy later claimed that they had reached an informal agree-
> ment: the EPIC movement would not nominate a candidate for con-
> troller. The Communists would run Anita Whitney, scion of an old
> California family, for that post, and not run anyone for governor,
> allowing their supporters to vote for Sinclair. At the party convention
> in early April 1934, Darcy presented his plan to the Politburo. He was
> rudely rebuffed. Browder instructed him to expose and denounce Sin-
> clair, and, in the bargain, to run for governor of California himself.[22]

And here is the lesson drawn by Gerstle from Darcy's "experiment"
in independent thinking:

---

[20] Gerstle, *Reviews in American History*, p. 562.

[21] Ibid., p. 563.

[22] Klehr, *The Heyday of American Communism*, p. 415.

What this episode makes clear is that party members voiced their dissatisfaction with the strategies of the Third Period and expressed their desire for a broadly-based radical alliance *before* the Comintern officially endorsed such sentiments in 1935 [*italics in original*].

The operation performed on Klehr's matter-of-fact story might serve as an object lesson in a seminar on how not to revise history. One Party member, Darcy, has been transformed into "party members." There is no evidence that Darcy was expressing a desire for a new general line of "broadly-based radical alliance" that would be applicable everywhere; the California situation was almost always sui generis and particularly at this time. Darcy evidently saw the possibility for a very good deal—a Communist state controller with EPIC votes in exchange for an EPIC governor with many fewer Communist votes. In fact, the Communists might have cost Sinclair more votes than they could bring to him. In any case, Darcy was not permitted to "experiment" with a popular front of his own; he never got that far. This episode makes clear that whatever dissatisfaction local leaders may have had with the pre–Popular Front line and whatever desire they may have expressed to change it prematurely, they were controlled by the top leadership and did what they were told to do. The moral is very different from the one that Gerstle seeks to draw from it.

In addition, Darcy in 1934 was maneuvering in a Communist transition period—the "united front from below" was giving way to the united front from above and finally to the Popular Front. Admittedly he was trying to do some independent tactical thinking beyond what was still permissible—a striking commentary on the notion of Professor Roy Rosenzweig that "party directives could be interpreted or reinterpreted according to local needs or conditions" by people in such fairly high positions as Steve Nelson or similarly Sam Darcy.[23] Yet Darcy could claim vindication when the line changed in Moscow the following year. To be premature was just as hazardous as to lag behind.

Darcy's story is even more complicated. Ten years later, he was something of a maverick again—in the opposite way. In 1944, he was the only one in the top leadership expelled for having openly opposed Earl Browder's transformation of the Party into an "asso-

[23] Rosenzweig, *International Labor and Working Class History*, p. 32.

ciation," a move that seemed to most Communists to follow from the organizational logic of the wartime ultra–Popular Front policy if pursued to the end. Thus Darcy might be cited as both a premature "rightist" and "leftist"—and was punished both times and vindicated both times only a year later by dictates from Moscow. Unlike many others, however, Darcy had had enough the second time.

Oddly, after having told us what to think of Darcy's earlier show of independent thinking, Gerstle apparently bethought himself that it might not be enough. He then brought forth his second witness, George Charney, the former Communist who, in his memoirs, tells us, more than three decades after the event, that he felt that the Popular Front "reflected what many of us really believed but could not articulate."[24] This inarticulate belief, whatever it was, was hardly the same as a "capacity for independent thinking." Nevertheless, Charney's belated articulation of the inarticulate suggests, according to Gerstle, that "some Communists sought to ground party activity in an analysis of American social and political conditions." Charney's vague unease has now been metamorphosed into an "analysis."

Charney also leads Gerstle to entertain the possibility that "American Communists in the mid-1930s could have seen themselves not only as faithful members of an international Communist movement but also as advocates of an authentic American radicalism." After which, Gerstle immediately adds: "The evolution of the Popular Front in this country increased the plausibility of this self-perception." Gerstle, it should be noted, had previously called for a new history that would "explore the extent to which American communism developed as an authentic expression of American radicalism."[25]

The technique of planting ideas, without accepting full responsibility for them, is fully displayed here. Some Communists undoubtedly thought that they could reconcile the "international Communist" and the "authentic American" aspects of the Popular Front. But, in the end, did they? Were the two really reconcilable? What is it worth to entertain a mere "possibility" of how American Communists "could have seen themselves"? And in but two successive sentences, "possibility" makes a jump to "plausibility." Gerstle

---

[24] Charney, *A Long Journey*, p. 59.
[25] Gerstle, *Reviews in American History*, pp. 561, 563–64.

is not the only new historian who resorts to such slippery methods to get across the idea of Communists as authentic American radicals during their Popular Front.

Why has so much significance been attributed to such marginal, isolated, dubious evidence as that provided by Darcy and Charney?[26] All pertain for good reason to the Popular Front. It is the rock upon which the new historians have built their airy castle of a Communist "authentic American radicalism." To bolster their case, the new historians like to point to two other aspects of the Popular Front— that it came as a relief to the American Communists, and that it brought many thousands of new members into the Party. On some of these matters the new historians are not wrong; they have merely interpreted them wrongly.

Anyone who was a member of the Communist Party for more than five years was almost certain to live through a change of line. If a line had been "sectarian," it suffered from lack of popular appeal but made up for that in excess of orthodoxy; if a line had been "opportunistic," it gained in popular appeal but suffered from seeming lack of orthodoxy. In these circumstances neither one nor the other could be altogether satisfying. By the time any one line had run its course, it tended to exhaust either its usefulness or its compatibility with Soviet policy. The new line could then be desired or rationalized because it provided one of the ingredients that the other had lacked. Thus came about the peculiarly Communist cycle of rejoicing at both the birth and death of any particular political line.

---

[26] I have found only one other alleged anticipation of the Popular Front. In his review of Klehr's book, Maurice Isserman wrote: "As early as 1932 Communist college students were reaching out to (or huddling together with) their socialist counterparts in common political enterprises" (*In These Times*, p. 18). This largely apocryphal tale refers to the Communist-led National Student League (NSL) of the early 1930s (I was editor of its magazine, *Student Review*, in 1934 and 1935). It was considered by the Communists to be a "front" organization and thereby enjoyed more leeway than an official Communist organization.

A National Student Anti-War Conference was held in Chicago in December 1932; it was dominated by pro-Communist delegates but some Socialists and pacifists, willing to follow the lead of the NSL, also attended. Some slight concessions were made to the Socialists in the "minimum program" adopted at the conference, and even these were promptly denounced by the leader of the Young Communist League. Communist and Socialist students continued to treat each other with varying degrees of suspicion and hostility until the American Student Union, a merger of the National Student League and the Student League for Industrial Democracy, was formed in December 1935. The "reaching out and huddling together" in 1932 is largely imaginary; in any case, the influence of Communist students in a front organization on the official Party policy was infinitesimal.

The Popular Front came after approximately five years of an exceptionally sectarian policy. Despite the greatest depression in modern times, the Party had made only modest gains in membership and influence. With the shift in tactics, a fresh wind seemed to blow through the Party's ranks; membership rose from about 7,000 in 1930 to some 26,000 in 1934 to 75,000 in 1938. From a small, besieged sect, Communists and fellow travelers (who may have increased Party influence by a factor of five or even more) found themselves welcome in places and organizations that previously had nothing to do with them and with which the Communists would have had nothing to do. It was a heady time.

Yet when the "shock" of the Nazi-Soviet pact changed the line again in 1939, the Party was able to retain most of its members. Then the anti-war, anti-imperialist, anti-Roosevelt line was itself reversed as soon as the Soviet Union was attacked in 1941. Again Party members rejoiced at the turn from one extreme to the other. The new pro-war, patriotic, pro-Roosevelt line enchanted Party members until they were told from abroad in 1945 that it was time to change again. It is the sequence, not merely any one point in it, that must be understood if the Communist movement is to be understood.

Those who stay through various changes of line do so because they have remained loyal to the Party, not to whatever it may temporarily stand for. The generation who were members between 1930 and 1956 stayed through all the changes of line because loyalty to the Party and to the Soviet Union had been burned into their minds and feelings. They had greeted the Popular Front with relief, but by the time it was strangled they owed their first loyalty to the Party, not to the Popular Front. Those who were brought into the Party by a policy would get out with the repudiation of the policy; some did get out, but not most of the generation of 1930–56; and then they got out because their faith in the Soviet Union was shattered, not because their cherished Popular Front had been betrayed.

Thus it is historically myopic to concentrate on how the Popular Front came in to the exclusion of how it went out, to take the Popular Front out of its context in the entire development of the Party, and to base a broad generalization on four of the sixty-six years of the American Party. Long afterward, it is true, the Communists who became disillusioned between 1956 and 1958 looked back to the

Popular Front and World War II "as a kind of golden era in which the party's political successes had grown out of the loosening of the rigid ideological bonds of earlier years." Still, seventeen years passed between 1939 and 1956; the time was too long for the 1956 crisis to have had "its roots in the Popular Front period," despite the nostalgia for the "golden era."[27] The 1956 crisis had its roots in the "implicit faith in the Soviet Union as the 'Land of Socialism,' " which, as George Charney finally understood, had been inculcated in the generation that was "a product of the 1930s."[28]

One of the things that attract the new historians to the Popular Front is the success it had in increasing the membership and influence of the Party. Just why it succeeded, and why it ultimately failed, seems to evade them. They might have found a good part of the answer in Steve Nelson's memoirs: "Tight discipline enabled us to be effective far beyond our numbers and to accomplish all sorts of good works, but it also made us more vulnerable to Stalinism."[29] The apparent paradox was that Communist organization and discipline paid off the most in the service of a policy that was most distant from orthodox Communist ideology. The Popular Front was a policy of the Communists but it was not a Communist policy. It was at its most extreme not even a radical policy, unless following in the wake of Franklin D. Roosevelt and John L. Lewis was evidence of radicalism.

Another paradox in the late 1930s was the circumstance that the Socialists stood to the left of the Communists, probably one reason that the former did not do so well. Socialism was put in cold storage by the Communists during the Popular Front. Communist trade unionism also followed fairly traditional lines. If the Popular Front had been permitted to run its course, it might well have turned out to be the forerunner of a non-Socialist reform movement somewhat to the left of the Democratic Party or even a left wing of the Democratic Party.

Some such goal was, in effect, Browder's implicit aim when he proposed transforming the Party into an "association" in 1944. He then carried almost the entire Party with him. It might have worked,

[27] Maurice Isserman, *The Socialist Review*, December 1981, pp. 77, 79.
[28] Charney, *A Long Journey*, p. 276.
[29] Nelson et al., *Steve Nelson: American Radical*, p. 416.

if he had had enough time to regenerate the organization and liberate it from dependence on the Soviet Union. His organizational reform never sank deep enough in the few months left to him as leader, and the dependence on the Soviet Union had sunk in too deeply over too many years to be rooted out quickly enough. As long as organizational discipline and submission to the Soviet Union remained, policy could still be turned on and off at the behest of the leadership—with Browder or without him.

For these reasons, the Communist-style Popular Front did not and could not develop into an authentic American Socialism or radicalism. One of the new historians' older mentors has lamented that the Popular Front "had no chance to realize its potential." Nevertheless, he claims that "it proved to be a highly effective instrument for a Marxist party" and "could serve as an example—suitably revised to fit changing circumstances—for socialist tactics in a strongly capitalist society."[30] This view has helped to mislead the new historians. The Popular Front did not serve as an example of "socialist tactics"; it used non-Socialist tactics in deference to a strongly capitalist society. The peculiar nature of the Popular Front derived from the fact that it was a tactical turn by a Communist Party with its chameleon-like faculty for changing the color of its political skin while remaining inwardly the same. This character enabled the Party to keep on a leash divergent strands of its makeup—loyalty to the Soviet Union (which was never tampered with during the period of the great Stalinist purges of the same 1930s), a disciplined, hardened leadership (which had survived several changes of line), and a fabulously opportunistic willingness to invoke Franklin D. Roosevelt and John L. Lewis as its involuntary leaders, the better to flaunt the banner of born-again Americanism. Those who see only the last in the Popular Front forget that it was the Popular Front of the Communist Party, not a Popular Front sui generis. That is why it could not realize its potential; the reason for its end in 1939 was consistent with its beginning in 1935.

The 1930s generation had its chance to show how different it was in 1939. It failed because its loyalty to the Party and its faith in Stalin and the Soviet Union were vastly greater than its attachment to the Popular Front.

[30] Max Gordon, *Radical History Review*, Spring 1980, pp. 134–35.

6

Broader questions of historical method have also been raised by the new historians. They blame the older historians as much for their methods as for their matter.

"Social history" is in; "political" and "institutional" history is out. The best thing that the new historians can think of saying about themselves is that they are "social historians"; the worst thing they can say about others is that they are political or institutional historians. The cult of social history is not limited to these new historians, but it has rarely been practiced so crudely and made to serve such tendentious political purposes.

For example, the first serious, large-scale history of American Communism, by Irving Howe and Lewis Coser, made a cogent analysis of its "totalitarian" character.[31] Now a new historian has hit back in this way:

> In the late 1970s a new generation of historians, influenced by the New Left and using the methods of the new social history, began to challenge Howe's and Coser's view that the Communist party was totalitarian. A number of social historians argued that such factors as race, ethnicity, and position in the party shaped the experience of individual Communists as much as did Stalinist indoctrination.[32]

This is another version of the "blend" theory. The first sentence refers to the Party; the second, to individual Communists. The experience of individual Communists was shaped by race, ethnicity, and position in the Party in some respects and by Stalinist indoctrination in other respects. The Stalinist indoctrination that persuaded most Party members from top to bottom to go along with the Nazi-Soviet pact at the expense of the Popular Front had little or nothing to do with race, ethnicity, and position in the Party; it had everything to do with loyalty to the Soviet Union and faith in Stalin's leadership.

Again and again reviews of Klehr's book by new historians indict it for going "against the grain of recent scholarship on the CP, which has emphasized its *social* history—the stories of the men and women who passed out leaflets, sold the *Daily Worker* on the corner, and

---

[31] Irving Howe and Lewis Coser, *The American Communist Party: A Critical History* (1957; reissue of 1962 edition by Da Capo, 1974), especially Chap. 11.

[32] Gerstle, *Reviews in American History*, p. 560.

marched in demonstrations."[33] This is an example of the special meaning given to this variety of social history. It invariably applies only to the Communist "rank and file" as if the middle and top leadership did not have a social history. By separating the rank and file from the leadership and calling for stories such as selling the *Daily Worker* on street corners, the new historians reduce the rank and file to people who perform only the most humble and menial tasks without regard for what was in the *Daily Worker* or what policy they were carrying out at the grass-roots level. Without seeming to realize it, the new historians adopt a most demeaning attitude toward the Communist rank and file. Or else they make it seem as if there were two Communist parties, one of the leadership and the other of the rank and file, each going its own way.

The effect of this type of social history is to depoliticize the most political of all political movements. The Communist Party politicized everything and made no secret of it. The Communist leadership spent most of its energies bearing down on the rank and file to carry out whatever policies or campaigns happened to be uppermost at the moment. By themselves, the commissioned officers of the Party would have amounted to little without the enlisted personnel. Any social history worthy of the name would study the Party as an organic or at least structured whole in which different tasks were carried out by different ranks in different circumstances. It is one thing to see the Party from the bottom up; it is another thing to see the Party only at the bottom.

The social history of the new historians is a cop-out. It is a dodge to avoid facing the political reality of American Communism by discrediting political history. The favoritism shown to the rank and file has the advantage of dealing with the people most removed from the making of Party policy and, therefore, seemingly most innocent of what was done in the name of the Party. But the Party could not have done without the service of the rank and file who year after year, often decade after decade, followed the Party line through all of its twists and turns. Rank-and-file Communists were not political neuters who merely passed out leaflets, sold *Daily Workers*, and marched in demonstrations. They recruited most of the new members through example and solicitation. Many of them were also the most rigid and fossilized element in the Party. George Charney noted that

[33] Rosenzweig, *Political Science Quarterly*, p. 759.

William Z. Foster's main base in New York in his successful struggle against 1956 "revisionists" was the garment district.

Charney knew this familiar type of Party member better than any of the new historians who romanticize it:

> It was a large section of several hundred members, who, with few exceptions, had belonged to the party since the twenties . . . Their dreams originated with the October Revolution and they never wavered in their devotion to the cause.[34]

Hosea Hudson eulogized the rank and file in these terms:

> The Party was a political party, and only the most developed, the most developed and class-conscious, the people who's willing to sacrifice, to take the sacrifice, to make the sacrifice and would be willing to accept the discipline of the Party could be members of the Party.[35]

Hudson at least took the Communist politics of the rank and file seriously, as the old-timers themselves did, or they would hardly have remained in the Party for so long.

Social history is not at issue; it has established itself as one of the major fields of the historical discipline. It is a protean form, not easily pressed into a single formula. Much depends on where, when, and why. What makes the new historians' exploitation of it reprehensible is that they seek to use it as a weapon against other types of history. Only social history, they imply, can unlock the deepest secrets of the Communist movement, as if it had a monopoly of the historical truth or reality.

Yet if there is one place where social history alone is inadequate, it is in the study of the Communist movement, a political movement par excellence. A social history of a Communist Party divorced from its political organization and institutional structure is so farfetched that it can be explained only by a "hidden agenda" to draw attention away from the organization and the structure. The new historians habitually blur or wipe out the distinction between the history of a Communist Party and the biography of individual Communists; these are undoubtedly related, but they cannot be treated in the same way, nor can one be made to substitute for the other. The Party takes its

---

[34] Charney, *A Long Journey*, p. 283.
[35] Painter, *The Narrative of Hosea Hudson*, p. 119.

political line from the leadership, and its institutional setup rests on the leadership, so that the leadership cannot be ignored or minimized in a Party history.

One young historian sagely advises that in studying the Communist Party we should not underestimate or ignore "who stopped over at one's house after dinner to play cards, listen to a ball game, sit on the porch drinking a beer, discussing the news," or "whom one could depend on to take care of the kids, lend one money, go shopping."[36] Yet everything about everyone is not necessarily significant or relevant, even in social history. What a historian underestimates or ignores depends on what the subject or problem is. Some Communists played cards or listened to a ball game; some did not. The information may be relevant to what we may want to know about such people, if we are sufficiently interested in their private lives; the same information may or may not be particularly relevant to the history of the Party as a political movement, which is how it saw itself.

Actually, neither Klehr's book nor mine neglects the social composition of the Party. *The Heyday of American Communism* contains two chapters on it, as well as chapters on agriculture, trade unionism, the unemployed, youth, Negroes, and intellectuals. *American Communism and Soviet Russia* also contains a chapter on "Party Life," together with sections on other aspects of the Party's social makeup. These books cover the history of the Party as a whole and, therefore, do not linger on individual rank-and-file Communists. Nevertheless, they clearly attempt to do justice to the political, institutional, and social components of the Party's history and in fact contain more social information than a somewhat similar book by one of the new historians—Maurice Isserman's *Which Side Were You On?*

What really irks the new historians is how the socialization of American Communists has been dealt with, not that it has been entirely missed. For example, the expression "malleable objects" in the book on American Communism by Irving Howe and Lewis Coser has been hotly protested. One might imagine that Communists were born, not made. All the ex-Communist memoirs cited by the new historians are records of human malleability, as well they might be.

---

[36] Paul Lyons, *Philadelphia Communists 1936–1956* (Temple University Press, 1982), p. 62.

If Howe and Coser had said that Communists were conditioned to become exemplary democrats instead of disciplined Stalinists, we may be sure that the word "malleable" would have been much less objectionable.

Klehr tried explicitly to distinguish between the many kinds of people who entered the Communist movement and their political conditioning in the Party:

> There was nothing unique or peculiar about Communists as people. They came out of all environments, had all sorts of motives for becoming members, and differed greatly in their commitment to the cause. But once a person entered the Party, and especially once in the leadership, only unconditional and unwavering loyalty to the dictates of Soviet policy, both foreign and domestic, enabled one to stay.[37]

This simple truism, borne out in 1929, 1939, 1945, and 1956, to cite only the most dramatic examples, does not sit well with the new historians. If giving unconditional and unwavering loyalty to the dictates of Soviet policy made American Communists into political puppets, so be it; the onus should not be on those who register the fact but on those who made it a reality. This does not mean that American Communists were puppets whose strings were pulled from Moscow every waking moment of their lives; they were, however, subject to the "general line," which was invariably set in Moscow, and they were expected to apply it to the best of their abilities.

It also does not mean that American Communists did what they were told to do because they were forced to do so. The drastic changes of line emanating from Moscow repeatedly confronted individual American Communists with anguished, sometimes heartbreaking, crises of conscience. If the voice of Moscow was obeyed, it was because loyalty to the Soviet Union and faith in Stalin were stronger than all other considerations, including those of national or individual self-interest. It is true, as Hosea Hudson said, that many Communists were "willing to sacrifice, to take the sacrifice, to make the sacrifice," but ultimately in the interest of the Soviet Union more than in their own or because they had made the Soviet interest their own. In this respect, they were not puppets; they acted of their own free will.

[37] Klehr, *The Heyday of American Communism*, pp. 415–16.

7

This fundamental and elementary nexus of American Communism and the Soviet Union has been hopelessly distorted and confused by some new historians, especially by those with pretensions of practicing social history.

One of them is Professor Mark Naison, the author of *Communists in Harlem During the Depression*. As is the vogue with the new historians, Naison's introduction immediately tells the reader that he has evolved "from student activist to college professor" and that working on this book enabled him to keep in touch "with a precious legacy of my '60s experience." He thereupon promises to present "a new historiographical image of the black-Communist encounter." As for the new image, the patient reader is bound to be disappointed. The book is largely a traditional history of Party work, made different only by its concentration on a single aspect in a single decade. From time to time, it forgoes its scholarly presentation and strikes out to promulgate the new orthodoxy on the Popular Front and the leadership-membership connection.

> When analyzing Popular Front Communism, it is important to discard the "totalitarian" model that dominates Party historiography: the image of an obedient and docile membership that jumps up and down in unison when the leadership snaps its fingers. The Party remained "bolshevik" at the core, making most of its key decisions without consulting the members; but it lost the power, and even the will, to reshape the total lives of its more prominent adherents, and much of the rank and file. The Party was run by a professional staff, but in other respects, it came to resemble a movement, with a free-floating group of members and sympathizers who publicly endorsed its basic objectives and agreed to follow the Party-line—but displayed considerable diversity, and even division in areas where the line did not apply.

This defense of Communist diversity concedes so much that it almost falls of its own weight. The new freedom, to be sure, applied only to the four years of the Popular Front, which makes one wonder how different it was before and after. But even during the Popular Front, only the "total lives" were not reshaped, and differences were tolerated "where the line did not apply." It is true that the Party and its members were much more freewheeling and permissive during the Popular Front; it was, after all, supposed to be not so much Communist as popular. To have been sectarian, ideologically narrow, and intolerant of all differences during the Popular Front would have violated that particular political line.

The Party in Harlem prospered. But then comes an unexpected revelation about a party that was not totalitarian and whose membership was not obedient and docile:

> The [Nazi-Soviet] Pact, and the Comintern's justification of it, forced Harlem Communists to repudiate many policies that had brought them into the mainstream of black life—it was an invitation to political suicide. Almost without exception, leading black Communists accepted the new Comintern guidelines, displaying their conviction that Soviet leadership constituted the essence of their movement, its ultimate energizing principle. But they came to this conclusion from an *American* political logic, a belief that only a Soviet-centered internationalism could give blacks the power and strategic insight to escape poverty and eliminate jim crow [*italics in original*].

And again:

> On issues where the Comintern spoke specifically, Harlem Communists, like their comrades in other places, changed their analysis at the drop of a hat, attributed extravagant moral purpose to Soviet territorial designs, and generally showed a lack of intellectual integrity and moral balance.[38]

What had happened to all that discarded totalitarianism, free-floating membership, and considerable diversity? Somehow, after four years of such latitudinarianism, Harlem Communists were herded into line by a ukase from Moscow. Instead of a snap of the fingers, there came the drop of a hat. The new historiographical image of the black-Communist encounter cannot in the end make good on its promise to do away with "the image of an obedient and docile membership." That membership was not obviously obedient and docile only so long as it was told not to appear to be obedient and docile, which was another form of obedience and docility. The Harlem experience is but another example of the fact that the Popular Front cannot be understood without taking into account how it died as well as lived—and was resurrected during the war in even more extreme form only to die again.

Another type of salvage operation, this time of Communist trade unionism, picks up many of the themes already noted. Roger Keer-

---

[38] Mark Naison, *Communists in Harlem During the Depression* (University of Illinois Press, 1983), pp. xi, xvi, 187–88, 289.

an's *The Communist Party and the Auto Workers Unions* also starts with the personal confession of faith that one comes to expect in this genre. It was his involvement in New Leftist "campus politics [that] sparked a curiosity about the history of American radicalism." This curiosity resulted in a doctoral dissertation which resulted in a book. A political pronunciamento in the guise of an introduction then tells the reader what to expect. We are immediately instructed, among other things, that the Communists were "legitimate" trade unionists.

This motif first appears in connection with what I have called the "blend" theory:

> The idea that the Communists were not legitimate unionists because they were agents of the Soviet Union and cogs in a disciplined, monolithic party is based on a simplistic view of the Communist party. The party's membership in the Communist International did not keep it from being the main expression of native, working class radicalism during the 30 years after 1919. The Communist party had a dual character. It was a blend of national and international radicalism.

It then reappears in this guise:

> The idea that the Communists' political ends (support for the Soviet Union, class struggle, and socialism) kept them from being legitimate trade unionists is not clear. If it means that the Communists lacked legitimacy, because they held beliefs that other workers did not share, the idea is unreasonable. That would mean that Socialists, Republicans, members of the Association of Catholic Trade Unionists, and others also could not have been good trade unionists.[39]

Some of this argument is bad factually, some bad politically. The Communist Party was not "the main expression of native, working class radicalism" for at least the first fifteen years after 1919; the Communists did not overtake the Socialists until about 1934. In any case, the Communists could still be agents of the Soviet Union, whether or not they were "the main expression of native, working class radicalism." A "dual character" would not exclude such a "blend." More to the point, it is assumed by Keeran that class struggle and socialism are political ends of the same order as "support for the Soviet Union." That support was a different kind of "political end." Socialist, Republican, and Catholic trade unionists may have differed in their political ends, but they differed according to the

[39] Roger Keeran, *The Communist Party and the Auto Workers Unions* (Indiana University Press, 1980), pp. ix, 3–4, 7.

preferences of their supporters, who were American workers. They did not change their line because the Soviet Union had changed its line. Keeran's apparent inability to see this distinction may be partially owing to his curious belief that the American Communist leaders had at times merely "an unhealthy deference towards the Soviet Union."[40]

It would be thankless and time-wasting to go through the entire accumulation of work by the new historians and others on American Communism. Those I have dealt with here are among the best and the most frequently cited by the new historians themselves.

8

What is going on here? The new burst of interest in the history of American Communism has its origins in a mixture of motives. Much of it apparently derives from the need of former New Leftists to find a new political home or at least a source of hope. Yet nothing in the present seems to offer the right combination of attractions. Thus a strange inversion has taken place. Radicals have usually preferred to behold their promised land in the future; these post–New Leftists have been impelled to find it in the past. They have invented a radicalism of nostalgia. The object of their affections, the Popular Front, came and went before most of them were born, but that is no obstacle if the radicalism takes the form of a doctoral dissertation, a book, and finally an academic appointment. No one has to do anything about this radicalism except to teach it to others. The Popular Front was just enough of a blend of different elements to lend itself to nostalgic radicalism. With a little effort and selectivity, it can be seen as the tactical line of a revolutionary party, a response to the temporary needs of the Soviet Union, a stepping-stone to socialism, a flight from socialism, a return to native roots, and even

---

[40] Another advocate of Communist trade union "legitimacy" is James R. Prickett, but he gets there by another route. Keeran thought that the Communists were both good trade unionists and good Communists; Prickett makes them good trade unionists but bad Communists, because they "abandoned the struggle for socialism, supported the New Deal, and made no serious or consistent attempt to challenge liberal ideology." To Prickett, "defense of the Soviet Union was a legitimate priority for working class radicals" ("Communists and the Communist Issue in the American Labor Movement, 1920–1950," doctoral dissertation, University of California, Los Angeles, 1975, pp. xi, 30). What matters least about the Communists, according to Prickett, is their "consistent support of the Soviet Union and the shifting attitudes toward the New Deal" (*Michigan History*, Vol. 57, No. 3 [1973], p. 186).

a success story. If ever a radicalism could be lived vicariously, it is this one.

Thus it is made to order for a peculiar type of academic radicalism. It is a safe haven for former New Leftists, who had to decide what to do with themselves and their political sympathies once the New Left illusion was taken away from them. Some of them chose careers that combine intellectual status, scholarly pretensions, professional rewards, and another kind of political outlet. Yet they have such a marked "party line"—of the partyless—that they are far from being independent in their research; the same themes in almost the same words appear again and again in their work; they cite one another in the same kinds of footnotes. Their "line" is distinguished by a certain bravado, as when they flaunt their New Left credentials, and by a special aggressiveness in their vendetta against their favorite targets. At times they exhibit an extraordinary combination of arrogance and ignorance.[41]

What has been going on here is a curious academic campaign for the rehabilitation of American Communism. It does not aim at total rehabilitation in all respects in all periods; the ostensible project is one of selective rehabilitation—Communists in the Popular Front, Communists in Harlem, Communists in the auto industry. The implicit political objective is shown by formulas such as "an authentic expression of American radicalism" or a "legitimate" force in the labor movement. The operation is carried on with a certain amount of academic discretion, for which the "blend theory" serves most handily. That theory makes it possible to admit the subservience of American Communism to the Soviet Union or the Comintern, while at the same time qualifying such "deference" or subordination out of existence in specific or local circumstances. The rank and file blots out the leadership; tactics supersede strategy; alleged single cases make dubious general rules. Above all the new orthodoxy refuses to face the history of American Communism in its entirety. The Party becomes like the elephant that seems to be a different animal depending on where it is touched.

---

[41] The prize for this combination would undoubtedly go to Paul Buhle, who denounced the "cretinoid intellectuals of Europe (such as Kautsky, Pollitt, and Althusser) who borrowed Marxism from Germany or Russia" (*Radical America*, November–December 1971, p. 73). Anyone who thinks that Karl Kautsky and Louis Althusser were "cretinoid," or that Harry Pollitt was an "intellectual," or that Kautsky had to borrow Marxism from Germany, can—as the Duke of Wellington once put it, when accosted by someone who addressed him as Mr. Smith—"believe anything."

There is also a popular side to this campaign of Communist rehabilitation that deserves brief mention. It goes back to a book put out by Vivian Gornick in 1977, *The Romance of American Communism*, the title of which tells what it is about. It is a sob-sister version of the later academic school, based mainly on interviews with old-time members of the rank and file. It is intellectually on the level of this statement by Gornick: "It seems to me the real point about the Communists is: they were like everybody else, only more so."[42] A more recent example of this genre is the documentary *Seeing Red: Stories of American Communists*, a film made by two veterans of the New Left. Much of it is a historical travesty of the American Communist story. The plain intent of the film is to show that Communists were ordinary Americans inordinately proud of what they had done as Communists until some of them were sorrowfully forced to leave in 1956 or after. The film presents American Communism in soft political focus, making just enough glancing concessions to some minimum of reality to avoid being recognized as outright propaganda.[43]

If the former New Leftists, academic or otherwise, continue to play these political games, they are bound to give "social history" a bad name. Curiously, two American scholars have recently shown how to do authentic, intelligent Communist social history. But they did their work on the present-day French Communist Party, not on the more distant American past. *The View from Inside* by Jane Jenson and George Ross is about what its subtitle says: *A French Communist Cell in Crisis*.[44] They have studied, at the closest possible range, a Communist "cell" in Paris in 1978 and 1979, and then intermittently until 1981, during a period of acute Party ferment. They attended meetings of the cell; listened to the hopes, anxieties, and confidences of its members; followed them step by step as they sought to reanimate the Party—and failed.

They have produced a remarkably vivid and convincing likeness of Party life at the bottom as it is influenced by Party leadership at the top. They succeed in bringing to life the reasons why the French Party has lost not only almost all of its intellectuals but a good part

---

[42] Vivian Gornick, *The Romance of American Communism* (Basic Books, 1977), p. 22. For more on this book, see my review in *The New Leader*, March 13, 1978.

[43] For reviews of this film, see *Dissent*, Fall 1984, and *Labor History*, Winter 1985.

[44] Jane Jenson and George Ross, *The View from Inside: A French Communist Cell in Crisis* (University of California Press, 1984).

of the rank and file. One of their most striking contributions is the story of how the leadership dealt with nascent feminist stirrings in the cell. Their social history is all the richer for being put in a fully realized political and institutional setting and for being informed by a high order of intellectual sophistication. There is nothing remotely comparable to it in the attempts at the social history of American Communism by the new historians.

Twenty-five years ago, I reflected that each generation would have to discover in its own way the nature of the relationship between American Communism and the Soviet Union. Unfortunately, that still seems to be true. The short answer to the question "What is going on here?" is: One illusion is being exchanged for another.

(*The New York Review of Books*, May 9, 1985, and May 30, 1985)

The "Class Struggle"

1

A POST–NEW LEFT professoriat has arisen out of the ashes of
the New Left student movement of the 1960s. It is a strange phenomenon in the midst of the Reaganite conservatism of the 1980s.
Faced with a choice of career after the rigor mortis of the New Left,
many of its former activists and sympathizers chose to get advanced
degrees and ascend the academic ladder to professorships in the
universities. By now a good many have gained tenure and many
more are on their way. The New Left is dead, and yet it is very much
alive in the very places where it was born.

An insider's view of how all this came to pass was given some time
ago by Ellen W. Schrecker, who now teaches American history at
Princeton University. In a now defunct post–New Left academic
journal, *Humanities in Society* (Spring–Summer 1983), she reported
the presence of "the largest and most important cohort of left-wing
scholars in American history." They were so numerous that "in
certain fields, American history for example, Marxism is the mainstream." They were said to "constitute the intellectual legacy of the
New Left, the political activists of the 1960s who turned to scholarship
in the 1970s in order to make sense of their own experience." She
explained that "the temptation to trade the frustrations of politics
for the pleasure of scholarship is strong, all the more so when the
professional rewards for such a switch are all too obvious."

In reality, it was not so simple a trade. The professional rewards have not been without some political compensations. They have taken the peculiar form of a minor academic industry devoted to the history of the American Communist Party. Books and dissertations have proliferated on this subject in recent years, after a long interval of virtual neglect. Instead of making sense of their own experience by confronting it directly, these post–New Left professors seem to want to make sense of it through the medium of an earlier generation. They have made the substitution as if it enabled them to feel that they are still keeping the faith by some mysterious process of political transference.

The latest example of this genre is the recent book *No Ivory Tower*, by the same Ellen W. Schrecker (Oxford University Press, 1986). It has received thoughtful reviews from Nathan Glazer and C. Vann Woodward, but they were mainly concerned with her treatment of the academic side of the story, summed up in her subtitle, *McCarthyism and the Universities*. This side is not my concern, for one reason because I am not competent to deal with it. I am interested, rather, in the other side of the story, which concerns the Communist professors caught up in the inquisitorial frenzy. I knew a good many of those Schrecker mentions by name, and I have no unpleasant memories of any of them. My concern is not with them as individuals, but with the mythical way they are portrayed as a group.

The nub of the matter is the singular political symbiosis that has taken place between the present generation of post–New Left academics and their Communist predecessors. This aspect of the book raises larger issues about the way the history of American Communism is now being presented by post–New Left historians. Even if we can believe everything Schrecker says about what went on in the universities in every unflattering detail, we need not believe everything she says about the Communist professors in every flattering detail.

2

Schrecker's professorial Communists often emerge in her pages as self-righteous, high-minded political innocents. They were, she assures us, "perfectly loyal, though politically unpopular, American citizens." They refused "to use their classrooms for purposes of indoctrination." They were committed to "objectivity and fairness."

They followed the Party line, because the Party happened to follow them. "While they were in it," Schrecker writes, "they did, it is true, follow the Party line; but they did so in large part because it was heading in the same direction they were. They did not let the Party interfere with their academic work and, in fact, consciously strove to keep their political activities separate from their scholarly ones." She implies that it was a sign of naïveté to ask a member of the Party whether he would "be loyal in a war between America and the U.S.S.R.," the implication being that he would, of course, in all circumstances, be loyal to America. One Cornell professor is approvingly cited: "We were intellectuals. We were scholars"—as if there were nothing more to it.

Much of this would have surprised and offended the Communist professors at the time. If there was anything they did *not* believe in, it was classless "objectivity and fairness." The merest Communist novice knew, or thought he knew, that these terms were products of bourgeois illusions and deceptions. Yet Schrecker wants the reader to believe that there was no intellectual difference between Communist professors and all the others. She gives assurances that the former "shared their colleagues' commitment to the standards of their calling, in particular its concern with objectivity and fairness." If so, those professors were remarkably ignorant of the most elementary Communist doctrines, or were remarkably successful in convincing Schrecker that they were not really Communist intellectuals and scholars. The Communists I knew in the universities would have been ashamed to admit that they thought the same way as everyone else, and that they did not know the class character of such bourgeois shibboleths as "objectivity and fairness."

To be fair to Schrecker, however, it cannot be said that she always represents the Communists as if they were political simpletons. She is sometimes saved from oversimplification by her own inconsistencies and contradictions. A case in point is her treatment of Communist indoctrination. The Communist professors, she says, "were almost unanimous in refusing to use their classrooms for purposes of indoctrination." She cites statements to that effect from three former professors, including Howard Selsam, a philosophy teacher at Brooklyn College, in whose class I sat in the early 1930s. At first Schrecker suggests that Communist professors, for reasons of professionalism and prudence, separated "their politics from their teaching." But on the very next page she writes:

Even though Communist professors generally refrained from outright proselytizing in class, this does not mean that their political beliefs did not influence their academic work. Naturally, scientists—and probably close to half of the academic Communists were scientists—had no problem keeping their politics separate from their scholarship. People in other fields, however, sometimes taught their courses from what they considered to be a Marxist perspective. Some, like the Brooklyn philosopher Howard Selsam, even taught Marxism. Taught, not indoctrinated. The distinction is important, for whatever the intellectual quality of the Marxism these teachers purveyed, they all struggled to present it in an unbiased way. Many went out of their way to let their students know that they were Marxists, if not Communists.

This passage is a good example of how Schrecker labors to make her Communists too good to be true and then backs away. She has just assured the reader that there was no political indoctrination or proselytization. But now it turns out that there was no "outright" proselytization. Professors in nonscientific fields even taught courses from a "Marxist perspective" or, as in one case, taught Marxism. Another Communist philosopher "who did discuss more controversial matters in class, always warned his students he was a Marxist"— as if that immunized them from his political influence. We are sternly instructed to see the distinction between teaching and indoctrinating, as if it were clear in practice. In any case, we are assured, Communists "struggled" to present their Marxism "in an unbiased way."

Was there really such a Chinese wall between their Marxism and their Communism that they could teach one without intimating the other? Have Communists never camouflaged themselves as "Marxists" and "socialists," on the unstated assumption that theirs is the only authentic Marxism and socialism? These questions seem never to have occurred to Schrecker, or, if they did, she has suppressed them in the interest of shielding her Communist subjects from the least suspicion of bias. If the Communists were without bias in the turbulent years of the 1930s, '40s, and '50s, it must be that there was no bias anywhere in the academy at that time—a state of academic grace rarely achieved.

Whether or not Communist professors proselytized students, they certainly proselytized other professors. When I was a student at Brooklyn College in the early 1930s, there was not a single Communist professor in the school. By the end of the decade there must have been at least twenty-five. The largest Communist unit at the College of the City of New York, or CCNY, according to Schrecker, numbered about forty. They did not grow by a process of spontaneous political combustion. Sympathizers were carefully spotted and cultivated. Open meetings were held to which likely candidates for membership were invited. "Shop papers" on local school matters and more general political issues were put out by Party units. These papers were not models of "objectivity and fairness." Schrecker, always tolerant of Communist "shenanigans" (her word), reports that "they were somewhat lacking in gentility as well as embarrassingly uncritical about the Soviet Union, but they were, nonetheless, the authentic voice of a politically significant segment of the academic community"—as if their Communist authenticity made up for their lack of gentility and embarrassingly uncritical defense of the Soviet Union. Elsewhere we learn that they were so lacking in gentility that some of the papers engaged in "scurrilous attacks on individuals" and that some of their editors later admitted that the attacks were "often irresponsible and in bad taste." Still, Schrecker was given the impression that the shop papers were "fun to read," despite the scurrility, irresponsibility, bad taste, and Party-line hackwork with which they were filled. The fun was certainly not shared by those on the receiving end.

3

The embarrassingly uncritical support of the Soviet Union was not a strange aberration on the part of these papers. The role of the Soviet Union was central in the Communist consciousness; the Soviet Union was then the embodiment of what Communism stood for, the guarantor of the true faith. This does not mean that every American Communist knew a great deal about Soviet Russia, or that what he thought he knew had much relation to reality. It was enough to believe that the "defense of the Soviet Union" was the first and foremost task of every Communist. The one sure way to get into trouble in every Communist Party in that era was to criticize anything that came out of the Soviet Union. Some deviations might be forgiven; that one, never.

Just how deeply the Soviet Union was embedded in the American Communist consciousness partially depended on when one entered the Party. During the first fifteen years, before the Popular Front, the Soviets were the Party's main political asset. One did not merely belong to a national Party; one belonged to an international movement of which the Soviet Union was the single success and guiding star. Without the support and prestige of the Soviet Union and the international movement, many a national Party, including the American, would have had very little vitality. The great crises that arose in the American and other Communist Parties were invariably set off by a change of line on the part of the Soviet Union. The workaday life of individual American Communists may have been spent coping with problems in factories, schools, and elsewhere, but the consciousness of being a Communist was inseparable from the political and psychological rapport with the Soviet Union.

One eminent mathematician protested to Schrecker that Party discipline was "scarcely shared with respect to matters of private thought by a very considerable number of people who have attached themselves to the group." How considerable they were may be a matter of dispute. But this apologia unwittingly reveals that the most indiscipline permitted was to keep nonconformist thoughts to oneself. Even so, it was not easy to keep a double bookkeeping system going for any length of time, one private, one public. Few remained in the Party for long who had to suppress their disagreements for a considerable period. Schrecker herself was convinced that "certainly they had reservations about some aspects of the Party line, but they supported most of it most of the time." Even those reservations were generally confined to "matters of private thought" in order to stay out of trouble with the Party's true believers. Only a cretin could have wandered into the American Communist Party and stayed in it for any length of time without knowing that fealty to the Soviet Union and its leader was unconditional and obligatory.

The Communist professors were no more immune to this and other imperatives of Communist good behavior than lesser mortals in the Party. The professors were not, as some of them may belatedly like to think of themselves, disembodied free spirits. In real life, Communist professors, like most professors, had limited areas of professional knowledge. Their Communist selves were for the most part outside their professional spheres and were largely political, in which area they generally knew as much or as little as most others. They deferred just as much as most others to the superior political wisdom and authority of the "cadre," the party's "functionaries" or full-time leadership.

Most Communist professors were no more likely to question major political decisions handed down from above than anyone else. Communist discipline was the same for professors as for all others. A sudden, unexpected change of line might confuse or trouble professors, but they soon found ways, like the rest, to adjust to it, or to get out. Few got out, until the 1950s. The notion that professors, because they were professors, behaved very differently in their political lives from other Communists is a myth. This is not to say that all Communist professors were the same, any more than all the others were the same; but there remained a political common denominator of ideology, faith, discipline, and loyalty that made up the core of what it meant to be a Communist, professor or proletarian.

Despite the myth of professional purity in Schrecker's book, inconsistencies and contradictions again appear unresolved. In only one short passage does she tell the reader what kind of Party these professors joined. The revelation happens to come in reference to the Popular Front of 1936–39:

> This new line, it must be noted, created serious contradictions within the CP. For, despite its apparent moderation, the Party still retained *its central commitment to Stalin's Russia* and attacked Trotskyists and other critics of the Soviet regime with all its old sectarian fervor. In addition, it retained its traditional *authoritarian structure* and expected its new recruits to follow its albeit less revolutionary line with the same unquestioning devotion older Communists did. [*Italics mine.*]

For once, some reality breaks through. But it is immediately followed by this:

> It is hard to tell whether the academics who embraced the CP during the Popular Front period would have done so had its line been more intransigent. Few of them were revolutionaries, nor were they even particularly interested in the Soviet Union. They joined the Party, almost all of them, because they thought it was the best way to fight fascism.

I am willing to believe that some—but not almost all of them—joined the Party during the Popular Front without quite knowing what they were getting into. In fact, that was true of a good many before the Popular Front. But in August 1939, these same nonrevolutionaries who were not particularly interested in the Soviet Union were faced with a sudden change of line. The Soviet Union had shatteringly made a nonaggression pact with the chief fascist state. The American Communist Party was no longer the best way to fight fascism; it was the best way to fight the embattled enemies of fascism. What did these professors do? Did they leave the Party in droves because it had betrayed what had originally drawn them into it? In fact, as Schrecker notes, very few left; the numbers could almost be counted on the fingers of one hand. The Nazi-Soviet pact could not have failed to make the Communist professors keenly interested in the Soviet Union. It was at the center of the crisis of conscience that beset many Communists in that period. If the professors were immune, they must have been intellectual nincompoops. Whatever makes people join a Communist Party, they do not remain the same once they have been in it for long. By 1939, the political education even of these professors must have progressed far enough for them to learn that the "central commitment" of their Party was to Stalin's Russia, and that they were bound intellectually to an "authoritarian structure." The new recruits were not so different from the old-timers after all.

Yet this is how Schrecker explains the change of line in 1939: "In the aftermath of the Pact, the Party, which had abandoned the anti-war movement in favor of collective security in 1935, returned to the cause of peace." Less than two years later, when Nazi Germany invaded the Soviet Union, the "cause of peace" was apparently abandoned in favor of the cause of war. Was it really the "cause of peace" that was embraced by the Communist professors from 1939 to 1941 and then the cause of war from 1941 to 1945? To describe Communist policy in the period of the Nazi-Soviet pact as the "cause of peace" without any qualification is to parrot the Party line of that period. The cause was obviously that of the Soviet Union whether it required a propaganda of "peace" or of "war."

Schrecker relates that a former Communist remembered his

> acutely embarrassing experience of telling people that the Soviet Union was justified in invading Finland in 1940, that the war between France and England on the one hand, and Germany on the other was an "imperialist war," and that it didn't matter who won.

That man was telling the truth; those things were what the Communist professors were saying. But it accords ill with the idea that they merely thought that Communism was "the best way to fight fascism" or that the Party had embraced the "cause of peace." After so many years, a historian might be expected to distinguish between propaganda and substance.

How, then, can we be certain that the Communist professors were "perfectly loyal, though politically unpopular, American citizens"?

Politically, they were American citizens who were "perfectly loyal" to the Soviet Union. Whether they would have betrayed their political loyalty and fought against the Soviet Union in a war with America is an open question. They were never called on to make such a decision. Some might have gone one way, some another. The only thing we can be sure of is that it is impossible to be sure how all of them would have reacted. If perfect loyalty is understood politically, however, it is absurd to make the categorical statement that they were perfectly loyal to America rather than to the Soviet Union.

4

I have gone into this aspect of Schrecker's book at some length because elsewhere she repeatedly resorts to ridicule to downplay the connection between American Communism and the Soviet Union or international Communism. At the very outset, she calls attention to the Communist coup in Czechoslovakia in 1948, the Berlin blockade that same year, and the "fall" of China to the Communists. Her dismissive comment is: "To give the American Communist Party any credit for these revolutionary changes was ridiculous." It is also ridiculous to think that anyone in his right mind ever did give them such credit. Something else was, however, not ridiculous—that the American Communist Party automatically and enthusiastically supported these changes, and that everyone in it was called on to do likewise (except perhaps in "private thought"), whether or not they were professors.

At another point, Schrecker discusses the obligation of the academic Communists to work in "front groups," to which she adds that the extent to which they were "dominated by the CP is unclear." The "fronts" were so called for good reason; Party policy openly dictated that they should be dominated—or led, as the Party more delicately put it—by Communists. This was abundantly clear to everyone at the time. But her next comment is: "But most of the Communist academics who joined such groups probably did so because they were concerned about the issue that the organization claimed to address, not because Stalin told them to." This gratuitous reference to Stalin is not as ridiculous as Schrecker thinks it is.

Stalin certainly did not personally tell the American professors to belong to Communist fronts. But the theory of the "fronts" or auxiliaries was first put forward by Lenin in a seminal work, *What Is to Be Done?*, as far back as 1902. Lenin had called them "transmission belts" to the Party. The international practice was then worked out in the Communist International in the early 1920s. When Stalin took control of the Comintern in 1928–29, the system was further developed, undoubtedly with his approval even if he also had other things on his mind. The American professors may not have belonged to fronts because Stalin told them to. But they belonged because the Party told them to.

Schrecker also sees fit to ridicule Arthur O. Lovejoy, a founder of the American Association of University Professors. Lovejoy had said:

> A member of the Communist Party is . . . engaged in a movement which has already extinguished academic freedom in many countries and would—if it were successful here—result in the abolition of such freedom in American universities. No one, therefore, who desires to maintain academic freedom in America can consistently favor that movement or give indirect assistance to it by accepting as fit members of the faculties of universities, persons who have voluntarily adhered to an organization one of whose aims is to abolish academic freedom.

Schrecker's sardonic comment is: "In other words, because there is no academic freedom in Russia, American Communists had no right to enjoy it here."

Whether they had such a "right" was a legal question. Whether they were right to espouse the cause of a Party with a "central commitment to Stalin's Russia," where academic freedom had long been stifled, was a political question. American professors who demanded a "right" for themselves that they were willing to see denied to professors in other parts of the world were hardly in a position to preach to others about academic freedom. They themselves did not believe in such an absolute right—for fascists, for example. American Communists may have had a "right" to enjoy academic freedom here, whether or not there was academic freedom in Russia. But a curious light is shed on their devotion to the ideal of academic freedom if they could belong to a Party that zealously supported kindred Parties that, on coming to power, had stamped out academic freedom. It does not seem to occur to the post–New Left historian that there is something intolerably one-sided about Communists who demand academic freedom in liberal societies and deny it to liberals in Communist societies.

How much illiberalism should a liberal society tolerate or defend? It is a most perplexing question. But Schrecker does not ask it. Instead she takes the easy way out and for the most part treats her Communists as if they were liberals.

5

One of Schrecker's prime exhibits is a mathematician at the University of Michigan who spent six months in jail in 1959 for defying the House Un-American Activities Committee. He deliberately chose to use the First Amendment after others found that they could safely refuse to testify by taking the Fifth. He appears to have been a person of unusual courage and conviction. Nevertheless, his case makes one wonder whether he could have been the kind of Communist that Schrecker says he was.

I knew his father slightly. He was a professor of economics who joined the Party back in 1931, in the most sectarian and rigidly extremist period in the Party's history. Ten years later, we are told, he was "something of a fixture at anti-war rallies around Boston during the Nazi-Soviet pact period, because he 'was looked on as someone who would present the Communist Party's point of view.' " He is said to have left the Party in the late 1940s "but was still an avowed Marxist," whatever that means. In effect, he had been a faithful, disciplined Party member for about two decades. I remember him as a sometime contributor to the *New Masses* when I was an editor in the late 1930s.

I offer this background only because his son, the mathematician, was, as Schrecker puts it, "a 'red diaper baby,' " that is, one brought up from childhood in a devout Communist family environment. He joined the Communist Party while a student at Harvard in the 1940s, and remained in the Party after having been hired by the University of Michigan in 1950. His ordeal began with his refusal to testify in 1954. "Though no longer officially a Communist at the time of his hearing," we learn, "he had never really broken with the Party, and he remained active on its fringes through his years in Ann Arbor."

Why did he refuse to testify? Because he was "the quintessential anti-authoritarian personality. Principled, tenacious, and fiercely independent, he had an almost innate predisposition for political dissent." He believed uncompromisingly in the principle of "the absolute inviolability of freedom of speech."

What are we to make of this rationale? After ten or more years in the Communist Party, during the expulsion of Earl Browder because he was no longer acceptable to Moscow, and a return of the Party line to the worst excesses of the past, this "quintessential anti-authoritarian personality" did not dissent from what Schrecker herself describes as the Party's "traditional authoritarian structure." He could not have been so naïve or ignorant that he did not know of the Party's "central commitment to Stalin's Russia." How in the world did he express his "anti-authoritarian personality," his principled independence, and his "almost innate predisposition for political dissent" in a Party with an "authoritarian structure"? Did he believe that one thing was right for Stalin's Russia and another for Truman's and Eisenhower's America?

The problem is not with him; it is with the historian who studies him. Hundreds of thousands of people have gone through the Communist movement, believing, as this man must have believed at one time, that it was the world's salvation. Many have regretted it or at best looked back on it as a useful political education. The first stone can certainly not be thrown by me. But anyone with a quintessentially anti-authoritarian personality and an absolute devotion to freedom of speech strains credulity to the breaking point if he also stays in the Communist Party for about ten years, during its most extremist, post-Browder phase, and after leaving it remains—for reasons we never learn—active on its fringes. Something is missing here.

Why indeed did all the Communist professors refuse to testify? The answer tells us something about their relationship with the Communist Party. Conceivably, some might have defied the committees in other ways. After all, the revolutionary tradition called for a different kind of behavior. It used to be expected of revolutionaries— and Communists still thought of themselves as working toward a revolutionary change in society—that they would stand up and speak out boldly for their cause. Some were so openly engaged in Party activity that they might have had little to lose by taking this course. But why was it so different in every one of these cases? Whether they should have been required to testify is a different question; I am here concerned with what the reason for their identical behavior tells us about them.

Every once in a while, as I have noted, Schrecker lets a breath of fresh air into her pages. At one point she comes out with the real reason for the solid front they presented to the various committees and investigations:

> The Party was, after all, a disciplined organization; the teachers who were involved apparently felt that they had to present a united front. Even people like the former CCNY instructor who claimed, "I didn't like the performance of the defense," nonetheless "did what everyone else did even though I wasn't part of any deliberative process." In retrospect, what seems most distressing about the behavior of these teachers was not their lying—which, given the no-win situation in which they felt themselves, may well have seemed to offer the only hope for keeping their jobs—but their willingness to let a small group of Party leaders make a decision that was to affect their own careers and livelihoods.

The comment does Schrecker credit; it reveals that she knew all the time that the Party, and not the professors, decided how they were going to behave. As usual, the policy was handed down from on high and was meekly followed by those below, despite the fact that these people were academics, scholars, and intellectuals. One academic active in Urbana, Illinois, even told Schrecker, who dutifully records it, that she could "never remember any situation in which we were told what to do, what to think, given a line and told to carry it out." She must have been a rare phenomenon; or, more likely, a victim of selective amnesia, an affliction frequently encountered in these pages.

Schrecker notes of her approximately seventy informants who left the Party that they chose afterward to be "neither Communists nor anti-Communists" and had "few regrets about their affiliation with the Party." We are told that many had simply left by the 1960s without "any specific disagreement with the Party but simply that they could no longer spare the time." Schrecker herself expresses scorn for "the flawed, but common, assumption that it was not possible for someone to be an ex-Communist without becoming an anti-Communist."

The point is worth considering. These professors prided themselves on their intellectuality. They probably read the Party press with more than ordinary care and frequency. Except for local matters, on which disagreement could go on for hours until the decision was made, they could have had no illusions about what would get them into trouble if they seriously disagreed with the line on major national and international issues. Party members with "an almost innate predisposition for political dissent" did not last long in this movement. Yet most of Schrecker's professors had stayed in the Party for years, through one or more somersaults of the Party line.

Were they such somnambulists that they could go in, stay in, and get out of the Party without reflecting on an experience that must have been one of the most meaningful in their lives? If they did reflect on it, could they have simply faded away without feeling some obligation, if to no one but themselves, to think about why it was they had left? Schrecker writes as if they deserve a badge of honor for having few regrets. She seems to be particularly eager to absolve them from the supreme shame of anti-Communism. Her attitude appears to be that Communism was a venial sin, for which one need have no regrets; but anti-Communism is a mortal sin, which cannot be forgiven.

But Communism was not something that one embraced for trivial reasons. It was also not something that one was likely to reject for trivial reasons. That so many of these professors are supposed to have left the Party as if it had been a social club trivializes their entire experience. Perhaps the whole experience is too painful for them to talk about. Perhaps some of them wished to avoid thinking that they had done anything wrong and so to continue to live happily ever after. But that is no reason for a historian to fail to look beneath the surface of these patently implausible and at best escapist rationalizations. Still, there is method in this mindlessness: it serves to make the Communist professors seem as innocent politically in going out of the Party as they had been in getting into and staying in it.

This post–New Left historian writes as if Communists were fallen angels and anti-Communists were the devil's own disciples. These two terms raise something of a problem. Communism is codified in its canonical literature; it is at any one time what the authoritarian Party says it is. In effect, one knows where one stands with orthodox Communism, especially in the period treated in this book.

Anti-Communism has no such distinct, determinable definition. It may be passive or active; it extends from the extreme right to the extreme left; it may be fascist, reactionary, conservative, liberal, social-democratic, Trotskyist, anarchist, and more. It is merely a

negation of Communism without a positive content of its own—
except to Communists, who prefer to lump all varieties of anti-
Communism together.

Thus there was no single anti-Communism that the Communist
professors had to turn to; they had plenty of political options to
choose among. They could even have remained Marxists—but not
the kind of Marxism that the Communists have misappropriated.
Yet, as Schrecker notes, most of the Communist professors left the
Party formally only to remain within its orbit, or without really changing their minds. Few of them, she says, can cite a specific incident
that disillusioned them, and most left the Party painlessly. If so, this
tells us something about the influence that Communism must still
have had on them.

If Schrecker is right and most of these ex-Communist ex-professors
still regard their Communist pasts without regrets and without self-
examination, that is just about the saddest thing she could say about
them. One wonders how many would really want the kind of absolution she gives them.

6

What is behind this mythification of the Communist professors?
Schrecker herself is clearly no throwback to the old-time Communists. From time to time she drops remarks that no Communist loyal
to the Party would make, even though she promptly goes on as if
these comments mattered little. In her generation of leftists, in
any case, it was not fashionable to be the type of Old Leftist that
the Communists represented. Something else explains this new
academic-political phenomenon.

The tie between these two quite different generations is based on
an assumed fellowship of the "left." It is an ambivalent kinship. The
post–New Left is both attracted to and unhappy with the Old Left,
as represented by the Communists. Schrecker shares this post–New
Left ambivalence; she accepts the Communists as an authentic part
of the "left" while establishing a certain distance from them. The
kinship with them is shown by her practice of using the terms "Communist," "left-wing," and "radical" interchangeably. On a single
page, she applies all three terms indiscriminately to a Tulane professor who was admittedly a Communist. The implication is that all
leftists, including Communists, belong in one political family and

have more in common than not. By neither entirely approving of the Communists nor rejecting them the post–New Leftists shift and slide between praise and blame, without ever resolving where they finally stand on fundamental issues. The one thing they cannot tolerate is anti-Communism, even as they make use of the most telling elements of the anti-Communist critique.

In this way Schrecker knowingly alludes, if only in an isolated passage, to the Communist Party's "central commitment to Stalin's Russia" and its "authoritarian structure." Yet she is willing to accept the Party's credentials as "left-wing" and "radical." Has there ever been an American left wing or radicalism worthy of the name that had a "central commitment" to such a foreign power and was based on such a structure? It was this kind of commitment that caused Charles de Gaulle to describe the French Communist Party as "East," not "left." Is it merely a peccadillo that a so-called left-wing party should be "authoritarian"? Are there no limits to what is acceptable in an American left wing or radicalism? What is bound to happen to such terms as "left-wing" and "radical"—and, in other contexts, to the term "socialism"—if they are stretched so far that they can be compatible with such a social monstrosity as Stalin's Russia and such a political disease as "authoritarianism"?

The New Left ambivalence is almost perfectly captured in the following:

> The American Communist Party, for all the emotion it once aroused, can now be studied; it is no longer necessary—if it ever was—to condemn or exonerate it. At its peak it was a dynamic and often effective movement for social change, yet it was also—and at the same time—a doctrinaire, secretive, and undemocratic political sect. Its main flaw, of course, was its uncritical relationship with the Soviet Union, a relationship that required its members to conform their political activities to the dictates of Stalin's foreign policy . . . There were other problems as well. As an ostensibly revolutionary organization, the CP enforced a type of disciplined and conspiratorial behavior that may well have stunted the development of a viable socialist tradition in America. And yet in spite, or perhaps even because, of these serious defects, the Party did make important contributions. It helped build the CIO, and it helped bring the problems of American blacks into the political agenda. The record is mixed. To view it in any other way is to distort the past.

Nothing gives away the peculiarly protective post–New Left attitude toward the Communist movement more than the singular idea that "it is no longer necessary—if it ever was—to condemn or exonerate it." Schrecker is evidently doubtful whether it was necessary "to condemn or exonerate it" even in its heyday, during which it was most subservient to the Soviet Union. What is there about American Communism that exempts it from condemnation or exoneration? If the same benevolence were extended to Schrecker's own subject, the universities during the McCarthyite period, she would be unable to condemn or exonerate anything done during those years. Yet her book is full of both study *and* condemnation. This counsel of selective condemnation is itself a form of tacit exoneration.

One might also imagine that Schrecker had used a mathematical instrument to calibrate the merits and demerits of American Communism. The aim of the entire exercise is to get to the apparently impartial verdict: "The record is mixed." Yet it might at best be considered "mixed" only if the alleged merits and demerits were commensurate. For example: the Party did not merely help to build the CIO. It also helped build itself in the CIO. It split the CIO. It sacrificed its own interests in the CIO as soon as conformity with the "dictates of Stalin's foreign policy" called for a break. But even this misses the main point. It is precisely the "mixture" of a central commitment to Stalin's Russia and an authoritarian structure with activity such as the participation in the CIO that is the source of the deepest culpability: the exploitation of idealism in the betrayal of ideals. The disruption caused by the Communists, when they have to obey their central commitment and structure, is incommensurate with the "help" they give, the main motive for which is to provide themselves with a "mass base." A summing-up that "the record is mixed" is a cop-out. The record of almost all movements, radical or otherwise, is mixed, but not in the same way or in ultimate outcome. A mixture that contains lethal "defects" is not an ordinary mixture.

This easy indulgence toward the Communist "mixture" comes out most revealingly in Schrecker's prescription for studying the Communist movement in America. It is an excellent statement of what has become the party line of the post–New Left historians:

> Though I am no believer in what is usually called "objective" scholarship, I am not sure that the history of the CP is served by judging every action the Party took. In addition, much of the current research seems to be asking the wrong questions. It studies the Party's top leaders instead of middle-level cadres and rank and file, and thus does not look at the most interesting aspect of American Communism: why

and how it came to dominate the American left during the 1930s and 1940s. To do that we will have to find out what ordinary Communists did on a day-to-day basis. That information may be harder to find than what line the Party leaders took on a specific issue, but it may well provide more insight into the role of the CP in American political life.

This credo comes strangely from one who has vouched for the Communist professors' "objectivity and fairness." Evidently Communists can believe in "objective" scholarship, but she cannot. Strangely, too, she objects to judging "every action the Party took" but wants to study "what ordinary Communists did on a day-to-day basis." Apparently the ordinary Communist's every action is more relevant politically than the Party's every action. This differentiation between the Party and ordinary Communists is another myth. It implies that what ordinary Communists did on a day-to-day basis was largely unrelated to the Party's own actions. The Party here becomes an empty abstraction, divorced from its membership. In fact, the Party was made up of its top leaders, middle-level cadres, and rank and file. To get anything done, the top leaders bore down on the middle-level cadres, and the cadres bore down on the rank and file. The shift in emphasis from the Party to its "ordinary" membership serves a political purpose: it atomizes the Party, thus disguising its essential nature by glossing over its admittedly top-to-bottom "authoritarian structure." As for judging *every* action of this or any other party, no historian can do that; the problem is always to judge the significant and relevant actions.

Why should a study of the middle-level cadres and rank and file be more interesting and provide more insight than a study of the top leaders? There is no reason to separate these ranks in the Party, as if there were two or three separate Parties. That none of these three categories spent every waking moment of their lives doing their Communist duty hardly needs saying. Another of the new historians, whose book Schrecker mentions with the reservation that he does not name names as she does, sagaciously advises students of the Communist movement to pay attention to "who stopped over at one's house after dinner to play cards, listen to a ball game, sit on the porch drinking a beer, discussing the news," and "whom one could depend on to take care of the kids, lend one money, go shopping." No doubt more important activities, such as working the mimeograph machine at a CIO local or distributing the *Daily Worker* at street corners, might be added. They may make a minor contribution to American social history, but they need not be politically significant or relevant to an understanding of American Communism. They cannot tell us for what ultimate ends such activities were engaged in, where the policies came from, why they were turned on and off.

If Schrecker had taken her own words about the "authoritarian structure" of the Communist Party seriously, she could never have asserted that studying the top leadership would be "asking the wrong questions" and studying the middle-level cadre and rank and file the right ones. The real reason for drawing so much attention to the middle-level cadre and the rank and file is to draw attention away from what was most Communist about them. They behaved as Communists precisely in their relationship with the top leadership, which would have been helpless without them, as they would have lost their political bearings without it.

The reductio ad absurdum of the academic inquisitions during the McCarthyite years is best shown by the change that has come over the university that drove out a truly great scholar, the late Moses I. Finley. The same department in the same university now has a tenured professor who regularly contributes to the theoretical organ of the Communist Party of the U.S.A. and specializes in personal vituperation against anyone who does not follow the full Party line.

Schrecker's book will not help those who seek some light on how and why the Communists in the academy in the 1930s and '40s gave way to the New Left movement of the 1960s, and the latter to the post–New Left professoriat of the 1980s. The book will make even more of a mystery of this confusing sequence by propagating so much muddle and mythology about the first of these. Whatever wrongs and "shenanigans" were committed against the Communist professors, there is no reason to make them into exemplars of objective scholarship, academic freedom, and civil liberties.

(*The New Republic*, January 26, 1987)

Soviet Reformers: From Lenin to Gorbachev

1

THE PAST—to use a phrase of Marx—"weighs like a nightmare" on the Soviet Union of Mikhail Sergeyevich Gorbachev. He is not the first Soviet leader to attempt to escape from the nightmare of Stalinism in order to make a radical change in how the Soviet Union functions. To understand the present effort, it is useful to look back historically at other such "reform" periods in Soviet history for what they can tell us about the general problem.

For this purpose, it is best to start with a brief view of Soviet history since the end of 1917. That history can be divided into five main periods, with a sixth now in progress.

First, there was War Communism for about three years, from 1918 to 1920.

Second, the first reform period of the New Economic Policy, or NEP, for about seven years, from 1921 to 1928.

Third, the Stalinist period of about twenty-five years, from 1928 or 1929 to 1953.

Fourth, after a brief interregnum or struggle for the succession, the second reform period, under Nikita Khrushchev, for about eight or nine years, from 1955 or 1956 to 1964.

Fifth, the reaction, headed by Leonid Brezhnev, for eighteen years, from 1964 to 1982.

Sixth, after another interregnum, headed by Andropov and Chernenko, the third reform period, inaugurated by Gorbachev in March 1985.

One thing may be noted immediately. The two full reform periods of the NEP and Khrushchev lasted from beginning to end for less than ten years. The periods that followed them, headed by Stalin and Brezhnev, lasted much longer, from eighteen to twenty-five years. In effect, the past reform periods did not succeed in making themselves irreversible; in fact, they were rather easily reversed and for lengthy periods.

2

The prototype of the species is the first one—the New Economic Policy, or NEP. It is particularly important at present because it has been a source of both inspiration and legitimacy for what Gorbachev is trying to do.

A key reason for the preeminence of the NEP period is that it is irrevocably linked with the name of Lenin. He introduced it in March 1921, defended it to his last breath, and died in January 1924, while the NEP was still untouchable.

Inasmuch as subsequent reform leaders have specialized in repudiating Stalin, they would be ideologically naked if they did not claim to go back to the pristine Communism of Lenin. In fact, some of the questions and answers have changed so little that they too go back to the NEP. This return to a NEP-type reform is particularly characteristic of the unfolding Gorbachev period; Gorbachev himself has invoked the precedent of the NEP, as if it gave him a license to do what he wants to do. Thus we are not straying too far from the present in paying special attention to the NEP period. NEP-type thinking is embedded in the present.

There is a second important reason for taking another look at the NEP. Most of the current attention to the NEP is almost wholly concentrated on its economic aspect. It also had, however, a political side of even greater long-term significance.

The NEP was adopted for a reason that is similar to that of subsequent reform periods, namely, the country was faced with some sort of crisis. In the case of the NEP, the crisis went back to the previous period of War Communism.

The economic system of War Communism was, as Lenin put it, "a direct transition from the old Russian economy to state production and distribution on communist lines."[1] It was, in effect, pure Communism, with no outlet for private initiative and the profit motive. At the root of the crisis was the refusal of the peasantry to produce a surplus to feed the rest of the population. The peasants went on strike, because anything they produced beyond their own needs was subject to confiscation. Moreover, there was little or nothing for peasants and workers to buy, even if they produced a surplus, because large-scale and small-scale production had almost completely broken down.

The crisis was so acute that "the revolution," as Lenin stated, "is on the brink of a precipice which all previous revolutions reached and recoiled from."[2] The precipice was marked by famine, drought, large-scale banditry, peasant revolt, abandonment of the factories, and, finally, the Kronstadt rebellion, which was put down bloodily at the very time the NEP was being introduced. The economics of War Communism was not the only cause of the crisis; the country had gone through three years of civil war and foreign intervention. By 1921, however, the civil war and foreign intervention had been overcome, and something still had to be done about War Communism.

The NEP was Lenin's strategy for withdrawing from the precipice to safer ground. It began with a reform of agrarian policy. Confiscation was abolished and a "tax in kind" substituted. The peasant could now produce as much as he liked; the surplus was subject to a small tax in kind; after paying the tax, he could sell the surplus for as much as the market would bear and take the profit for himself.

This shift in agrarian policy was the foundation of the NEP. Other innovations, such as joint enterprises between the Soviet state and foreign businesses, were introduced later. Throughout the NEP period, however, freedom to trade was limited to small-scale producers and the state retained a monopoly of large-scale or heavy industry. Toward the end of his life, Lenin came to believe that the basic solution to the economic problem lay in the organization of coop-

---

[1] Lenin, *Collected Works* (Moscow: Progress Publishers, 1966), Vol. 33, p. 61.
[2] Ibid., p. 67.

eratives, but the culture of the people, he complained, was so low that it would take "a whole historical epoch" for a cooperative economy to take hold in the entire country.[3]

We may call the NEP "reformist," because that is just the word used by Lenin for it.[4] He also called it other things that reveal what its practical function was intended to be—a "respite," an interval of time "in which the old and worn-out forces can 'recuperate,' " a partial reversion to "capitalism," a "flanking movement," a "retreat to a form of state capitalism, to concessions, retreat to trade," a "breathing space," and a product of "sheer necessity." Lenin's "reformism" was a tactical retreat to enable the Soviet regime to go on the offensive again at a later time when the "reform" had exhausted its usefulness. Lenin himself put it this way: "We are retreating, going back, as it were; but we are doing so in order, after first retreating, to take a running start and make a bigger leap forward."[5]

The NEP period was foreseen by Lenin as quite long, sometimes very long, though on this point he was not altogether consistent. He once said that the NEP would have to last "for a long time, but, of course, as has been correctly noted, not forever." He also mentioned that the NEP would give way to the new, fully Communist society "twenty years earlier or twenty years later," as if the time factor did not matter. Still later, he said that catching up with capitalist countries would take only "several years." And he foresaw that putting the entire population into cooperatives would take "a whole historical epoch."[6]

Economically, the NEP did serve its immediate purpose. It rescued the Soviet regime from the danger of possible disintegration and collapse. The peasantry soon began to produce surpluses of grain and food. The famine was relieved after only one year of the NEP. By 1925, agricultural production had approached the prewar level.

But, as I have noted, the NEP also had a political side to it. If the victory of Stalin in 1928–29, which brought about the demise of the NEP, is to be understood, Lenin's NEP-inspired politics was a significant contributing factor. The political NEP was far from being a democratic "reform"; in fact, it was just the opposite.

[3] Ibid., p. 470.
[4] Ibid., pp. 109–10.
[5] Ibid., p. 437.
[6] Ibid., pp. 160, 177, 392, 470.

The monolithic Soviet party-state was not born in 1917; opposition groups and parties continued to exist for some time inside and outside the main Bolshevik Party. Inside the Party, a "Left Communist" faction, whose main spokesman was Bukharin (later to go over to the other extreme), had sprung up in 1918 but did not outlast that year. By 1920, two more serious Communist opposition groups had arisen—the "Workers' Opposition," made up mainly of trade unionists, and the "Democratic Centralists," mainly intellectuals. The former was critical of War Communism as a reflection of widespread working-class discontent; the latter was primarily interested in greater democracy within the Party.

The monolithic Party was officially ordained in March 1921 at the same time as the NEP—and both at the behest of Lenin. A resolution on "party unity" denounced these two groups as "syndicalist and anarchist deviations" that were incompatible with Party membership. The effect was to make official a policy of banning opposition groups or tendencies at least in principle, though it did little to inhibit the factional struggles later in the decade. The ultimate beneficiary was Stalin, who succeeded in imposing his own type of "party unity" prescribed by Lenin.

Lenin had little difficulty getting the better of opposition within the Party, but the other two parties still functioning, if against increasing repression—the Left Socialist-Revolutionaries and the Mensheviks—were more formidable obstacles in the way of the monolithic party-state. The Left Socialist-Revolutionaries drew their support mainly from the peasantry; not so long ago they had been allies of the Bolsheviks and had even collaborated in the dissolution of the Constituent Assembly in January 1918. The Mensheviks were largely urban and particularly influential in the surviving trade unions, where they had more proletarian backing than the Bolsheviks. Both had long criticized War Communism as unnecessarily extremist and self-destructive.

Now the NEP appeared to justify their opposition to War Communism and put the Bolsheviks on the defensive as having belatedly agreed with them. Thus Lenin was faced with an acute political as well as an economic crisis after the Tenth Congress. Lenin's tactics were brutal in the extreme. He denounced the Left Socialist-Revolutionaries and Mensheviks as pure and simple counter-revolutionaries, mainly because they had dared to criticize War Communism prematurely and were likely to benefit from his late conversion. "All the White Guards, headed by the Mensheviks and Socialist-Revolutionaries," he said, "wax jubilant and say, 'Aha, you are retreating!' "[7] This crime brought out the most bloodthirsty language from Lenin. Because the Mensheviks and Socialist-Revolutionaries were allegedly saying, "The revolution has gone too far. What you [Bolsheviks] are saying now we have been saying all the time; permit us to say it again," Lenin replied: "Permit us to put you before a firing squad for saying that."[8] He also spoke of using machine guns against the Mensheviks and Socialist-Revolutionaries for their crime of saying: "You say you are retreating towards capitalism, and we say the same thing; we agree with you!"[9]

Thus there were two faces to the NEP—one opened the Soviet regime to temporary, limited economic experiments of a quasi-capitalist nature; the other imposed a full totalitarian, monolithic political order by officially wiping out all types and degrees of political opposition or driving it underground. By 1922, little or nothing remained of opposition in or out of the Party. And it was in that year that Stalin became general secretary of the Party and systematically put his henchmen in key posts in the Party apparatus, an advantage that stood him in good stead during the internal Party struggle later in the decade.

Stalin owed his victory, at least in part, to the political system Lenin had put in place beginning in March 1921. Lenin legitimated the monolithic Party with a monopoly of power in the country, and Stalin took the next step of giving himself a monopoly of power in the Party and, through it, in the country. In this respect, the political side of the NEP—the elimination of all political opposition—was a necessary, though not a sufficient, condition for the rise of Stalinism, whether or not Lenin himself would have gone all the way down the same road if he had lived long enough.

Two years later, after Lenin's final stroke, his so-called Testament called for the removal of Stalin as general secretary on the ground that Stalin was "too rude" for the job, but it was too late.

This complaint about Stalin's "rudeness" refers at least in part to a telephone conversation during which Stalin spoke insultingly to Krupskaya, Lenin's wife. Lenin seemed to recognize that "rudeness"

[7] Ibid., p. 220.
[8] Ibid., p. 283.
[9] Ibid., p. 313.

would appear to be a "trifle" to other Bolsheviks and, therefore, sought to bolster his case by relating it to the rivalry between Stalin and Trotsky. The entire passage suggests that Lenin was something less than firm in his demand for Stalin's removal as secretary-general:

> Stalin is too rude and this defect, although tolerable in our midst and in dealings with us Communists, becomes intolerable in a secretary-general. That is why I suggest that the comrades think about a way of removing Stalin from that post and appointing another man in his stead who in all other aspects differs from Comrade Stalin in having only one advantage, namely, that of being more tolerant, more loyal, more polite and more considerate to the comrades, less capricious, etc. This circumstance may appear to be an insignificant trifle. But I think that from the standpoint of safeguards against a split and from the standpoint of what I wrote above about the relationship between Stalin and Trotsky it is not a trifle, or it is a trifle which can assume decisive significance (January 4, 1923).

And what if the comrades could not find some paragon among them having the only advantage mentioned by Lenin? Elsewhere Lenin had already found flaws in all the other contenders. That Lenin, for personal as well as political reasons, wanted to remove Stalin from that particular job, not yet considered to be predominant in the party hierarchy, is a noteworthy historical sidelight, but that the others did not take his advice all that seriously and preferred to keep Stalin in charge of the organization is surely equally or more significant. In any case, Lenin's political contribution to the ultimate benefit of Stalinism is hardly negated by this belated, somewhat equivocal criticism of Stalin's personality.

When the Testament was revealed to members of the Central Committee some months after Lenin's death, the proposal to remove Stalin was turned down with the help even of some, such as Zinoviev, who at that time were considered particularly close to Lenin and were later to live to regret their lack of foresight—and to die for it.[10]

As for the still hotly debated question of how much Lenin's legacy was responsible for Stalin's ultimate power, my own belief is that there are two types of errors to avoid—that Lenin had everything to do with it and that he had nothing to do with it. Without Lenin's imposition of a one-party totalitarian state, there is some chance that

---

[10] For an excellent account of this episode, see Robert Tucker, *Stalin As Revolutionary* (Norton, 1973), pp. 270–73, 288–91. A still indispensable treatment of the Leninist period is Leonard Schapiro's *The Origin of the Communist Autocracy* (Bell, 1955; new edition, Macmillan, 1977).

Stalin's imposition of a personal dictatorship through a Stalinized Party might have been avoided—or at least made far more difficult. This does not mean that Lenin if he had lived long enough would necessarily have been indistinguishable from Stalin. In fact, it is hard to see that any other Bolshevik leader of the 1920s would necessarily have been indistinguishable from Stalin, but that does not absolve them of all responsibility for Stalin's ascendancy. Politically, Lenin's decision in 1921 to suppress all opposition was bad enough in its consequences without going so far as what Stalin did with it.

The social basis of Stalinism was largely, if inadvertently, brought about by Lenin. He was almost singlehandedly responsible for the decision to go ahead with the seizure of power by reversing the Marxist sequence of revolution—to take power in the name of Communism or socialism and create the social and economic conditions necessary for it afterward. Once this move was successfully made, he let loose a social upheaval that increasingly went out of control. Lenin himself had finally reached a stage of disorientation by resorting to the Napoleonic maxim: *"On s'engage et puis . . . on voit,"* which he freely translated as "First engage in a serious battle and then see what happens."[11] Improvisation was substituted for principle. Stalin took Lenin at his word that the NEP could not go on forever or even for very long and imposed the order of a concentration camp and extermination chamber on the increasingly recalcitrant Soviet reality. If the Soviet Union had not been driven to make good on Lenin's miscalculations, of which not the least was his expectation that a European revolution was about to rescue the Soviet Union and put it back on the orthodox Marxist path, it could well have been spared the Stalinist furies.

In any case, the Leninist legacy of "reform" through the NEP was far more complex and double-edged than it is usually made out to be. In its main outline, it was a daring maneuver. Its essence was to use capitalists and capitalist methods against capitalism, to use capitalism against itself.

---

[11] Lenin, *Collected Works*, Vol. 33, p. 480. This statement appeared in the comment "Our Revolution," written in January 1923 in reply to Nikolai Sukhanov's well-known *Notes on the Revolution.* The entire piece shows that Lenin was haunted to the end of his days by the argument with the Mensheviks over the prerequisites of a socialist revolution and finally admitted that the Bolsheviks had decided to "create the fundamental requisites of civilization in a different way from that of the West-European countries."

This strategy followed from Lenin's reasoning, which went as follows: The necessary condition for a full Communist economy was the growth of large-scale industry, which in turn was the necessary condition for a growing proletariat. The only way the new, weak Soviet state could get large-scale industry was to get capitalists, Russian and foreign, small and large, to create it for the ultimate benefit of the Soviet state. This was the rationale for inviting foreign capitalism into Soviet Russia in the form of mixed enterprises and economic concessions.

Lenin once put it this way: "Get down to business, all of you! You will have capitalists beside you, including foreign capitalists, concessionaires and leaseholders. They will squeeze profits out of you amounting to hundreds percent; they will enrich themselves, operating alongside of you. Let them. Meanwhile, you will learn from them the business of running the economy, and only when you do that will you be able to build up a communist republic."

The "proletariat" for which Lenin claimed to speak at this time, October 1921, was admittedly a fiction. In this same speech, Lenin acknowledged that "the proletariat has disappeared." He also said scoffingly: "Forgive me, but what is the proletariat? It is the class which is working in large-scale industry. Where is your large-scale industry? What kind of proletariat is it? Where is your industry? Why is it at a standstill?" With virtually no proletariat, it was the Party, not the proletariat, or at best the Party self-appointed as the representative of the proletariat, that was "the ruling class." But Lenin also said, in March 1922, of the Party: "If we do not close our eyes to reality we must admit that at the present time the proletarian policy of the party is not determined by the character of its membership, but by the enormous undivided prestige enjoyed by a small group which might be called the Old Guard of the party." Ironically, the Mensheviks had to be suppressed because, with their preponderant influence in the trade unions, they were far more "proletarian" than the Bolsheviks.

But Lenin always returned to the theme that the capitalists could be permitted to operate only on condition that they should be strictly controlled: "The proletarian state may, without changing its own nature, permit freedom to trade and the development of capitalism only within certain bounds, and only on condition that the state regulates (supervises, controls, determines the forms and methods of) private trade and private capitalism."[12] He also spoke in this vein: "We shall make as many concessions as possible within limits, of course, of what the proletarian *can* concede and yet remain the ruling class."

All this freedom to trade and develop a limited amount of capitalism was temporary and provisional. Lenin actually anticipated Stalin's campaign against the peasantry by warning that the day of retribution was coming. In 1922, when conditions showed signs of improvement, he already looked ahead to the next, post-reformist stage: "Permit me to say this to you without exaggeration, because in this respect it is really 'the last and decisive battle,' not against international capitalism—against that we shall yet have many 'last and decisive battles'—but against Russian capitalism, *against the capitalism that is growing out of the small-peasant economy, the capitalism that is fostered by the latter. Here we shall have a fight on our hands in the immediate future, and the date of it cannot be fixed exactly"* (*emphasis added*).[13]

There is still a dispute over Lenin's basic attitude toward the NEP. Was it a tactical retreat to last only as long as it provided the necessary preconditions for an advance toward an orthodox socialist economy, or was it itself "the road to socialism" and, therefore, not to be cast aside as soon as it had exhausted its usefulness? An article, "The Importance of Gold Now and After the Complete Victory of Socialism," published in *Pravda*, November 6–7, 1921, has been interpreted as bearing out the latter sense, because it cautions that revolutions are doomed if it is believed that they "can and must solve all problems in a revolutionary manner under all circumstances and in all spheres of action." But the emphasis in this article is on the particular circumstances of the time to justify a reformist "retreat"— a key term in this article—which Lenin says "is coming to an end." Far from having given up "revolutionary methods," Lenin looked forward to getting back to them as soon as the lack of "sufficient strength" had been overcome.

The same problem has been posed by one of Lenin's last articles, "On Cooperation," of January 1923. It made cooperative societies a further advance of the NEP and maintained that they were "all

[12] Ibid., p. 185.
[13] Ibid., p. 277.

that is necessary to build a complete socialist society." Since Lenin here equated cooperatives with socialist enterprises, there seems to be little more than a change of terminology, inasmuch as he eliminated the difference between them "if the land on which they are situated and the means of production belong to the state, i.e., the working class." In any case, the prospect was put far off, because "it will take a whole historical epoch to get the entire population into the work of the cooperatives through NEP." To get the overwhelming mass of peasants into cooperative societies, however, required a "cultural revolution" among them—a term unexpectedly introduced in this context and hardly one to be expected in the foreseeable future.

This visionary article cannot be easily assimilated in the corpus of Lenin's previous writings. After Lenin's stroke in May 1922, he was entirely cut off from all active participation in Party work and appears to have given himself over to speculations uncharacteristic of Marxist thought. One was that the final outcome of the world struggle for socialism "will be determined by the fact that Russia, India, China, etc., account for the overwhelming majority of the population of the globe," rather than by the proletariat in the more advanced industrial countries. Thus Lenin's brooding in 1923 cannot be taken as necessarily representing his view of the NEP in 1921–22, when he was still fully engaged in promoting it. In any case, as he admitted, few "practical workers" in the Party appreciated the "exceptional importance" of cooperatives, which had to wait for the present Gorbachev period to be taken up again, if as yet on a small scale, with official approval.

It was left to Stalin to decide on the date and the method, but it was Lenin who had set forth the basic strategy. The NEP, then, was peculiarly two-faced in its economic policy as well as in its political policies. It was to be a period of undetermined duration during which certain freedoms were officially encouraged—the peasants to produce as much as they could for their own profit, small-scale private manufacturing and trade to increase, foreign and domestic capitalists to build up Soviet trade and industry, factory managers relieved of undue interference by the party and trade unions. It was also a period that looked forward to the day when a "last and decisive battle" would be fought against the very same peasants, small-scale manufacturers and traders, factory managers, and foreign and domestic entrepreneurs.

The NEP was a remarkably ingenious and even grandiose gamble—this much, I think, must be conceded. And it largely succeeded. What it has to tell us for the future is that the Soviet system was, at least in Lenin's time, far from being as rigid and inflexible as it is sometimes thought to have been. Lenin showed how much it could compromise, twist and turn, retreat and advance, without losing its essential character. That is why every reform period goes back to the cult of Lenin against that of Stalin, not so much because Lenin was a permissive Communist and Stalin was not, but because the conditions that faced Lenin demanded a strategy of flexibility, compromise, concessions, indirection, partial retreat, and a breathing space.

Finally, the NEP anticipated future NEP-type reforms by generating a fierce intra-Party factional struggle. By 1926, such a struggle broke out between a faction headed by Bukharin and Stalin, who were then allies, and a so-called United Opposition that temporarily brought together Zinoviev and Trotsky. Much of this struggle turned ideologically on the future of the NEP. The Bukharin-Stalin faction argued that the NEP had been such a success that it deserved to be continued; the Zinoviev-Trotsky Opposition held that the Soviet economy was losing its socialist character, that it had favored the peasantry too much, and that it was now necessary to emphasize industrialization. The complexities of this struggle would take too long to unravel—it is enough to say that it took Stalin, who now had effective control of the Party machine, only about a year to get rid of the leaders of the Opposition, who were expelled in late 1927. Having rid himself of Zinoviev, Trotsky, and their followers, with Bukharin's help, Stalin turned on Bukharin and finished him off.

By 1929, Stalin was supreme. He then turned around again and adopted much of the program of the former "Left Opposition" by pushing through a policy of increased collectivization and rapid industrialization. That was how the short, happy life of the NEP came to an end.

If the NEP was a precedent for later periods of Soviet reform, we should expect to meet again with the encouragement of private initiative in a controlled economic environment, with a temporary improvement in economic conditions, and with an immanent intra-Party struggle over how far the reform movement should go.

3

Khrushchev will probably be remembered most gratefully for two things—his so-called Secret Speech at the Twentieth Congress in 1956 exposing the evils and crimes of the Stalinist epoch, and the liberation from the gulag and its camps of hundreds of thousands of prisoners, many of them former Party members and even staunch Stalinists. Except for these blessings, little seems to remain of Khrushchev's policies, for one reason because they were inconsistent and even self-contradictory.

For example, it was a time of cultural "thaw"; Solzhenitsyn's *One Day in the Life of Ivan Denisovich* was published in 1962 to much rejoicing and acclaim. Yet Pasternak was persecuted in that very same period.

Khrushchev gave the peasants more leeway in the disposition of private surpluses, as the NEP had done three decades earlier. But Khrushchev was also a devotee of the pseudoscientific agronomist Lysenko.

By extricating the Party from the dead hand of Stalin's vengefulness, Khrushchev gave Party members a new sense of security from that terror. But he also upset the Party by attempting to tinker with it. At the Twenty-second Party Congress in 1961, he pushed through changes in the statutes to provide that top officials could hold their jobs for a maximum of fifteen years and middle-ranking officials for only six years. This sort of Party reform apparently created a sense of threat in the ranks and later served to turn the whole Party against him from top to bottom.

Khrushchev's final fate was easily as significant as anything else that happened in his relatively short-lived period. The most notable thing about his removal was the ease with which it was accomplished. He was apparently completely isolated; Brezhnev took over without a struggle. Khrushchev himself became a nonperson; not even an obituary was published at his death in 1971. Khrushchev contributed one invaluable precedent for the benefit of the Gorbachev effort— Khrushchev showed that it was possible to repudiate at least the worst excesses of the Stalinist heritage and die in bed.

Still, even Khrushchev's liberation of Stalin's prisoners is not without a shadow. Here was a system that had to put hundreds of thousands into the gulag in order for Khrushchev to liberate them. When one thinks of their liberation, even if so many of them came out wasted and broken, one must rejoice; but when one thinks of the system that put them into a hell on earth, one is almost driven to despair.

Among the great powers today, it is only in the Soviet Union that a leader can appear to be a liberator by not subjecting his people to the inhumanity, the barbarism, of his predecessors. If a German chancellor tried to claim credit as a humanitarian for not putting millions of people, including little children, into gas ovens, we would consider him to be a moral monster.

Soviet "liberators," such as Khrushchev, liberate within a system that, unless it is dismantled, requires more liberating. Khrushchev left enough of the system intact so that Gorbachev has plenty of liberating work left to do. We will know that the system has achieved the goal of "a qualitatively new state of Soviet society" only when there is no more need for such Soviet liberators.

4

If we look at the present period under Gorbachev from a historical perspective, we might well ask: How original or innovative have Gorbachev's economic policies been?

The answer, I think, must as yet be: Not very. In economic policy, which is the main arena of the present reform, Gorbachev's changes have been remarkably reminiscent of the NEP. For example, a new law has given individuals and families the right to go into private business to manufacture consumer goods such as toys and souvenirs and perform services such as repairing cars and garden tools. This measure of limited private enterprise goes right back to the NEP and, in addition, merely legalizes what has been going on unofficially if not illegally for years.

In theory, much of Gorbachev's program was put forward as early as 1965, soon after Khrushchev's overthrow, by Alexei N. Kosygin, then the Chairman of the Council of Ministers. Kosygin proposed the decentralization of management, the simplification of central planning, the improvement of productivity and efficiency, with the increasing use of such economic "levers" as profits, prices, incentives, bonuses, loans, and credits.[14] Also in the mid-1960s, the economist

---

[14] At the Central Committee plenum in September 1965 (*Pravda*, September 28, 1965, cited by Hanson Leung C.K. *Studies in Comparative Communism*, Winter 1985, pp. 231–32).

Professor Liberman attracted a good deal of attention by advocating decentralization of controls and the replacement of quantitative production quotas with an emphasis on quality and price.

The essential Gorbachev ideas for the Soviet economy are hardly new or original. What is striking is that it has been so hard to carry them out before. What is new is the urgency with which they are now being advanced.

Why the urgency? The reason given by Gorbachev and his lieutenants is that the Soviet Union fell back disastrously during the Brezhnev era. Gorbachev himself has said: "One cannot help seeing that since the early 1970s certain difficulties in economic development have begun to make themselves felt."[15] Gorbachev has also spoken of the Brezhnev era in the most scathing terms. In one recent speech, he castigated Party members who had "engaged in embezzlement, bribe-taking and report-padding," "manifestations of spiritual emptiness and skepticism," "a scornful attitude towards laws, hoodwinking, bribe-taking and the encouragement of servility and glorification," "banality, primitive tastes and spiritual emptiness."[16] The rot came from the top: "Many party members holding leadership posts were not subject to supervision or criticism, which led to failures in work and serious violations of party ethics."[17]

One of Gorbachev's most outspoken associates, later ousted and repudiated by Gorbachev, Boris Yeltsin, went somewhat further in assessing the blame:

> Why do we raise a number of the same problems Congress after Congress? Why has the obviously alien word "stagnation" appeared in our party lexicon? Why have we been unable for so many years to eradicate from our life bureaucratic excess, social injustice, and abuses? Why, even now, is the demand for radical changes getting bogged down in an inert stratum of timeservers with party membership cards? In my opinion, one of the main reasons is that a number of Party officials lack the courage to promptly and objectively assess the situation and their personal role, to tell the truth, even if it is bitter . . .[18]

If we may take Gorbachev at his word, the present crisis is so profound that it is systemic. He has gone so far as to say that the

---

[15] *Pravda*, June 12, 1985. (All translations from *Pravda* hereafter are taken from the *Current Digest of the Soviet Press*, published weekly at Columbus, Ohio.)

[16] Ibid., January 28, 1987.

[17] Ibid.

[18] Ibid., February 27, 1986.

present crisis demands nothing less than some sort of *revolutionary* change. In Khabarovsk in the summer of 1986, he said: "I would equate the word restructuring with the word revolution."[19] In January 1987, he reiterated that the new leadership had in mind "truly revolutionary and comprehensive transformations in society."[20] And in February of the same year, he told an audience of over nine hundred people, mainly foreigners, at the so-called International Peace Forum: "You have arrived in the Soviet Union when essentially revolutionary changes are under way."[21]

The term "revolution" need not be taken literally. If Gorbachev meant "revolution" literally, he would be committed to overthrowing the allegedly existing proletarian state and putting a new class in power—at least he would have to do so from a Marxist point of view. His second in command, Yegor K. Ligachev, recently entangled himself in the same Marxist contradiction. "The process of restructuring that is now unfolding is revolutionary in nature—both in scale and in content," he said. "Needless to say, this does not involve changing the essence of our social system."[22] Needless to say, there can be no revolution, for a Marxist, that does not change the essence of a social system. As if he thought that he had gone too far, Gorbachev himself gave assurances that his shake-up would not result in "disorganizing society."[23] How he could lead a revolution without shaking up and disorganizing the existing society, he did not say.

Nevertheless, the very use of such a term as "revolution" for what Gorbachev & Co. want to do is most revealing. It suggests that the changes they want to bring about are so far-reaching that they must resort to rhetorical overkill to make the bureaucracy and the people aware of the full seriousness and basic nature of their plans for a renewal of the entire system.

How basic the changes will actually be is something for the future to decide. As Gorbachev has repeatedly stressed, only a start has yet been made. Nevertheless, it would be a gross mistake to scoff at the whole enterprise.

[19] Ibid., August 2, 1986.
[20] Ibid., January 28, 1987.
[21] Katrina vanden Heuvel, *Nation*, March 7, 1987.
[22] *Pravda*, November 7, 1986.
[23] *The New York Times*, February 26, 1987.

5

The shift has been most marked in the cultural and journalistic fields. Plays have been put on, books published, films shown, and articles printed that were never before permitted. *Glasnost*, or openness, is the latest miracle cure for whatever ails Soviet society—poor harvests, infant mortality rates, alcoholism, drug abuse, prostitution, earthquakes, shipwrecks, hijackings, airplane crashes, even traffic accidents, classified as state secrets.

Thus far, intellectuals have benefited the most. This is all for the best and no one would begrudge the Soviet intellectuals their newly increased freedom of expression. One reason for this favoritism may well be that this second cultural thaw pays off the most in foreign appreciation. Another reason may be that the new cultural policy is least likely to cause trouble in the Party and in the economy. Most of all, the renewal of the system requires scientific inventiveness and intellectual creativity, which cannot be obtained without greater freedom of expression and experimentation.

As yet, the Soviet Union is still in the stage of getting special commendation and reward for permitting a play or book that would be permitted as a matter of course in most Western countries. The Soviet intellectuals' new freedom looks good only against the backdrop of the cultural horrors of the past, not as it might be judged by any standards that Western intellectuals recognize as minimally acceptable. One of the odd things about the stir that the new intellectual permissiveness in the Soviet Union has aroused is that it implicitly assumes that anything better than hard-core Stalinism or soft-core Brezhnevism is a great advance in the history of human freedom.

The emphasis on *glasnost* suggests that, if only the people knew how bad things are, they would move to correct them—as if people did not already know how bad things are. *Glasnost* is also a means of showing how bad Gorbachev's predecessors were. New Soviet leaders invariably tear down the old ones—Stalin tore down Lenin's closest co-workers who opposed him, though not Lenin himself; Khrushchev tore down Stalin; Brezhnev tore down Khrushchev; and Gorbachev has been busy tearing down Stalin and Brezhnev. Thus *glasnost* is being practiced in almost every sphere of Soviet life at the expense of past leaders and does nothing to threaten Gorbachev's own record or prestige. One wonders how much *glasnost* there may be for anyone who wished to criticize Gorbachev.

Despite these caveats, the determination of Gorbachev & Co. to shake up the Party, to make it enter a new economic and technological age, should not be in doubt. Just how far they really mean to go—or how far they will be able to go—may be debated, but that they sincerely believe that something is deeply and dangerously wrong—and that something drastic must be done about it—cannot, in my opinion, be denied. This is not like any reform movement of the past; it certainly goes further than anything that Lenin or Khrushchev ever thought of proposing.

What, then, is driving Gorbachev's team to such extremes with such urgency?

The question can be answered at least partly with what the new leadership itself has said. It is apparent that something happened sometime in the 1970s that caused the rising generation of Soviet leaders to become acutely apprehensive of the future.

In the past, the Soviet economy had moved forward "extensively," that is, by using up more natural resources, building more factories, and multiplying the labor force, with little or no modernization of the means of production. If more machinery was turned out, it was a replica of the old machinery. But now natural and human resources cannot be stretched any further; the crisis of the 1970s came about as a result of diminishing returns from the same industrial base.[24] For one thing, the rate of economic growth had begun to fall in the 1970s and continued to fall in the early 1980s. One figure revealed by Gorbachev will do to show the depth of the Soviets' economic retrogression. "Over the past three five-year plans [that is, a period of fifteen years]," he disclosed in January 1987, "the growth rates of national income declined by more than 50 percent."[25] The lesson that the present leadership has learned is that extensive, quantitative

---

[24] "Through inertia, the economy continued to develop to a large degree on an extensive basis, oriented toward drawing additional labor and material resources into production. As a consequence, the growth rate of labor productivity and certain other indices of efficiency dropped substantially. Attempts to rectify the problem through new construction exacerbated the problem of balance. The national economy, which has vast resources, ran into resource shortages. A gap formed between social requirements and the achieved level of production, between effective demand and the amount of goods available to meet that demand" (Gorbachev, *Pravda*, February 26, 1986).

[25] *Pravda*, January 28, 1987.

exploitation of resources, natural and human, must be replaced by intensive, qualitative development.

By the time Gorbachev came to power in March 1985, the full force of this critical economic state of affairs had hit the top leadership. It realized that a scientific and technological revolution had taken place in the rest of the world but had bypassed the Soviet Union. If any one factor may be said to have shaken the leadership out of its accustomed self-satisfaction and inertia, it is this—the failure to meet the competition of what Gorbachev has referred to as "the capitalism of the 1980s, the capitalism of the age of electronics and informatics [*sic*], computers and robots."[26] It was not simply that the Soviet Union had fallen behind the United States or Western Europe in the new technology; it could not produce what Japan, South Korea, and even Taiwan were turning out in mass production and with which they were flooding world markets.

The shock was all the greater if we recall the ambition and pretension that the Soviet leadership had once had. Back in 1961, at the Twenty-second Party Congress, Khrushchev had boasted of overtaking the United States by 1970 and building a full Communist society by 1980. Gorbachev is making no such promises; the problem now is to catch up and make up for lost time, not to overtake and overcome.

Once the urgency of the task had sunk in, it was realized that there was no shortcut to the new era. The whole Soviet system was not prepared for it; the whole system had to be reshaped—or as the current slogan has it, "restructured"—to advance to a higher scientific and technological level. The "scientific and technological revolution," as Gorbachev has put it, "is linked with the improvement of social relations, the restructuring of thinking, the cultivation of a new mentality, and the establishment of dynamism as a way of life, as a norm of existence."[27] All this is a rather tall order—technological, social, ideological, and psychological. If taken seriously, it implies that the entire Soviet order desperately needs redoing from top to bottom.

What can possibly account for this extraordinary sense of crisis? The impetus has certainly not come from below. There is no evidence

[26] Ibid.
[27] Ibid.

that the Soviet leadership is responding to mass unrest. On the contrary, the leadership is making feverish efforts to stir up the masses, to make them more responsive to change, to shake them out of their accustomed ways, and to bring the utmost pressure to bear on them to change their habits of thought and work—habits instilled by the previous six decades of Communist rule.

Gorbachev's revolution will not succeed if it remains "from above." It must set the broad masses in motion, and therein lie both its promise and its peril. A major transformation from top to bottom can release huge energies hitherto held back by enfeebled leadership and enervated bureaucracy. But once the masses of people get the idea that they have been released from automatic Party tutelage and obedience, they may take things into their own hands and test the limits of Gorbachev's invitation to democratize and initiate from below. Limits there almost certainly are and will be, but no doubt the present leadership considers them to be something to be worried about if and when they have been reached.

My own belief is that the new Soviet leadership has been shocked into action primarily by the prospect of a precipitous decline in prestige and power on the world stage. The Soviets have struggled for decades to obtain a position of accepted parity with the United States in a world of only two superpowers, with all other nations trailing behind.

Now that position has been threatened by two main developments.

One may be described as ideological or cultural. The Marxism-Leninism of the Soviet Union had become an ideology to be scorned, when not ignored. Culturally, the Soviet Union had been turned into a wasteland from which creative writers and artists had fled or been driven out. Such creative minds as were left had their freedom of expression stifled or suppressed.

The best proof that Soviet cultural or intellectual status had sunk abysmally is what has happened in France. Two or three decades ago there was hardly an influential intellectual who was not a member of the French Communist Party or at least a fellow traveler. Today there is hardly one who is. The term "Communist intellectual" has become virtually an oxymoron.

I would not underestimate the cost to Soviet prestige and influence of this worldwide phenomenon. I would imagine that it helps to account for the zeal with which the Gorbachev leadership is trying to revive Soviet culture and give it some free air to breathe in.

But by far the greatest threat to the Soviets' world position has come from its scientific and technological retrogression. A country that cannot hold its own technologically with South Korea or Taiwan has reason to worry if it also claims to be one of the world's two superpowers. It has even more reason to worry if its leaders finally realize that they cannot go on in the old way, that the rules of the game were changed while they were not looking.

At the very outset of his regime in 1985, Gorbachev struck this note: "The country's historical destiny and the positions of socialism in today's world depend in large part on how we handle matters from now on"—by which he meant "making broad use of the scientific and technological revolution and bringing the forms of socialist economic management into line with present-day conditions and requirements."[28] A year later, in the summer of 1986, he put the same thought this way: "We should, we simply must, make socialism stronger, a dynamically developing system that competes successfully with capitalist society in all parameters. This requires, above all, complete and effective use of the truly inexhaustible possibilities that are opened up by the scientific and technological revolution."[29] That scientific and technological revolution is almost an obsessive theme in Gorbachev's speeches. The international, military, economic, and social implications of falling so far behind must be equally obsessive.

6

Another indication of how serious the present leadership is in its determination—one might almost say its desperation—to pick itself up by its scientific and technological bootstraps is the amount of resistance the program is said to be encountering. One of the peculiar aspects of the present Soviet scene is the anxiety of Soviet spokesmen to stress how great the internal resistance is. Hardly a visitor to the Soviet Union these days comes back without having been regaled with tales of the extent of such resistance throughout the huge bureaucracy.

Gorbachev is said to have unburdened himself privately to a group of some thirty Soviet writers in June 1986:

[28] Ibid., April 24, 1985.
[29] Ibid., July 1, 1986.

Between the people who want and long for changes and the leadership that encourages them, there is the administrative staff of the party apparatus and the ministries who do not want changes . . . Take Gosplan [the State Planning Committee]. As far as Gosplan is concerned, there is no authority, there is no General Secretary, no Central Committee. Its officials do whatever they want . . . The transformation is going ahead . . . But if you only knew with how much anguish all this is proceeding . . ."[30]

Pravda itself reported that at a meeting with the writers Gorbachev had said:

It [restructuring] is not coming easily. Conflict situations are showing up, and various stands are being fully revealed. In the process that is under way we are encountering everything imaginable—from wait-and-see philosophy to a lack of forethought and rashness.[31]

But where is the resistance coming from—and why? Here again we can learn a good deal from what Gorbachev and others have said publicly about the difficulty they are having pulling and pushing the Party into the new age.

At just about the time Gorbachev is said to have complained bitterly to the Soviet writers, he made much the same charges—if less emotionally—at a plenum of the party's Central Committee in mid-June 1986. He complained that "the restructuring itself is proceeding slowly so far . . . old approaches pull us back, and inertia is still strong . . . The turn to quality, efficiency and new methods of leadership is taking place painfully and with difficulty."

Gorbachev blamed various types of resistance. Quite a few Party members, he said, "have a political understanding of the need to work in a new way but simply don't know how to do this in practice." Others "take a wait-and-see attitude or do not believe in the success of the economic and political breakthrough planned by the party." Still others claim "that the directives voiced at the [Twenty-seventh] Party Congress [in February 1986] apply to the sphere of high-level policy, while practical work should take its normal course, following beaten paths. It must be said that such moods are still common among party personnel."[32]

Three months later, in September 1986, Gorbachev made more

---

[30] First published in the Italian newspaper *La Repubblica*, October 7, 1986, cited by Stephen F. Cohen, *Nation*, November 15, 1986.

[31] *Pravda*, June 21, 1986.

[32] Ibid., June 17, 1986.

serious charges about the nature of the resistance. He now accused "quite a few people who understand very well what restructuring is" but do not accept it, because "their main concern is to preserve the old, outmoded ways, to preserve their privileges, even though this is not in accordance with our principles, laws and morality or with our current policy." Among these people were workers and peasants, he said, but his real targets were "executives and administrative personnel" as well as "some among our intelligentsia." His wrath was mainly directed at "executives [who] are set in their ways, and . . . don't want to change their old thinking." In this speech, Gorbachev saw fit to evoke the memory of the NEP "when V. I. Lenin had to exert considerable effort to prove the need for a new economic policy," as if Lenin's effort was similar to and justified his own.[33]

Gorbachev has given an even more serious reason for another type of resistance. There are still people, he said, who "often see not what it [restructuring] in fact contains but [what is to them] all but a shaking of foundations, all but a renunciation of our principles." These are people who "have difficulty in accepting the word 'restructuring' and who even sometimes can pronounce it only with difficulty." The present political line, he protested defensively, "is aimed at fully disclosing the potential and advantages of the socialist system," not at renouncing or betraying it.[34]

This latter line of opposition implies, ironically, that Gorbachev might be charged with trying to carry through a counterrevolution, not a revolution—a counterrevolution, that is to say, against the kind of society that Communism had come to represent in the Soviet Union for most of its past. This recalls the same type of accusation by so-called Left Communists against Lenin's NEP. There is, however, a difference. Lenin frankly described the NEP as a "retreat," "respite," "breathing space." Gorbachev and his supporters use none of these terms.

In any case, we can now identify at least three types of resisters:

Those who are unprepared to adapt or are incapable of adapting to the new line;

Those who do not wish to adapt to it owing to its threat to their vested interests;

[33] Ibid., September 20, 1986.
[34] Ibid., October 24, 1986.

And those who see the new line as threatening the "socialist" foundations of the Soviet political and economic system.

One clear lesson would seem to be that it is premature to pronounce upon the ultimate fate of this effort. Gorbachev himself has frequently said that it is just about getting started. Inasmuch as Gorbachev has revealed that the Central Committee meeting in January 1987 had to be postponed three times, presumably because the leadership was not sure of its backing, there is reason to believe that the resistance extends into the higher, if not the highest, echelons of the party. At any rate, the leadership is not taking any chance of promising too much too soon. It has given itself fifteen years, to the year 2000, to achieve "a qualitatively new state of Soviet society," instead of the usual one or two five-year plans.[35]

Gorbachev has sufficiently reconstructed the top leadership so that he probably does not have to fear being overthrown from that quarter soon. In this respect, he seems to have learned the lesson of Khrushchev, who was easily removed because he had not been able to put his own men into the Politburo. But Gorbachev appears to have far more support in the top ranks than down below. His main problem is with the party and ministerial bureaucracies. *What happens in the Party is more than anything else going to decide whether he succeeds or fails.*

There is an obvious reason why the whole Party is not overjoyed with his grandiose plans. The Soviet Party has long been accustomed to controlling all the levers of power, large and small. The Party has now been put on notice that the economy cannot enter the new era unless it surrenders a good many of its former prerogatives. One of the prime aims of the new leadership is to decentralize the economy and to give more decision making to the managers of individual and group enterprises. Gorbachev and his lieutenants have made clear that decentralization cannot be accomplished unless the dead hand of Party bureaucracy is removed from non-Party economic and other types of organizations.

Toward the end of 1986, Gorbachev declared:

The foremost task today is to radically improve the style, forms, and methods of party organizations' work . . . To this end, it is necessary to be more resolute in doing away with the practice of supplanting economic, soviet, and public organizations, to increase their indepen-

---

[35] Ryzhkov, ibid., March 4, 1986.

dence and responsibility, and to dispense with the technocratic approach to solving political and social problems."[36]

It should not be hard to understand why this kind of talk strikes some elements in the Party as subversive of all they had been taught and had practiced for decades, why it should appear to them as "shaking the foundations" and "all but a renunciation of our principles."

How Gorbachev & Co. propose to accomplish this delicate operation of decentralizing will be most interesting to observe. The traditional means at hand are basically persuasion, force, or a combination of both. He could succeed by persuasion alone only if he commanded the support of the overwhelming majority in the Party and country. This seems at present to be unlikely, or there would not be so much talk about the strength of the resistance. But Gorbachev has cut himself off from the use of force, Stalin-style or anything like it, precisely by trying to put so much distance between his type of rule and Stalin's. If he resorts to force, he will make a mockery of his repeated professions of seeking to open up the Soviet system to increased democratization, and he will undercut his populist appeal.

Stalin accomplished a bloody revolution from above; Gorbachev would obviously like to accomplish a bloodless revolution from above, though on condition that it should succeed in enlisting mass approval and support from below. The future tactics of Gorbachev's revolution may depend on the resistance it encounters; the more the resistance, the more likely the pressure from above to overcome it. In any case, revolutions from above are notoriously treacherous; what can be set off from above can also be reversed from above.

One can sympathize with Party members and ordinary bureaucrats who have seen these campaigns and slogans come and go, knowing full well that what comes from the top can go from the top. The paradox is that Gorbachev's main political mechanism for change is the habit and enforcement of Communist Party discipline; he needs Party discipline in order to loosen Party control, but the loosening of Party control may well threaten the Party's unity and even lead to a factional struggle resembling that of the late 1920s or to his abrupt removal à la Khrushchev.

Can Gorbachev succeed? The answer depends on what success is

[36] Ibid., October 24, 1986.

thought to mean. He can, to my mind, certainly make the present system work better, if only by such means as the campaign against drunkenness and absenteeism. This sort of thing may be called reforms within the system. But, if we are to take seriously Gorbachev's analysis of what ails the Soviet system and what must be done to cure it, he needs to accomplish more—much, much more.

There is a basic problem with evaluating what Gorbachev is doing or plans to do. It is that we must consider not only what is changed but what is left unchanged. Thus far almost all emphasis has been put on the changes, most of which are still in the realm of intention or experiment rather than of accomplished facts. We will not know how to draw up a balance sheet of Gorbachev's "restructuring" for quite a while, and for that we will have to know what he has not changed as well as what he has.

If the real trouble is with the system, and it actually requires some sort of "revolution," my advice to anyone waiting for the outcome would be: Don't hold your breath.

(Dissent, Summer 1987)

HISTORY
OR
FICTION?

Journalistic History

STROBE TALBOTT'S new book, *Deadly Gambits: The Reagan Administration and the Stalemate in Nuclear Arms Control*, has introduced something new to the literature of nuclear arms policy-making. It has been praised by distinguished reviewers. It seemed important and authoritative enough for Walter Mondale to recommend it twice in his second television encounter with President Reagan in 1980. It is the work of an experienced and well-informed journalist, who was diplomatic correspondent for *Time* magazine from 1977 until recently, when he became Washington bureau chief. Much of his book makes fascinating reading. I even happen to share his general views, insofar as they can be inferred from his book.

Why, then, should I be acutely troubled by *Deadly Gambits*? Why does it present "journalistic history" at its most problematic? The feature that troubles me most is also what makes the book most fascinating. *Deadly Gambits* sets out to reconstruct how the Reagan Administration made nuclear arms policy during its first three years. It is the inside story of the "bureaucratic politics"—Mr. Talbott also calls it "bureaucratic warfare" and the "cutthroat marketplace of ideas"—that went into the formulation of the "zero option" of the Intermediate-Range Nuclear Force (INF) talks and the Strategic Arms Reduction Talks (START).

The book begins conservatively, with an expository chapter on the basic elements of the nuclear arms problem. Mr. Talbott knows his subject and has a rare ability to clarify and simplify its most baffling and intimidating aspects. But the book quickly shifts from being a nuclear arms primer to being a blow-by-blow account of rivalry, intrigue, and skulduggery in the top levels of the bureaucracy. More than any other book of its kind, it is made up of direct quotations attributed to its leading characters. Without the word-for-word dialogue, the book would lose much of its know-it-all seductiveness. We are not only there with the principal bureaucratic cutthroats; we know exactly what they said and how they said it. Mr. Talbott writes as if he had been a fly on the walls of even the most closely guarded rooms in the White House and Pentagon, hearing all, knowing all, recording all.

Previous books of this sort were far more restrained. John Newhouse's book on the Strategic Arms Limitation Talks (SALT I), *Cold Dawn*, published in 1973, was also much admired but had hardly any of the direct quotations and novelistic effects that abound in *Deadly Gambits*. Mr. Talbott's own previous book on SALT II, *Endgame*, published in 1979, had some of these embellishments but so few they did not call much attention to themselves. In *Deadly Gambits*, however, Mr. Talbott reconstructs scene after scene, confrontation after confrontation, word for word, sometimes gesture for gesture. Two questions arise: How could such verbatim information have come into his hands? And why should the rest of us have to find out what our nonelected officials do and say on matters of incalculable moment and urgency through the medium of a single, nonelected journalist?

In the foreword to his book, Mr. Talbott warns: "Official records of many events here will remain classified, and participants constrained from freely discussing their roles, for years to come. Therefore I cannot, here or in the pages that follow, acknowledge the sources that allowed me to keep a running account of events as they unfolded." This explanation is somewhat disingenuous. Mr. Talbott's book reads as if the many participants were not at all constrained from freely discussing their role with him, often to the exact language and facial expressions employed. If we are to believe Mr. Talbott's revelations, we must assume that the words came from the participants—the very participants who would otherwise be constrained from freely discussing their roles for years to come.

Their constraint therefore applies only to the people whom they are supposed to represent, who pay them, and who will suffer the consequences of their words and actions. Indeed, if official memoirs are any indication, these same participants are most unlikely in years to come to tell us as much as they have presumably told Mr. Talbott.

The participants are among the most highly placed officials in the United States government. They are charged with conducting policy in a field that is second to none in its gravity. Yet these participants are not shown engaging in high-minded discussions of the issues. They are portrayed as cutthroat rivals and shabby intriguers. The book gets much of its tension from a bureaucratic version of a shoot-out at the O.K. Corral.

We are in the presence of something more than journalistic history; this is novelistic journalistic history. It does to journalism what Truman Capote did to the novel in *In Cold Blood* and Norman Mailer did in *The Executioner's Song*. They experimented with nonfiction fiction or fictional nonfiction by the imaginative reconstruction of circumstantial details and invented dialogue. But they were professional novelists working with nonfiction material; Mr. Talbott is a professional journalist working with recent historical material. We are not accustomed to giving journalists the same leeway we give novelists. The novels of Capote and Mailer were essentially biographical, focusing on the lives of single persons. Mr. Talbott's book is ostensibly historical, dealing with a large cast of important official characters and a subject of singular moment. The two subjects are incommensurable, yet their treatment has been converging.

The line between journalism and fiction has become blurred. Even without the novelistic aspect, journalistic history is at best a hybrid. It does not obey the rules of history, and it stretches the conventions of journalism to the breaking point. In becoming novelistic, journalistic history runs the risk of becoming unrecognizable as either journalism or history.

The problem of anonymous sources is already present in daily and weekly journalism. Even individual stories based on unnamed officials open themselves up to manipulation and misuse. A politician or official who is anonymous cannot be held accountable. In politics, as the saying goes, information is power. Information gives officials power over journalists. The tables might be turned if all journalists went on strike against informants who insist on anonymity and unaccountability. It would be highly imprudent to wait for this to happen. But a single newspaper story is as nothing to a book full of apparently exact quotations from dozens of highly placed anonymous officials. The one says to the reader, "This is as much as we can learn at the moment"; the other says, "This is history." A newspaper can report one thing one day and revise or revoke the report the next day; a book makes a promise of much longer duration and far greater authority. The scale and presentation make a vital difference.

In both cases, officials who hide behind anonymity are guilty of serious malfeasance. They treat official information as if it were their private property; they profit from it in their memoirs. *Deadly Gambits* is full of references to the most highly classified material. When the government pleases, it prosecutes those who divulge such information without authorization. Yet the highest echelons of government habitually break the law without the slightest twinge of conscience or threat of retribution.

The plot of *Deadly Gambits* centers on a struggle between bad guys and good guys. If there is a villain, it is Richard Perle, the assistant secretary of defense for International Security Policy. If there is a hero, it is Paul H. Nitze, the negotiator with the Russians on nuclear arms in Europe. Somewhat harder to place is Richard Burt, at first director of the State Department's Bureau of Politico-Military Affairs and later assistant secretary of state for European Affairs. These three are the leading actors in a large cast of characters that includes President Reagan; Secretary of State George Shultz; former Secretary of State Alexander Haig; Secretary of Defense Caspar Weinberger; the under secretary for Policy in the Defense Department, Fred Iklé; the former director of the Arms Control and Disarmament Agency, Eugene Rostow; the negotiator on strategic arms control, General Edward Rowny; and many others. From beginning to end, they are at one another's throats, which makes for high drama and low chicanery. Most of the action takes place between the third-echelon assistant secretaries, Mr. Perle and Mr. Burt, or on the part of the two negotiators, Mr. Nitze and General Rowny, because the principals, Messrs. Reagan, Weinberger, and Shultz, are portrayed as too uninterested or incompetent to deal with the problem of arms control.

Judging from what Mr. Talbott has them say, these are not very nice people, or at least they are not very nice to one another. Some of the things they are quoted as saying will give some sense of the seamier side of bureaucratic politics that was revealed to Mr. Talbott. The august figure of Paul Nitze comes in for some of the choicest abuse. Mr. Perle accuses Mr. Nitze of having been deceptive and even dishonest. He denounces him for "an act of intellectual and political cowardice." Not to be outdone by his rival, Mr. Burt is reported to have said, "Nitze's utterly spooked; he's gone around the bend; he's panicking; he's falling apart." Mr. Rostow's deputy, Robert Grey, laments, "Paul's lost his mind." Mr. Nitze, always the gentleman, merely charges Mr. Perle with talking "rubbish," raising "phony" problems, and trying to "torpedo" his negotiations. Someone must have told Mr. Talbott just what insults were used, because he almost invariably puts them between quotation marks.

Mr. Talbott also knows just what was said in the most unlikely places. He takes us into the Situation Room in the White House. At a meeting there, Mr. Perle is supposed to have snapped, "Nitze doesn't deserve a damn thing." Mr. Talbott is also privy to just what was said at the equally hush-hush National Security Council meetings. A report of a discussion there goes on for two pages. An even more startling account is given, with the inevitable quotations, of a meeting at the National Military Command Center, which Mr. Talbott helpfully tells us is "known as the 'Tank,' the inner sanctum where the Chiefs [of Staff] hold their most important and sensitive deliberations." We are told exactly what one official, Admiral Jonathan Howe, said to Mr. Perle and vice versa in a telephone conversation. Nothing very significant passes between them, but it all adds up to more of the dialogue that gives this book its unique distinction.

No document is safe from Mr. Talbott. He tells us about one report that received "a code-word classification, higher than top secret, and was never issued even as an inter-agency paper within the government." No quotation this time, but he claims to know who prepared it and what was in it.

One of the more entertaining features of the book is that it tempts the reader to play the guessing game "Who Told What?" Someone, for example, must have told Mr. Talbott just what was said before and during the celebrated "walk in the woods" by Mr. Nitze and the Soviet negotiator, Yuli Kvitsinsky, on July 16, 1982. Only the two of them were there. Previously, we are told, they had indirectly assured each other there would be no listening devices. It would thus appear most unlikely that the exact words uttered by them could be reproduced, especially *in extenso*. Yet that is just what Mr. Talbott has apparently achieved. Who could have told him? We can hardly believe that it was Mr. Kvitsinsky. That would leave only Mr. Nitze. After all, our choices at this juncture are extremely limited. Whoever told him, however, will still be constrained from freely discussing his role for years to come, at least as far as everyone but Mr. Talbott is concerned.

But even if we assume that Paul Nitze was the source, could he have reproduced his conversations with Mr. Kvitsinsky so exactly? If Mr. Talbott's informant did not have a listening device with him, he must have been endowed with total recall. It would be interesting to know whether this is one of Mr. Nitze's little-known gifts.

Here is the conversation after a dinner for the two delegations between Mr. Nitze and Mr. Kvitsinsky about guarding themselves against listening devices:

> Later in the evening, Kvitsinsky and Nitze stepped outdoors for some fresh air and privacy. Kvitsinsky had relaxed somewhat, but his attempts at being light-hearted still exposed both barbs and raw nerves. "How confident are you," he asked Nitze, with forced humor, "that everything we're saying isn't being overheard?"
>
> Playing along, Nitze replied: "Pretty confident. But somebody may have put a listening device up there"—and he gestured to a rolled-up awning.
>
> "Right," said Kvitsinsky. "Better to meet in the woods"—as Shchukin and Nitze had done during SALT I.
>
> With the thinnest of smiles, Nitze objected: "But how could either of us be confident that the other didn't have a listening device in the sole of his shoe?"
>
> Kvitsinsky's comeback was prompt, and it was exactly what Nitze wanted to hear. "If that happened," said the Soviet, "each would know that the other was responsible."

This kind of thing, with its "forced humor," "playing along," and "thinnest of smiles," might appear in a spy novel, which is exactly how some of *Deadly Gambits* reads. Whoever told Mr. Talbott about this conversation must have been able to recall the slightest, least essential details. Mr. Talbott also quotes Mr. Nitze during the "walk in the woods" in passages of astonishing length. One runs on for four consecutive sentences totaling sixty-seven words, another for four sentences of fifty-four words. If no listening device was used, someone must not have needed it.

Or take the conversation Mr. Burt and Mr. Perle had as they came down an escalator in the Pentagon. Mr. Burt had just conferred with the Joint Chiefs of Staff without Mr. Perle's knowledge.

> Perle hailed him and asked what he'd been doing.
> "Just seeing some people."

"About what?"

"Oh, a number of things."

"Aha!" exclaimed Perle, "I'll bet you've been briefing the Chiefs on START!"

Burt looked pained. He avoided a direct answer and was obviously all the more eager to get to his car. Perle went back to his own office and ordered his aides to find out whom Burt had been seeing. His suspicions were confirmed. Perle said to [the Chairman of the Joint Chiefs of Staff, General David Jones] he was upset to discover that the Chiefs were paying more attention to a State Department official than to Perle himself, who was, after all, an Assistant Secretary of Defense. Jones gave Perle a stony stare and told him to have a nice day.

Here within a few lines we are given the chance to play our guessing game twice. In both cases, only two characters were involved. Did Mr. Perle or Mr. Burt or both tell Mr. Talbott what they said to each other at the bottom of the escalator? Did Mr. Perle or General Jones or both make Mr. Talbott privy to their dramatic little scene? Or was there a third person with an infallible memory always present? Do such highly placed informants inform in such petty detail? Do they talk as if they were writing publishable dialogue? We can only guess.

Mr. Talbott exhibits uncanny knowledge of the innermost secrets and slightest movements of his characters. "In keeping with a by-now fairly well-established pattern," we are told, Mr. Burt "left the dirty work to be done by his deputies." The new Chairman of the Joint Chiefs of Staff, General John Vessey, "was angry at the way Perle persisted in riding roughshod over professional soldiers, abusing them both behind their backs and to their faces. But he suppressed his anger." (Mr. Perle is said to have been convinced that the Chiefs were "pushovers and patsies for whoever leans on them the last, the longest and the hardest.") At a National Security Council meeting, "Haig pursed his lips and looked down at his notes." Mr. Burt and his principal deputy, Robert Blackwill, "were sitting around in Burt's office with their feet up." Mr. Perle and James Woolsey, a key member of the Scowcroft Commission on Strategic Forces, "ran into each other at a neighborhood swimming pool," and Mr. Woolsey had Mr. Perle "over to his house for coffee with Scowcroft." Mr. Nitze once snapped at Mr. Rostow, "Well, you sure pulled the rug out from me in there"—on the way back to their car.

The Reagan Administration, for all its sanctimony about leaks, has virtually institutionalized leaking as the modus operandi of bureaucratic politics. In his recent memoirs, *Caveat*, former Secretary of State Haig told of his experiences as if he had just arrived in Washington and knew nothing of its peculiar folkways:

> Line-by-line quotations from my report to the President on a conversation with the Soviet ambassador were put in the hands of a television commentator in time for the evening news on the very day they were delivered to the White House. A story in *Newsweek* contained direct quotes from deliberations in the National Security Council. An NSC decision on Libya appeared in the papers on the day it was made. Plans for covert action in Central America were leaked to the *Washington Post*, then backgrounded to the major media. A secret submission to the NSC by James L. Buckley, the under secretary of state for security assistance, was leaked. I learned that my memoranda to the President were being transmitted by a hidden hand to Senator Helms and, thereafter, were being made available to reporters in a method of leaking-by-proxy that suggests the Byzantine complexity of the methods involved in the craft of leaking.

Mr. Haig attributed much of his difficulty with the White House to these Byzantine methods. At least some of the leaks of which he complains must, then, have come directly from within the White House. This game can be played only by officials highly enough placed to know what to leak. This much is no mystery.

I once tried to break through the conspiracy that permits officials to use classified material in their memoirs but denies ordinary citizens and even historians access to the same materials. The occasion was the publication of Henry Kissinger's memoirs, which were bursting with classified material. As National Security Adviser and Secretary of State, Mr. Kissinger had probably set a record for briefing journalists anonymously, even on planes, where the disguise was transparent. When I asked to see the documents Mr. Kissinger had used, my request was rejected on the ground that these documents had never been declassified; only the portions used by Mr. Kissinger had been. By means of this dodge, no one else could gain access to the documents to determine what the context of the isolated quotations was or how faithfully they were used. In this and other ways, nonelected officials are not only enabled to make policy, they are permitted to control the history of their policy-making. The result can only be the corruption of journalism, the corruption of history, and the corruption of the democratic process.

Journalism and history do not—or should not—compete with each other. They have different functions, so they cannot fairly be compared. The one works close to the event with whatever information may be immediately available. The other works from a longer perspective and with much richer materials. The immediacy that gives journalism its irresistible morning-after advantage cannot be challenged by historians. Journalists write for a mass audience with varied interests and backgrounds; historians, especially serious ones, write partly or wholly for other historians, or at least they must obey rules set by their peers.

The difference comes out most sharply in the way sources are used. Journalists have long been accustomed to conceal their sources if they choose to do so or cannot help themselves. Historians may not hide behind sources that cannot be checked by other historians. They may find new materials, but no other historian would accept them without the exact provenance of the discovery. That is why historians tend to read notes and sources at least as carefully as they read texts they refer to; one cannot judge the reliability of a text without knowing where it came from. The reporter, however, is not responsible for authenticating what his source says, only for reporting it accurately. If the source is anonymous, the intelligent newspaper reader is—or should be—put on guard, and this to some extent mitigates the ever present risk of misinformation or propaganda.

The crucial questions raised for and by journalists who write history are: How much and what kind of license should they have? Is it right to put words in the mouths of participants in the story? Should a blanket of silence be permitted to shield highly placed officials from accountability for their words and actions? Is it best in a democratic society for a single journalist to become the chosen instrument of interested officials? What is the price that a democratic society pays for permitting such officials to evade the responsibility to report openly and fully to the people they ostensibly represent and instead to hide behind a screen of anonymity and unaccountability?

The line between journalism and history is not easy to draw. It is clear, however, that journalistic history that is also novelistic goes too far. It is time for journalists, editors, publishers, reviewers, and leak-prone officials to examine their consciences in this matter. Political and journalistic hygiene demands it.

(*The New York Times Book Review*, December 9, 1984)

Author's Note

The New York Times Book Review subsequently published a number of unusual letters in connection with my article. I had sent Secretary Weinberger and arms negotiator Nitze inquiries about the roles ascribed to them in *Deadly Gambits*. Weinberger replied with one letter, Nitze with two. My original article was also sent to Mr. Talbott to give him an opportunity to reply. My letters of inquiry to Assistant Secretary of Defense Perle and Assistant Secretary of State Burt were not answered. Herewith are the letters from Weinberger, Nitze, and Talbott, with my reply to Talbott.

Weinberger's Letter

November 6, 1984

Thank you for your letter of October 30 and for allowing me the opportunity to advise, at least one person, of the facts concerning the matters about which Mr. Talbott writes so erroneously but with such certainty.

You asked me about the quotations on page 59 of his book. I sent out for copies of those quotations and therefore am able to tell you that the whole series of quotations on page 59 were never said by me, nor felt by me, and because they are put in direct quotation marks, I feel perfectly free in describing them to you, or anyone else who might ask, as complete lies. It still amazes me how many writers are perfectly willing either to rely on somebody else's inaccurate statement without bothering to check the source (Mr. Talbott never checked with me, nor have I ever seen him) or are perfectly willing to make up a story out of whole cloth and print it as fact.

For further information about my attitudes, you might want to consult some of my colleagues in NATO and various members of congressional committees before whom I have actively supported our own involvement in NATO and associations with Europeans, and actively opposed such proposals as the Nunn Amendment, which would reduce our commitment to Europe.

You also asked about the quotation on page 227 which I have also obtained. I did not find a quotation on page 227, but there is a series of quotations on page 226 that purport to quote an exchange with me at an NSC [National Security Council] meeting. To the best of my memory, reinforced by my notes of those meetings, no such exchange ever took place, and the quotations attributed to General Jones [General David Jones, then Chairman of the Joint Chiefs of Staff] are totally unlike the style and manner of any comments I ever heard him make.

You further asked how direct quotations from an NSC meeting could be "available to Mr. Talbott." The answer is they could not be, and that Mr. Talbott simply had to make them up or rely on statements made by some people who thought it served their interests to attribute remarks that were never made to various participants.

In any event, I appreciate your giving me the opportunity to respond to your questions.[1]

Nitze's Letters

November 7, 1984

You ask for my comments on the quotations in Strobe Talbott's *Deadly Gambits*.

It is my understanding that during the Carter Administration, Strobe arrived at an agreement with David Aaron [then deputy to the National Security Adviser] and Les Gelb [then head of the State Department's Bureau of Politico-Military Affairs], which may have been approved by Cyrus Vance [then Secretary of State] as well, that Strobe would be provided with day-to-day information on all the developments concerning the negotiations of SALT II, but would not use any of that information unless and until the negotiations succeeded or until they definitively broke down. I believe this followed a pattern originally begun by Henry Kissinger [then President

---

[1] The allusions in Mr. Weinberger's letter require some explanation. On page 59 of *Deadly Gambits*, Mr. Weinberger is said to have spoken privately "of being fed up with European 'hangups' and 'moaning and groaning.' He sometimes described the task facing the U.S. as a combination of therapy and trickery: 'We've got to make them think that what we're doing is good for them. Not just that, but we've got to make them think that they're going to *like* it, and that it's what they've been asking us to do.' " On page 226, Mr. Weinberger and Richard V. Allen, then the National Security Adviser, are said to have claimed at a meeting of the National Security Council that the Strategic Arms Limitation Talks (SALT) obstructed needed United States weapons programs. General Jones is said to have disputed this claim; the direct quotations attributed to him include three sentences that run on for thirty-two words.

Nixon's National Security Adviser] with John Newhouse, which resulted in [Mr. Newhouse's 1973 book] *Cold Dawn*. Strobe's SALT II arrangement ended up with [his 1979 book] *Endgame*. Many of the sources Strobe developed during SALT II were also prepared to cooperate with Strobe during the START [Strategic Arms Reduction Talks] and INF [Intermediate-Range Nuclear Forces talks] period using the same ground rule, even though doing so had not been approved by higher authority in the Reagan Administration.

As a result of those arrangements Strobe obtained a great deal of information from a number of sources with respect to the INF and START negotiations. When Strobe indicated to me what he had already been told by others about the "walk in the woods" [when Mr. Nitze met privately with his Soviet counterpart and reached an informal agreement on "a joint exploratory package" for limiting the deployment of medium-range missiles in Europe], I decided it would be better that he have the facts straight rather than having them wrong. I therefore did my best to help him get the sections dealing directly with me right. I tried not to add information on subjects [on] which he had not already been informed or misinformed.

Therefore, to answer your specific questions, I believe the sections of Strobe's book dealing with matters of which I had personal, first-hand knowledge are substantially correct. I am not in a position to comment on the accuracy of quotations of things said when I was not present.

November 19, 1984

I am not a journalist, so I am reluctant to comment on questions regarding what is proper procedure in that profession. I am much more interested in whether the substance is substantially correct than with the procedures, although I imagine procedures can also be important. I imagine the choice as to procedures is between dry-as-dust precision or the color and immediacy necessary to make a book readable.

Most of the conversations between [Yuli] Kvitsinsky [Mr. Nitze's Soviet counterpart in the INF talks] and myself were taken down by translators and carefully checked for accuracy. With respect to those occasions when we talked without translators, I would write down notes to aid my memory while riding back from the discussions in my car and then dictate as close to a verbatim memorandum of conversation as possible. Such dictation usually took longer than the original discussion. I imagine there were some deviations between the words actually used and what I dictated; I would be surprised, however, if such deviations changed the substance.

Talbott's Comments

Mr. Draper's article is a constructive, forceful contribution to public discussion of a number of important issues and a number of difficult dilemmas faced by both journalists and their readers. He raises the very legitimate question of how the public can evaluate the accuracy of information and the validity of judgments offered in a book like mine when the author does not (because he cannot) identify sources. This is a problem, I would suggest, that is inherent in journalism, since those of us who practice that profession are able to learn what is going on only if people directly involved in events will be, in private, more candid and comprehensive in their revelations than either they or their institutions can be in public. In exchange for their candor, these sources expect—and are explicitly assured—that they will not be identified. The fact that this journalistic technique is so common does not make it any less problematic than Mr. Draper suggests; but the fact that it is so problematic does not make it any less indispensable to the practice of the profession and to the fulfillment of the journalistic mission, which is to inform the public of things that various institutions, including the government, frequently do not want known.

Historians have both an advantage and a disadvantage in this regard. Their sources are for the most part out of harm's way, as it were; they cannot be reprimanded or fired by their bosses for leaking, so they can be cited without jeopardy. The disadvantage, of course, is that the historian does not have the chance very often to follow events day by day, as they unfold, remaining in close contact with the shapers of those events. The journalistic observer is able to discern what people thought they were doing at the time they were doing it and thus to recognize revisionism and self-serving forgetfulness when, as they often do, they arise later. I've seen enough of the official record of what transpired in SALT II, INF, and START to know that future historians—when they have access to the full record and are in the enviable position of being able to identify sources in footnotes—will still be in some danger of being misled on certain points precisely by that record. Indeed, one purpose I hoped to serve in *Deadly Gambits* was to give future historians an additional resource to help them in evaluating other disclosures that will then be available to them.

My book, in short, is very much a work of journalism, which is, by definition, not the last word on an event. But it is very often the first—and freshest—word and, as such, valuable both in the present and in the future, especially if every care is taken to assure that it is accurate. That brings me to another theme in Mr. Draper's essay.

While I accept Mr. Draper's general point about the difficulties of journalism as history, I differ with him on what he characterizes as a tendency in my book and others to resort to novelistic or even fictional devices for the sake of a good story. That is not something I have done, and I agree with him that it is not something others should do in the name of journalism or history.

He places great stress on the extensiveness of the quotations in my book, particularly those at closed-door encounters. Let me say a word about how I assembled my chronicle of INF and START in *Deadly Gambits* (and, before that, of SALT II in *Endgame*). Early on, I approached a wide variety of people involved in, or likely to be knowledgeable about, the deliberations within the United States government and the negotiations with the Soviet Union. Many agreed to speak to me on two conditions: (a) that I would not identify them as sources, and (b) that I would withhold publication in *Time* and in a book until, by my lights, the story could be said to be over.

I began work on *Deadly Gambits* literally the day after the 1980 election. For the next three years and some months, I made the rounds of sources, week in and week out. I frequently saw people very soon after a meeting in Washington or a negotiating session in Geneva had occurred—sometimes on the very same day, often within a few days. My sources' accounts of what transpired were based not just on very fresh memory but often on notes taken in meetings, on memorandums of conversations, on talking points, on reporting cables, and on other documents. Moreover, I had numerous opportunities to check, recheck, and triangulate with different participants their recollections of what was said and done.

It was by this method that I was able, with confidence and I believe with accuracy, to use fairly extensive quotations. I did so only when sources with firsthand, immediate knowledge of what was said offered me direct quotations, and in many cases I was able to verify those quotations with others who had been present.

When the Soviet Union withdrew from both INF and START at the end of 1983, I notified my sources that—again, by my lights—the story I had set about to tell was over. Many but not all agreed with my determination. The one constraint that remained and that still remains is that I would not, in this book or elsewhere, identify exactly who had provided me with the information necessary to produce the chronicle—and who would have done so only on the condition that they not be identified. Mr. Draper is free to play what he calls his "guessing game" about who told me what when, but I cannot join in, as a player or as a referee.

A briefer comment, if I may, on Secretary Weinberger's letter:

His records and recollection may show that he never said what I attributed to him; the recollections of others—offered to me and confirmed by additional sources close to the time of the event described—convince me that he did, although I have no desire to reciprocate his charge of lying. I suspect we have here an example of the kind of revisionism and selective memory I was referring to above. I'm sorry that Secretary Weinberger does not recall the occasions on which we met, but he is quite right that I did not meet with him when well along with my project in order to check quotes directly with him. The records of his public affairs office should confirm that I attempted to do so but was turned down more than once.

My comment on Ambassador Nitze's [November 7] letter is even briefer. He includes a conjecture about the arrangements and the sources that led to my earlier book, *Endgame*. Mr. Nitze was out of the government at the time (although he was an extremely important figure in the public debate over SALT II), and he does not know exactly whom I relied on as sources for that book, although he—like Mr. Draper in the case of *Deadly Gambits*—is free to speculate.

Draper's Reply

My article tried to make three main points—the problematic nature of "journalistic history"; the even more serious problem of "novelistic" journalistic history; and the ominous collusion between anonymous officials and favored journalists, together engaged in surreptitiously feeding the public a version of events for which no one can be held accountable. Mr. Talbott deals mainly with the first point, barely touches the second, and has nothing to say about the third.

We do not disagree on everything. Mr. Talbott agrees that a book full of anonymous sources and quotations is a "problem." But, he pleads, it is a problem "inherent in journalism," and his book "is very much a work of journalism."

I had already pointed out in my article that a book of this nature comes on as far more than daily or weekly journalism. It rather belongs to journalistic history, which is something else. A reader cannot go through more than 350 pages, spanning three years of nuclear arms policy, with a large cast of important official characters, without getting the impression that it is more than a "work of journalism."

Even experienced journalists have taken *Deadly Gambits* to be more like history than like ordinary journalism. In a column in *The New York Times* of November 13, 1984, Flora Lewis wrote that "the book documents a distressing story of non–decision making." Yet there is not a shred of documentation in the book. She also called it "a rigorous, objective study." The book may have a number of virtues, but rigor and objectivity are not among them. On November 16, 1984, Tom Wicker referred to the book as "authoritative," another wildly misused term for a book which never cites any "authorities." Yet these seasoned journalists were apparently so impressed by the pretension of omniscience that they treated the book as if it were accredited history rather than customary journalism.

The best defense that Mr. Talbott can muster is that he was the victim of journalistic necessity. I never doubted that, though it seems odd that Mr. Nitze, for one, should have no compunctions about coming forth in his letter to me as the source of Mr. Talbott's version of the "walk in the woods." I had no intention of tracking down all Mr. Talbott's sources, but even the slightest effort confirmed one of his most important sources. In any case, one wonders why so many participants who, as Mr. Talbott puts it in his foreword to *Deadly Gambits*, will remain "constrained from freely discussing their roles, for years to come," were not constrained from freely discussing their roles with him.

The perils of total anonymity and unaccountability are shown most strikingly by Secretary Weinberger's letter. He is referred to no fewer than fifty-five times in the book; he is quoted directly at least ten times and indirectly many more times. On occasion, Mr. Talbott even claims to know what was in Mr. Weinberger's mind. Mr. Weinberger's role in the book is that of a villain second only to Richard Perle, the assistant secretary in Mr. Weinberger's department. It is no small matter for the Secretary of Defense to denounce two of the direct quotations attributed to him as "complete lies." Mr. Talbott falls back on the recollections of anonymous informants who may be just as guilty of "revisionism and selective memory" as he implies Mr. Weinberger is.

The point is that the reader has no way of knowing how to find his way through this tangle of alleged errors or lies so long as he does not know who told Mr. Talbott all those unflattering things about Mr. Weinberger. One does not have to be an admirer of Mr. Weinberger's policies (I myself have disagreed with him sharply and publicly) to recognize that this sort of anonymous tale telling without checking with its victim can easily make the journalist a transmission belt for personal vendettas and political smears.

There is little to say about Mr. Talbott's novelistic effects, because he says so little about them. He merely denies them and virtuously disapproves of the practice. I cited typical passages of a novelistic character; they cannot be passed off with a bland disclaimer. Even Mr. Nitze can say no more than that Mr. Talbott is "substantially correct" about matters of which Mr. Nitze had firsthand knowledge. I never had any doubt that Mr. Nitze was Mr. Talbott's source in this case, but I wondered how the exact language that runs on for four consecutive sentences of sixty-seven words or another four of fifty-four words could be safely attributed to Mr. Nitze. I can understand that Mr. Nitze told Mr. Talbott the substance of his conversations; that substance, however, was "novelized" in Mr. Talbott's version. This relatively simple case might be forgiven, but there are far too many others of a far more serious nature, such as the quotations attributed to Mr. Weinberger and others.

Mr. Talbott also seems to want to brush off the paragraph in Mr. Nitze's letter about the deals made by officials with John Newhouse and Mr. Talbott himself. Mr. Nitze is no innocent in these matters and must have had some basis for what Mr. Talbott calls his "conjecture." Here again, the ordinary citizen cannot be sure of anything because Mr. Talbott stonewalls, and those officials would be guilty of malfeasance in office if they admitted their complicity. Not only do these officials make policy; they also seek to control the history of their policy-making. Significantly, officials of the stature of Mr. Weinberger and Mr. Nitze were willing to answer my inquiries quickly and frankly, but my letters to Richard Burt and Richard Perle, the two assistant secretaries most prominent in *Deadly Gambits*, were not answered at all, as if they had something to hide.

The practice of anonymity and unaccountability has become so widespread that it is accepted as if it were preordained. When a system of public information that is so open to abuse is taken for granted, that is the time to worry the most about it. The present system is diseased, yet our most highly placed officials and respected journalists go on spreading the infection. *Deadly Gambits* is only one of the deadly symptoms in recent years.

I suspect that reviewers of *Deadly Gambits* were beguiled by its relentless exposé of the Reagan Administration's ineptitude. I don't object to that, but there is something larger at stake. If too many of us condone the present license when it is practiced in behalf of views we favor, what will we do when it is practiced in behalf of views we abhor?

(*The New York Times Book Review*, December 16, 1984)

To Quote or
Not to Quote

1

WE ARE NOW GETTING the first wave of books on the Iran and Contra affairs. I use the plural, because there was no Iran-Contra affair, as the title of the congressional investigation had it. There were an Iran affair and a Contra affair, which most of the time were separate and distinct. They intersected at a point usually called the "diversion," and some of the same characters, notably Oliver North, appeared in both affairs. Nevertheless, it was never one affair, but two, and each had its own raison d'être.

The first wave of books on an important historical event has virtues and vices peculiar to itself. It is necessarily closer to journalism than to historical scholarship. It falls somewhere between news and history, not as hot as the first, not as cold as the second. Since there is never a final stage, what we are doomed to get is successive waves or stages, each with its distinctive virtues and vices.

The first wave of books on the Iran-Contra affairs has been peculiarly unlucky. The books have largely based themselves on the public hearings of the select congressional committees in May–August 1987. What was not to be expected was the appearance in the meantime of the private testimony, or depositions, given to the joint committees in preparation for the public hearings.

These depositions are in many respects richer and more detailed than the public hearings. Many of these depositions are critical for a full understanding of the events. Most were given by participants who did not testify in the public hearings. Since the depositions were not televised, they did not suffer from the pressures of time and publicity that plagued the public hearings. Their early publication was unexpected, because the testimony had ostensibly been given with assurances of secrecy. For example, the former chief of staff, Donald Regan, gave his deposition on the assumption that it was "Top Secret." But now we have almost two hundred pages of it in print.

Anyone working on the Iran-Contra affairs would today be confronted with the following:

Twenty-seven volumes containing 202 depositions, for a total of 31,458 pages

Twelve volumes of public hearings, for a total of 9,902 pages

Three volumes of documents, for a total of 4,751 pages (hundreds of other documents are also contained in the volumes of depositions and hearings)

Five volumes of a Testimonial Chronology, Witness Accounts, Supplemented by Documents (of which three volumes, for a total of 2,529 pages, have appeared)

One volume of Chronology, with 194 pages

One volume of the *Report of the Congressional Committees Investigating the Iran-Contra Affair*, with 690 pages

One volume of the *Report of the President's Special Review Board* (Tower Report), with 285 pages

And, as if these were not enough, hundreds of thousands of documents stored in the committees' archives in Washington, D.C., not available in print

The task of studying at least 50,000 printed pages is alone daunting. The editing of these volumes leaves much to be desired. There are no indexes in the volumes themselves (Appendix D to Volume 1 contains a cumbersome, all-inclusive index). Documents often seem to have been thrown together without any perceptible order. The job was clearly a hasty one, which probably accounts for the early appearance of most volumes. A good deal has been blacked out and cannot be read at all. Nevertheless, the entire collection is of inestimable value to the serious student, and future accounts must be largely based on it.

This enormous mass could not be carefully studied—the depositions and documents least of all—by the writers of the first wave.

This does not mean that these early books have nothing of value to tell us. They represent a preliminary survey and interpretation from different vantage points; they contribute additional details and sidelights; and they warn of prejudices and pitfalls. The five books that I have chosen to examine exhibit all of these traits.

2

While the public hearings could hardly fail to be informative, they left much to be desired. Why this was so is the main interest in *Men of Zeal* by the two senators from Maine, Republican William S. Cohen and Democrat George J. Mitchell, an unusual combination of authors.[1]

Cohen and Mitchell reveal that the congressional hearings were shockingly improvised and politicized. Twenty-six members were patently too many for the joint committee, but the opportunity to get on prime-time national television day after day was too much for too many to resist. The staff did not have enough time to prepare adequately for the hearings; many staff members were not cleared quickly enough; a few senior lawyers had to cope with more than 300,000 documents and over 1,000,000 pages with very little assistance. The deadline set for the entire inquiry was too short, with the result that time limitations and lack of resources forced the committee's lawyers to concentrate on some issues and neglect others. The CIA ignored requests for months and otherwise showed its contempt for the committee's work.

The decision to turn the hearings almost wholly over to the lawyers was not necessarily wrong in itself; it was what the lawyers did that was wrong. This abdication of responsibility by the congressmen is explained by Cohen and Mitchell on the ground that they were too busy with their other congressional work to prepare adequately. Whatever the reason, the politicians could not have done worse than their lawyers, especially the chief counsels, Arthur L. Liman for the Senate and John W. Nields, Jr., for the Representatives.

Cohen and Mitchell virtually admit that Liman and Nields were not equal to the occasion. They attribute Liman's troubles to his thinning hair and accent, Nields's to his long hair and mannerisms. They report that thousands of letters, telegrams, and phone calls,

[1] Viking, 1988.

many of them viciously anti-Semitic, came in denouncing Liman in the first week; Senator Cohen himself, not Jewish, received letters expressing the desire to hang him along with "that Jew, Liman"; Liman once sent Cohen a letter of appreciation with the grimly humorous comment "But why does your name have to be Cohen?"

It may well be true that television was unkind to Liman and Nields. But I do not think that was the real reason for their unsatisfactory performances. In fact, the authors undercut their own analysis by observing that committee members, "no matter how artful or photogenic, did no better than Liman." Cohen and Mitchell cite John Mortimer, the British barrister and author, on how to deal with witnesses: "The art of cross-examination . . . is not the art of examining crossly." This maxim was repeatedly violated by Liman and Nields. They too often behaved as if they were less interested in eliciting information from witnesses than in arguing with and getting the better of them. They made themselves into would-be star performers showing off their vaunted superiority. It would have been bad enough if they had been successful; it was much worse when they were something less than brilliant tangling with recalcitrant witnesses such as former General Richard V. Secord and Oliver North.

It was not so much their hair and accents that did them in as their failure to succeed in their self-assumed roles. When Nields went after Secord, the first public witness, he immediately plunged into the intricacies of the Iran-Contra bank accounts. As Cohen and Mitchell point out, this line of questioning was wrongheaded for two reasons: the practical result of linking the two affairs from the outset was "to blur the edges of each," and Secord, "an aggressive, combative witness," could not be effectively challenged "because crucial evidence was still being held up by Swiss authorities and others." Nields seemed to start in the middle "of a complicated and confusing story."

The major fiasco was the interrogation of Oliver North by both Nields and Liman. The committee had already made humiliating concessions to North's lawyer, Brendan Sullivan, who was permitted to set the conditions for North's testimony. During the hearings, Sullivan was permitted to bully and browbeat as if he were dealing with juvenile delinquents. The chairman, Senator Daniel K. Inouye, permitted him to get away with the most offensive outbursts. On one occasion, Sullivan burst out, "Don't answer the question. Next question. The question, Mr. Chairman, won't be answered." Sullivan was particularly insolent with respect to Liman. Sullivan shouted at Liman, who had just asked North a question, "That is none of your business . . . Get off his back." Cohen and Mitchell say that Sullivan actually succeeded in intimidating members of the joint committee.

North was a shifty, often unresponsive witness. His most effective moments came when he answered a question with a patriotic, self-serving speech that had little or nothing to do with the question. Cohen and Mitchell give one of many examples of a speech by North in response to Nields, who had asked a simple question about a fence or security system at North's home: "Were you aware that that security system was paid for by General Secord?" North went on for almost fifteen minutes about Abu Nidal, the Palestinian terrorist. He read from *The Christian Science Monitor* about Abu Nidal and mock-heroically offered to meet him on equal terms anywhere in the world. He kept going on about his eleven-year-old daughter and how proud he was of his five and a half years at the National Security Council, before finally admitting that he had falsified documents about the payment of the fence.

Cohen and Mitchell comment sardonically: "We shook our heads in disbelief. That fence might keep out the neighborhood dogs or some anti-Contra activist who had poured sand in his car's gas tank. But Abu Nidal? Hardly. Still, the theater was far more compelling than our doubts."

They also note that North had many apologists on the committee, one of whom was Representative Bill McCollum, Republican of Florida. He said on June 25, 1987, that North was one of those who were guilty of "deliberately deceiving and lying" and were responsible for "one of the most treacherous things that has ever occurred to a President, it seems to me, in our history." But after learning how North had gone over with the television audience, McCollum saluted him on July 14 as having "served your country admirably" and having been "a dedicated, patriotic soldier," which he and the country were grateful for "and will remember forever, regardless of anything else."

Cohen and Mitchell unobtrusively convict Vice President George Bush of tampering with the truth in his recent autobiography. Bush pretended that he had known nothing about the arms-for-hostages deal until he had been briefed by Republican Senator David Durenberger of Minnesota almost a month after the story had been made public in November 1986. "What Dave had to say left me with the feeling," Bush wrote, "I'd been deliberately excluded from key meetings involving details of the Iran operation."[2]

The senators have no trouble tearing away Bush's mask of ignorance. They list the dates of high-level meetings at which Bush was present and at which detailed reports were made and discussions held about the various deals. Bush was present at meetings on August 6, 1985, at which National Security Adviser Robert C. McFarlane reported that Iran wanted one hundred TOW missiles from Israel in exchange for four hostages; on January 6, 1986, when McFarlane's successor, John M. Poindexter, told about a plan to exchange four thousand TOWs for hostages; on January 17, 1986, when President Reagan signed the finding that authorized the shipment of arms to Iran; and on July 29, 1986, when Bush, in Jerusalem, was fully briefed on the entire matter by Amiram Nir, the Israeli Prime Minister's adviser on counterterrorism. That Bush was not deliberately excluded and must have known a great deal of what was going on can be unmistakably demonstrated; our next President's record in these affairs suggests that he has not been clever enough to tell an untruth that could not be easily exposed.

In the end, Cohen and Mitchell imply that the way the joint committee held its public hearings was gravely flawed. Among other things, they advise against future joint hearings and recommend a maximum of eleven members if a future joint hearing should be unavoidable. They warn against permitting witnesses or their lawyers "to seize control of or manipulate the proceedings." They reject fixed deadlines in such investigations. They seem to be less certain about the wisdom of having granted North immunity. They point out that the joint committees might have waited to grant immunity to North until after the independent counsel had determined whether he had committed an indictable offense; but they immediately note that such a delay would have extended the hearings well beyond Reagan's term of office. And they call on Congress to "take into account the power of television" and yet resist "(as the Committee did) the pressure to conform its behavior to television's demand." The authors, however, elsewhere admit that the committee did not resist the pressure of television. This formula may merely betray the senators' idea of heaven as a place where they can always have it both ways.

---

[2] George Bush with Victor Gold, *Looking Forward* (Doubleday, 1987), p. 240.

As for the Iran-Contra story itself, the authors have produced a useful primer that is as critical of the Congress as it is of the Executive. Both senators were among the few impressive participants in the hearings, and for that they deserve our gratitude.

3

Oliver North is a dangerous type in a democracy. There is an adventurist, fanatical streak in him; he admittedly regards obedience to a President as if he were serving a czar or dictator; a cause to which he gives himself justifies all manner of evil, especially lying on a grand scale and deceiving even close colleagues. Mixed with all this is a talent for crowd-tingling demagogy, a predilection for patriotic bathos, and a self-sacrificial zealotry. The televised hearings gave him an audience of millions and one that was particularly vulnerable to his exhortations. In fact, the chances are that much of what most people remember of the hearings came from him.

Anyone who wishes to know more about North can begin with Ben Bradlee, Jr.'s *Guts and Glory: The Rise and Fall of Oliver North*.[3] It is a popularly written account that contains a store of information about North not available in such detail elsewhere. North refused to be interviewed for it, but his classmates, fellow Marines, and later associates seem to have talked about him willingly and mainly admiringly.

About half the book is devoted to the Iran and Contra affairs. The account is more detailed and far livelier than that in the Cohen-Mitchell book. The story is told more or less straight until the last fifteen pages, in which Bradlee offers his own views, of which the following indicates his final verdict: "North's tragic flaw was that in his sincere zeal to promote democracy, he helped subvert it; in his desire to protect and defend the Constitution he swore to uphold, he trampled some of its most fundamental precepts."[4]

Bradlee fills four pages with a catalogue of North's lies—to the National Security Council, to Congress, to Secord, to the Iranians,

[3] Donald I. Fine, 1988.

[4] The constitutional implications of the Iran-Contra affairs have been analysed with remarkable acuteness and scope by Professor Harold Hongju Koh, "Why the President (Almost) Always Wins in Foreign Affairs: Lessons of the Iran-Contra Affair," *The Yale Law Journal*, June 1988, pp. 1255–1342. If all members of Congress were required to read and ponder this study, they would be less proud of themselves.

to friends and co-workers. North must have been keenly aware of his record of deceit when he flauntingly testified that he was going to tell the whole truth—"the good, the bad, and the ugly." If North had not lied so much and had not been caught lying, he would not have had to admit so readily that he had lied and would not have needed to promise that he would lie no more. Yet one of North's most sensational revelations rests only on his say-so and suggests the danger of relying solely on the public hearings.

Bradlee, Cohen and Mitchell, and others make much of North's statements that the director of the CIA, William Casey, wanted to create an overseas "off-the-shelf," "self-financing," "independent of appropriated monies," "stand-alone," "full-service covert operation." The senators even plead in favor of the concessions made to North on the ground that his testimony was crucial, "if only because he disclosed the existence of the so-called off-the-shelf covert capability that is so inimical to our concept of democracy" (p. 307).

But all we knew from the public hearings about the "so-called off-the-shelf covert capability" was what North told us. Now that we also have the private depositions, there is no more reason to trust North on this than on anything else.

One of the most important depositions was given by John N. McMahon, Casey's deputy director until his resignation in March 1986. McMahon had spent over thirty-four years in the CIA. He was made deputy director in 1982 and had thus worked more closely with Casey than anyone else in the Agency. His office adjoined Casey's; the door between them was always open; he was privy to all that went on, as deputies are supposed to be. He was an honorable man, who demanded a Presidential "finding" as soon as he found out, in Casey's absence, that CIA officials had engaged in unlawful cooperation with North in the ill-fated transport of arms from Israel to Iran in November 1985—the "bit of a horror story," as North called it.

McMahon gave the "off-the-shelf covert capability" a quite different interpretation. He said that Casey wanted to build an intelligence capability outside the established CIA mechanism "but all part of the Central Intelligence Agency, nothing on the shelf or as described by Colonel North." McMahon maintained that Casey's idea was to be funded by congressionally appropriated funds, not North's unappropriated funds, and in compliance with U.S. laws requiring Presidential findings and notification to Congress, not North's outlaw version of it. The following exchange took place:

> *Counsel*: As I stated before, I don't believe we have any corroborative evidence of Colonel North's testimony on this particular point, and what he did relate were conversations that he had and discussions he had with the Director apparently one on one in this area.
> *McMahon*: Casey never related that or even gave a hint to me that anything like that was fermenting in his mind.[5]

McMahon was not the only one mystified by North's off-the-shelf story. Robert M. Gates, McMahon's successor as deputy director, was read North's testimony on the subject, after which he was asked whether Casey had ever said anything to him about it. Gates replied: "No. He never said anything that would have even suggested that he was thinking about such a thing." To Gates's knowledge, no such entity was ever discussed by anyone at the Agency. Gates said that he would have resigned if the off-the-shelf notion had been pursued and, anyway, he thought it was "fundamentally unnecessary."[6]

The least that can be said about the testimony of McMahon and Gates is that it should be taken into account in any consideration of North's off-the-shelf story. North asks us to believe that Casey had confided in him alone about a palpably unlawful, unconstitutional scheme that could not have been put into effect by Casey and North alone and would have had to draw in others in the Agency as high up as McMahon or Gates. Casey was guilty of all sorts of shady practices, but this plot is inherently implausible; it was feather-brained, and no one has ever accused Casey of that particular imperfection. Unfortunately, the details of Casey's idea, as McMahon knew it, have been partially blacked out in his deposition. The story should not be permitted to persist without a full disclosure of what others knew about it.

In fact, the only such off-the-shelf scheme of which we can be certain was concocted and carried out by North and Secord; it was already a reality by the time North attributed it to Casey as a plan for the future.

North had lied so much and was so deceptive in his testimony that it is a sound rule to take nothing for granted that rests solely on his

[5] Deposition of John N. McMahon, Appendix B: Vol. 17, pp. 178, 182, 270.
[6] Deposition of Robert M. Gates, Appendix B: Vol. 11, pp. 964–67.

word. He was notorious for his fabrications, self-aggrandizement, even fantasies.

North's co-workers knew all about his propensity for make-believe. McFarlane said that he had had "four or five years experience of reading things [by North] which I knew to be not compatible with the realities of things." Asked whether North was "a bit of a dramatist, prone to hyperbole at times . . . even a romanticist perhaps on certain occasions with respect to facts and the way he would brief people on subjects," McFarlane agreed.[7]

The CIA's Dewey R. Clarridge described one side of North as "sort of boyish and boastful, and it would be in character for him to say I won't be here tomorrow, I will be down South, and then for him to say, yes, it was a quick trip and I flew all night and I came back and I haven't slept for 48 hours, always complaining about how busy he was and how terribly overworked."[8] Another high CIA official, Clair George, was asked: "Did Ollie ever tell you things that weren't true?" George replied: "Yes—for instance, his endless conversations with the President, and other such minor details." Question: "Did he frequently exaggerate?" George: "Sure, he did."[9] Constantine C. Menges, who worked on both the CIA and NSC staffs, once told Assistant Secretary of State Elliot Abrams: "I urge you, never take *any* important action based solely on what Ollie tells you."[10]

Yet much of what has been written about him is based solely on his testimony and might just as well have been written by himself. A careful historian or journalist would do well to warn the reader whenever North is the only source of a particularly juicy story.

One aspect of Bradlee's book concerns journalistic ethics, and I wish to point to it briefly because it arises much more seriously in connection with the book by Jane Mayer and Doyle McManus to be discussed later. Bradlee tells the reader that all the quotes in his book come from interviews or documentary sources; he admits to

---

[7] McFarlane testimony, p. 144.

[8] Clarridge deposition, Appendix B: Vol. 5, p. 923.

[9] George deposition, Appendix B: Vol. 12, p. 149.

[10] Constantine C. Menges, *Inside the National Security Council* (Simon and Schuster, 1988), p. 280. Menges's article "The Sad, Strange Mind of Col. North," in *The Washington Post*, November 27, 1988, based on his book, contains more such personal experiences on how North "was regularly exaggerating and reshaping events."

only one exception—that he decided "to recreate dialogue" in the case of former National Security Adviser Robert C. McFarlane's trip to Tehran in May 1986.

Bradlee does much more re-creating of dialogue than he is willing to admit. Here is one example: on November 25, 1986, the National Security Adviser, John M. Poindexter, saw President Reagan to submit his resignation. Poindexter's testimony reads:

> And the President responded and said that he had great regret and that this was in the tradition of a Naval officer accepting responsibility.[11]

This is the version of Chief of Staff Donald Regan, who was present:

> And the President nodded and said, "I understand." He said, "This is a shame that it has happened this way, that a man with your great naval record," and so on, "has come to this end," but he said, "That is it," and there was a sort of awkward silence.[12]

And this is the way Bradlee has it:

> "Well, John," the President responded, "it's really a shame that it had to end this way, and what you're doing is in the great tradition of a naval officer accepting responsibility."[13]

The differences between the three versions are relatively innocuous. The fact remains, however, that what Bradlee made the President say was not really what he had said. It is a collage of some words from Poindexter and some from Regan, with some touches by Bradlee.

Is there any good reason why an author should take such liberties with a source or sources, apart from making his readers believe that they are getting the exact words, as if he were present? This re-created or doctored dialogue creates a kind of fictionalized journalism or popular history, as if the untainted facts would be too onerous for readers to bear. It is open to such abuses that I shall discuss it more fully in connection with the Mayer-McManus book, which makes use of such dialogue on a much larger scale.

[11] Poindexter testimony, p. 121.
[12] Regan testimony, p. 34.
[13] *Guts and Glory*, p. 4.

4

The Israeli connection has never been fully clarified. One reason is that we have known about it mainly from the American side and far less from the Israeli. An Israeli chronology of events that was submitted to the congressional committees has not been made public, though snippets of it are cited in the committees' Iran-Contra report. As a result, the promised revelations from Samuel Segev, an Israeli journalist, in his book *The Iranian Triangle*, with the subtitle *The Untold Story of Israel's Role in the Iran-Contra Affair*, could be awaited with more than usual anticipation.[14]

The book does not quite live up to its promise. Much of his story is not "untold." The entire section dealing with how Israel and the United States came to enter into a kind of partnership in the "Iran initiative" in 1985 is based on two U.S. sources, the Tower Report and the congressional committees' Iran-Contra report. This section retells the story of the early efforts of Adnan Khashoggi, the Saudi money man, and Manucher Ghorbanifar, the Iranian middleman, to interest Americans in an arms-for-hostages deal; the intervention of the part-time consultant Michael Ledeen (of which more later in connection with Ledeen's own book); and the joint efforts of Israel and the United States in 1985 to make contact with allegedly "moderate" elements in Iran and to gain the cooperation of Iran to obtain the freedom of the American hostages in Lebanon by sending arms to Iran.

In the 1985 phase, Israel had acted as it had understood its own long-term interests and as an American surrogate. Both roles were interconnected, inasmuch as serving U.S. interests whenever possible was also an Israeli incentive.

The Israel–United States connection came about in this case because the ubiquitous Ghorbanifar had sought to get in touch with the United States through two Israeli intermediaries, Adolph (Al) Schwimmer, the founder of the Israel Aircraft Industries and latterly a private businessman, and Ya'acov Nimrodi, a former Israeli army representative in Iran and now a wealthy entrepreneur. This approach of Ghorbanifar had been reported to National Security Adviser McFarlane by David Kimche, the director general of the Israeli Foreign Ministry. Kimche, according to McFarlane, had reported

---

[14] Free Press, 1988.

the contact with Ghorbanifar as if the latter represented Iranian officials, and Kimche had asked whether McFarlane would approve an attempt to "influence the captors of the United States and other countries' hostages in Lebanon to release them."[15]

As the United States–Israel collaboration increased, it was convenient for the Americans to let Israel take the lead, for one reason because an American participation behind the scenes through Israel lent itself to a plea of "plausible deniability." At this stage, the Israelis mainly involved were Kimche, Schwimmer, and Nimrodi. The latter two had no official status, but they stood to gain financially from any arms deals in which they participated. They were now brought in because the Israeli government was also anxious to mask its collusion in a scheme to send arms to Iran.

Schwimmer was the Israeli in charge of delivering the eighty U.S.-made Hawk missiles owned by Israel to Iran in November 1985. At this point in his narrative, Segev does have an untold story of Israel's role. Unfortunately, it would have been better left untold, because it is a demonstrably fictitious account to save face for Schwimmer. The crux of the matter is the trouble that Schwimmer had getting the missiles out of Israel.

According to Segev, Schwimmer was asked by private charter companies for a guarantee of $50 million to charter Boeing 747 cargo planes to transport the missiles from Israel to Iran, owing to the risks in making such a delivery. The sum was too much for Schwimmer and Nimrodi, and the Israeli government did not want to take official responsibility for the project. Schwimmer desperately appealed for help to the Israeli Defense Ministry, which appealed for help to the Israeli defense minister, Yitzhak Rabin, who happened to be in New York. Rabin called National Security Adviser McFarlane, who was in Geneva for the first Reagan-Gorbachev summit conference. McFarlane called North in Washington and told him to find a way to help.

At this point, Segev's story gets into trouble. North, in Segev's version, sent Secord to Israel, where Secord hit on a plan for Israel to send the eighty missiles to Lisbon on an Israeli plane rather than on a chartered plane. Secord undertook to obtain landing rights for the Israeli plane in Lisbon, where the missiles were to be transferred to three other planes chartered by Secord. But Secord failed to get

[15] McFarlane testimony, p. 43.

landing rights in Lisbon, thereby becoming primarily responsible for the fiasco that followed. Schwimmer and Nimrodi, Segev claims, "suddenly realized that the people the White House had assigned to the project were incompetent."[16] Poor Schwimmer, according to Segev, was blameless; Secord's "mishandling of the arrangements" was entirely responsible.

The curious thing about this tale is that Segev's notes give as its source the joint congressional committees' Iran-Contra report. The story told there is quite different. The report clearly says that Secord did not first go to Israel. The problem, according to the report, had arisen because "the government of Country 15 [Portugal] was unwilling to grant the special clearances" for an Israeli plane to land in Lisbon. Secord went directly to Lisbon, where he tried without success to get the clearance.

It was Schwimmer, not Secord, who had caused the original problem by failing to make sure that he had a suitable plane and a Portuguese clearance. Subsequently, an Israeli El Al plane had actually taken off for Lisbon only to be called back for lack of permission to land. Schwimmer afterward telephoned North to say that he had released three smaller planes in order, as North reported scornfully, "to save $." North then went to high CIA officials for help and succeeded in getting a CIA "proprietary" in Germany to provide Secord with a plane, which flew a first installment of eighteen Hawk missiles directly from Israel to Iran, thereby avoiding the Portuguese problem. This delivery proved to be worse than nothing at all when the Iranians bitterly complained that they had received the wrong missiles.

Only now was Secord sent to Israel by North to find out what had gone wrong. Segev has the whole sequence of Secord's presence in Israel muddled, so that Segev can make Secord responsible for all the trouble from the outset. The wrong missiles were not Secord's fault; as Secord reported, "Schwimmer and Nimrodi had promised Ghorbanifar that the missiles being provided could shoot down high-flying Soviet reconnaissance planes and Iraqi bombers," whereas in reality they were intended for low-flying planes.[17]

On both the American and Israeli sides, this contretemps had far-reaching consequences. North's resort to the CIA for a proprietary

---

[16] *The Iranian Triangle*, pp. 201–2.
[17] Congressional report on the Iran-Contra affairs, pp. 176–87.

plane led to the need for the retrospective Presidential finding that set in motion much of the turmoil the following year. In Israel, Kimche, Schwimmer, and Nimrodi were removed from the entire affair and replaced by Amiram Nir, Prime Minister Shimon Peres's adviser on counterterrorism.

I have gone into the difference between Segev's version of the November 1985 fiasco and that in the congressional report in some detail, because it tells much about the tendentiousness of Segev's "untold story." An account that purports to be based in large part on the congressional report is nothing of the kind. It is full of mis-statements and distortions, with the intent of absolving Schwimmer and Nimrodi of all blame and of heaping it all on Secord. Nir, who took over from them, thereupon becomes Segev's main Israeli villain; he never does anything right. Peres does not come off well, because he was responsible for imposing Nir. The Americans were altogether hopeless.

However dubious a guide Segev may be to the Israeli side of the story, he has much to learn about the American side. On a single page, he is capable of committing three glaring blunders. He has CIA Director William Casey instigating the replacement of James Baker by Donald Regan as the White House chief of staff. This explanation will come as a surprise to Regan, who told about the incident in his recent book, *For the Record*, in which it is candidly described as Regan's own idea.[18] Segev also has McFarlane resigning as National Security Adviser because Regan tried to block his "free access to the Oval Office"; McFarlane as National Security Adviser had a regularly scheduled half hour with the President at 9:30 a.m. every working day and needed no access from Regan in order to see the President. Finally, Segev puts North in Turkey in 1980 as an officer in the backup Marine force during the abortive attempt to rescue the hostages; in 1980, North was spending part of that year at Camp Lejeune in North Carolina and the rest at the Naval War College in Newport, Rhode Island, nowhere near Turkey.[19]

Segev's version of what went on within Israel is hard to judge because he rests most of his inside information on "interviews with participants or their aides and on government papers not yet officially declassified." No doubt Schwimmer and Nimrodi were among his

[18] Harcourt Brace Jovanovich, 1988, pp. 219–29.
[19] *The Iranian Triangle*, p. 190.

main informants. Unfortunately, we may never get Nir's side of the story; he was reported on December 1, 1988, as having been killed in a plane crash in Mexico.

For reasons that mystify me, Segev's book has been praised by Abba Eban for its "lucid and objective spirit," by former Ambassador Samuel Lewis for its "authoritative detail," by former Under Secretary of State Joseph J. Sisco as "an illuminating book for both experts and non-experts," and by others in a similar vein. It is enough to make one lose any remaining faith one may have in blurbs on book jackets.

5

Michael A. Ledeen's new book, *Perilous Statecraft*, is a different kind of book, but with some of the same problems.[20]

Ledeen is the only author in this group who actually participated in the Iran affair. As a result, his book is mainly an apologia for himself, not for someone else. It is lively, opinionated, and unrepentant, whatever else it may be.

Ledeen has the distinction of having been "present at the creation" of the affair, at least in its American aspect. As a part-time consultant to National Security Adviser McFarlane in 1985, he says that he was "asked" to meet with "one of the smartest and most experienced intelligence officials in Western Europe."[21] When Ledeen asked him how "we could be usefully involved in Iranian affairs when we knew nothing about the country," this unnamed official told him, "Talk to the Israelis, they know all about it."

Ledeen came back to Washington and reported what he had been told to McFarlane, who agreed to his suggestion that it would be a good idea for him to go to Israel and meet with Prime Minister Peres. Ledeen was given no other mission except to find out what the Israelis knew about the situation in Iran. It turned out that one of the "smartest and most experienced intelligence officials in Western Europe"

---

[20] Charles Scribner's Sons, 1988.

[21] *Perilous Statecraft*, p. 100. Presumably McFarlane would have had to ask him to meet with this official, but McFarlane implied in his testimony that Ledeen had come to him with a report of this meeting without having been asked to arrange it (McFarlane testimony, p. 177). Ledeen himself had previously told about the meeting as if it had occurred during a number of discussions early in 1985 (Ledeen deposition, Appendix B: Vol. 15, p. 950).

had been wrong; Peres told Ledeen that "Israeli intelligence was not particularly good" and that he was "personally dissatisfied with it." Yet a false lead and a disappointing meeting with Peres enabled Ledeen to insert himself into the still nascent "Iran initiative."

Soon Ledeen became acquainted with Kimche, Schwimmer, and Nimrodi on the Israeli side and through them with the two main connivers, Adnan Khashoggi, the Saudi money man, and Manucher Ghorbanifar, the Iranian middleman. Ledeen is particularly high on Schwimmer, whom he describes as the "ideal Israeli counterpart" of Khashoggi and as Peres's closest personal friend. In a short time, Ledeen's connections with the Israelis and his rapport with Ghorbanifar became his chief stock-in-trade in Washington. He himself, after all, knew as little as everyone else in Washington about what was happening in Iran, but he had the advantage that he could always bring back allegedly hot intelligence from the Israelis or Ghorbanifar, the latter an inexhaustible source of whatever the Americans wanted to hear.

When Ledeen comes to tell the story of the November 1985 shipment of Hawks from Israel to Iran, his version is like Segev's in that it favors Schwimmer—and it is just as mythical. "In the first half of November," Ledeen writes, "North undertook to commission a jumbo jet that would carry the eighty HAWKs from Israel to Iran."[22] In fact, North did not get into the act until Rabin on November 17 had called McFarlane for help and McFarlane had called North to do what he could for the hapless Israeli organizers.[23]

In his book, Ledeen is still soft on Ghorbanifar, who, he laments, "was accused of many things of which he is almost certainly innocent, from having been an agent of Israel to inventing lies at key moments of the initiative."[24] Ghorbanifar most probably was not an agent of Israel, though the Israelis also had an important stake in him, but that he invented lies at key moments is as close to a certainty as anything in this affair. In any case, Ledeen must be the only American who still thinks that Ghorbanifar told no lies.

One key instance of Ghorbanifar's lying occurred on the occasion of the mission to Tehran headed by former National Security Adviser McFarlane in May 1986. Ghorbanifar was blamed for having de-

---

[22] *Perilous Statecraft*, p. 151.
[23] McFarlane testimony, pp. 52–53.
[24] *Perilous Statecraft*, pp. 192–93.

ceived both sides about what each was prepared to do, which caused much unnecessary misunderstanding and prejudiced the meeting from the start.

In his deposition, Ledeen had been somewhat more forthcoming. He had attested to Ghorbanifar's reliability and had told how he had come to believe that "Ghorbanifar was indeed a person with whom we could and should work." Ledeen had urged the CIA to deal with him "because of his contracts and his knowledge and sources." Ledeen had thought that Ghorbanifar could do "things" for the United States "which, so far as I could tell, nobody else could, and that we just could not walk away from such a useful character."[25]

All this has been toned down in his book. Others in a position to know how Ledeen promoted Ghorbanifar have been less reticent. Charles Allen, the CIA's chief intelligence officer for counterterrorism, who was able to observe Ledeen in this period and who figures in Ledeen's book, first learned about Ghorbanifar from Ledeen. Allen recalled: "He [Ledeen] said that Ghorbanifar was a good fellow, praised Ghorbanifar to the hilt."[26] Another high CIA official, Clair George, the deputy director for operations, related that the Israelis said that "Ghorbanifar was the greatest thing since bagels" and Ledeen told Casey that Ghorbanifar was "a great guy."[27]

In effect, if Ghorbanifar was responsible for much of the havoc caused by the Iran initiative, Ledeen was responsible for being his most ardent American sponsor. Ledeen's latest effort to rehabilitate Ghorbanifar is consistent with his past attachment to the Iranian con man.

In his book, Ledeen has some difficulty explaining what his role was. As a part-time consultant for McFarlane, he was merely supposed to "listen, ask questions, and then inform the policymakers in Washington."[28] If he had restricted himself to listening and informing, he would hardly have played an important enough role to devote a book to himself. But Ledeen sometimes forgets that he was only supposed to be a messenger and lets on that he engaged in more

---

[25] Ledeen deposition, pp. 1006, 1008, 1284, 1309.

[26] Allen deposition, Appendix B: Vol. 1, p. 464. Allen also said that "each time Mr. Ledeen met with me or Mr. [Dewey R.] Clarridge [CIA chief of the European Division] or anyone else he always praised Mr. Ghorbanifar, and I anticipated that he would strongly urge that Mr. Casey endorse Mr. Ghorbanifar's efforts" (p. 510).

[27] George deposition, p. 99.

[28] *Perilous Statecraft*, p. 121.

substantive discussions. For example, we are told: "At a day-long discussion in a suite at the elegant Prince de Galles Hotel in Paris the second week of September [1985], Ghorbanifar, Kimche, Schwimmer, Nimrodi, and I looked at possible paths of action."[29]

At such sessions in the elegant Prince de Galles Hotel and in the less elegant suites of official Washington, Ledeen argued forcefully for a policy that would downplay arms-for-hostages and instead stress the long-term strategic interest in an Iran–United States understanding. This much seems true; it is vouched for by others. Yet he based his belief that a serious negotiation was possible at that time on very tenuous grounds.

Ledeen's claim rests primarily on a meeting in October 1985 between himself, Ghorbanifar, Schwimmer, Nimrodi, and a so-called Senior Iranian Official, whose identity he still conceals, supposedly in order to protect him.[30] This Iranian, however, was neither senior nor official. He was, according to Segev, Ayatollah Hassan Karoubi, said by Ghorbanifar, who produced him, to have been "Khomeini's 'right-hand man' "—undoubtedly one of Ghorbanifar's imaginative improvisations.[31]

We have three versions of what happened at this meeting. Karoubi, according to Ledeen, bitterly complained against the Israeli-U.S. policy of sending weapons to Iran and instead pleaded for other types of assistance to the Iranian "moderates" to change the regime

---

[29] Ibid., pp. 133–34.

[30] Ledeen adopts this title on the ground that it was used by the Iran-Contra committees (*Landslide*, p. 138). The committees' report actually designates him merely as the "First Iranian" (p. 170). In his deposition, Ledeen said that Ghorbanifar had described him as "a senior Iranian official" (p. 1020). The term thus goes back to the ubiquitous Ghorbanifar.

[31] This Karoubi or "First Iranian" had originally come to the attention of Theodore G. Shackley, the former CIA official who resigned in 1979 owing to his ties with Edwin Wilson, another former CIA official who was convicted of illegally exporting high explosives and other dangerous weapons to Muammar al-Qaddafi's Libya. Shackley met Karoubi and Ghorbanifar in Hamburg, West Germany, in November 1984 through the good offices of former General Manucher Hashemi, the former head of the counterespionage department of SAVAK, the Shah's secret police. Shackley described this meeting in his deposition (Appendix B: Vol. 25, pp. 141–50) without naming Karoubi; he is identified as the "First Iranian" in the Iran-Contra report, p. 164. It was at this meeting with Shackley that Ghorbanifar first let the Americans know that he was interested in getting TOW missiles for Iran. The story is too intricate to be told here, but it is significant that both Ghorbanifar and Karoubi owed their first appearance in the "Iran initiative" to the shadowy Hashemi. I have been told that Karoubi was a mullah, of much lesser rank, not an ayatollah.

or influence the post-Khomeini succession.[32] Karoubi's word was all that Ledeen had to go on to promote the idea that a basic realignment of Iran was to be taken seriously.

Segev tells a very different story about Karoubi. He is said to have demanded 150 Hawk missiles, 200 Sidewinder missiles, and 30 to 50 Phoenix missiles. Segev also says that Ledeen did far more than merely listen. Ledeen allegedly told Karoubi that the United States would be willing to enter "a new era of relations with Iran" and provide it with arms, intelligence, technicians, and advisers in various fields after the liberation of all the hostages.[33] The Israelis recorded one of their discussions with Karoubi and may also have a record of the October meeting in which Ledeen took part.[34]

In this case, Segev appears to be more trustworthy than Ledeen. Unluckily for Ledeen, we have one more version by him on what happened at that meeting. It was given by Ledeen himself to Oliver North on October 30, 1985, soon after Ledeen's return from Geneva. North's notebook contains jottings that Ledeen had told him that Karoubi "wants to be U.S. ally—has support in Tehran." In order to get the hostages out, Ledeen advised North, Iran demanded a "blanket order" of 150 Hawk missiles, 200 Sidewinder missiles, and 30 to 50 Phoenix missiles. The deliveries of hostages and missiles were to be staggered, with a hostage to come out first, then missiles sent, another hostage out, more missiles sent, and finally a third hostage released.[35] The version in Ledeen's book is so far from Segev's and from what he told North soon after the event that one cannot help but wonder how Ledeen came to be so unreliable about an incident that he himself makes so critical in his entire experience in the Iran affair.

Ledeen took Karoubi so seriously that he had promised—without authorization—an official U.S. response in thirty days. McFarlane, to whom he reported the great news about Karoubi, never took it seriously and let the thirty days pass without responding. Ledeen forever after considered that the failure to follow up on Karoubi's views was the "great blunder" of the Iran initiative.

[32] *Perilous Statecraft*, pp. 140–41.

[33] *The Iranian Triangle*, pp. 183–84.

[34] Segev publishes almost four verbatim pages recorded by the Israelis at a meeting with Karoubi in Hamburg in July 1985 (pp. 157–60).

[35] North Notebook Excerpt, October 30, 1985, in Appendixes to Parts 1 and 2, Part 3, p. 327. The same reading is given in the Iran-Contra report, p. 175.

One of the strangest aspects of the affair during 1985 is that Ledeen, a part-time consultant without diplomatic or other official status, was the sole American at these various meetings, usually with three Israelis and the ineffable Ghorbanifar. McFarlane evidently did not take these efforts very seriously or was busy with other things. Secretary of State Shultz and the State Department were left entirely in the dark. Yet Ledeen was professedly trying to play down the hostages, who were President Reagan's main concern, and to set up a fundamental turn in Iranian-U.S. relations.

Ledeen came to the end of his short run soon after the November 1985 "horror story." In McFarlane's absence, he went to see John M. Poindexter, who was taking McFarlane's place, and was abruptly dismissed from the project. Ledeen speculates that Poindexter considered him to be "unreliable, incompetent, or both." Poindexter himself explained that he was "never completely comfortable with Mr. Ledeen," because "he talked too much and I didn't think he was a particularly discreet emissary to be using" and "we were concerned with Ledeen not really being very knowledgeable about what he was dealing with."[36] It surely was "perilous statecraft" for McFarlane to have entrusted the first six months of the Iran initiative to a part-time consultant with a minimum of supervision.

In the end, Ledeen was grateful to Poindexter for having saved him from being further implicated in the Iran affair. Thanks to Poindexter, Ledeen had the last laugh.

6

I have left for last another recent book on the Iran-Contra affairs, *Landslide*, by two journalists, Jane Mayer and Doyle McManus, because it raises a question of journalistic ethics.[37] Before I get into that, however, the book itself is worth considering.

This time the main character in the drama is President Reagan, as the subtitle, *The Unmaking of the President, 1984–1988*, indicates, though the supporting cast of North and others necessarily comes in for much attention.

The real subject of the book is the political character of Ronald Reagan and his Administration. The first three pages start off with

[36] Poindexter deposition, Appendix B: Vol. 20, pp. 1356–57.
[37] Houghton Mifflin, 1988.

the report allegedly given to the new chief of staff, Howard Baker, by a trusted, politically experienced confidant, Jim Cannon, who was asked by Baker to "scout out the territory" before he took office. Cannon is said to have interviewed the President's aides, who told him "how inattentive and inept the President was. He was lazy; he wasn't interested in the job. They said he wouldn't read the papers they gave him—even short position papers and documents. They said he wouldn't come over to work—all he wanted to do was to watch movies and television at the residence."

For about four hundred pages, Reagan never gets any better. The authors' condemnation of and contempt for him are ceaseless and implacable. They see him unsparingly: "He moved in a world of myths and symbols, not facts and programs . . . Despite his position and power, Reagan often appeared to be living in contented isolation . . . The line between fact and fiction, or accuracy and expediency, was one Reagan crossed early."

They give him credit for getting through his first term successfully only because the troika—Chief of Staff James A. Baker, deputy chief of staff Michael Deaver, and White House counselor Edwin Meese—saved him from himself. They attribute many of his troubles in the second term to his new chief of staff, Donald T. Regan, who comes off in their account as power-hungry, small-minded, and politically incompetent. No one does well in this theater of absurd fecklessness, but Reagan and Regan get the worst notices.

This relentless case for the prosecution might be harder to believe if much of it had not already appeared in books by those who had formerly worked for Reagan—Office of Management and Budget director David Stockman, press secretary Larry Speakes, Deaver, and Regan. They essentially tell the same story of Reagan's indolence, ignorance, and incompetence. The difference is that Mayer and McManus have exhibited them against the background of a detailed, running account of the Iran and Contra affairs, which Speakes, Deaver, and Regan merely touched on.

The subtitle of the book, *The Unmaking of the President, 1984–1988*, must be charged to premature wishful thinking. The most remarkable thing about President Reagan's role in the Iran and Contra affairs is that he came out of them without anything more than a temporary dip in his political standing. As *The Economist* of November 12, 1988, noted after the recent election, Reagan "has ended up hugely popular." He probably helped considerably to elect President Bush. It would take us too far afield to speculate on why Reagan has been able to make his successors pay for his sins of omission and commission, but this is the real question of his Administration, not the premature announcement of his "unmaking."

Like so many books of this genre, this one mixes the true, the probably or perhaps true, the dubious, and the indefensible. The authors have put together a racy, headlong story at the price of some tampering with their sources. They sometimes get their facts wrong, but these mishaps tend to be minor and not enough to be seriously troublesome.[38]

What is more troublesome concerns a question of journalistic ethics. I have already alluded to the "re-created" dialogue in Bradlee's book. Whatever his lapses may be, they are nothing like those of Mayer and McManus. Page after page in their book abounds with dialogue, some of it hyped up—whether or not the intention was to dramatize rather than to hype up—so flagrantly that a question must be raised: How much of this dissimulation is permissible?

The authors tell the reader in a note on sources: "Where dialogue is presented, the quotations have been derived either from contemporaneous notes or from interviews with several participants. No dialogue has been reconstructed from secondhand sources."

It is impossible to check the dialogue from their interviews, but the dialogue from contemporaneous notes is open to question. Of the many cases that I have noted, the following three are typical and should give some notion of what the problem is.

1. "In August 1985, Israel went ahead with a shipment of 508 TOW missiles in Iran—with no explicit U.S. approval, McFarlane said. 'No one in [the] U.S. government . . . had contact with Israel' on the shipment of those TOWs, he said" (*Landslide*, p. 329).

The book's notes direct the reader to a handwritten record made by Charles J. Cooper, an assistant attorney general, in *Select Committee Documents*. There are about five thousand pages of these

---

[38] Reagan did not say "But visiting hours are Thursday" at a meeting on December 7, 1985 (*Landslide*, p. 179). Shultz attributed it to Weinberger (Shultz testimony, p. 32), though Weinberger denied saying it (Weinberger deposition, p. 491). North did not invent the term "Project Democracy" (*Landslide*, p. 147). It appeared as early as March 21, 1983, in a memorandum from then National Security Adviser William P. Clark to Charles Wick (Deposition of Walter Raymond, Jr., Appendix B: Vol. 22, p. 433). Carl R. (Spitz) Channell did not agree to give $50,000 to David Fischer for every meeting with President Reagan (*Landslide*, p. 202; Channell deposition, Appendix B: Vol. 4, p. 161).

printed documents; without a volume and page reference, the note is virtually useless to all but the most curious and tenacious of knowledgeable readers.

In any case, the relevant source for McFarlane's alleged statement reads:

> M[cFarlane] knows of no one in U.S.G[overnment]. who had contact w[ith] Is[rael]. re transfer of 508 TOWs.[39]

In *Landslide*, McFarlane is made to say explicitly that no one had contact with Israel about the shipment of the TOWs. In the original, McFarlane merely said that he *knew* of no one in the U.S. government who had had such contact. There may have been someone, but he did not know of anyone.

Yet this metamorphosis is relatively innocent.

2. *Landslide* contains an account of the interrogation of Oliver North by Attorney General Edwin Meese in the presence of three of the latter's aides during which North was first confronted with the "diversion" memorandum. This account fills almost three pages, virtually all in dialogue form.[40]

It is based on six different sources. Mayer and McManus have made a collage of phrases from all of them, put together in such a way that the reader would be led to believe that the dialogue flowed in just the sequence given by the authors. In fact, they have stitched together phrases out of different contexts from the six different sources.

The entire account is too long to be given here, but part of the Mayer-McManus version is enough to show how it was concocted:

> How did it happen? Meese asked.
> "The Israelis, in January 1986, approached us," North said. "They arranged to take residuals from these transactions and transfer them to the Nicaraguan resistance." [*Landslide*, p. 338]

One reference to the Israelis appears in the handwritten notes taken by William Bradford Reynolds, an assistant attorney general, who had discovered the diversion memo. The relevant portion reads:

---

[39] Appendix B, Vol. 7, p. 598.
[40] *Landslide*, pp. 337–39.

Nir – Jan 1986
> Meeting with O[liver] N[orth] – Nir said Israelis would have taken funds from residual acc't and transfer to Nicaraguan acc't.[41]

When Reynolds was asked to explain this reference, he said:

> He [North] said—in—his statement was the Israelis came up with the idea of taking residual funds and transferring them to Nicaragua for the contras.[42]

It will be noticed that Reynolds's original note used the conditional—"would"—and his later explanation referred to nothing more than an Israeli "idea." Yet Mayer-McManus have North saying that the Israelis had arranged for the diversion to the Contras as if it were an accomplished fact.

Another version, which may have been the primary source, was given by John Richardson, the Attorney General's chief of staff. It reads:

> *Nir*: Israelis, in Jan 86, approach w[ith]/2 ways to help—Arrange to take residuals from these transactions to N[icaragua].[43]

Another reference by him to the Israelis reads:

> Israeli suggest[ion] to sweeten pot?
> – Disc[ussed] Israeli help gen[era]lly –
> N[orth] & R[abin]
> Don't recall asking them.
> Israeli offers.[44]

Thus Richardson's version on this point agrees in essence with Reynolds's—North did not say that the Israelis had actually arranged to transfer the residuals to the Contras, and at most he may have said that they had offered to do so. The trouble would have been avoided if the authors had simply quoted what Reynolds or Richardson had said. By "re-creating" their own version in dialogue form,

---

[41] Deposition of William B. Reynolds, Appendix B: Vol. 22, p. 1285.

[42] Ibid., p. 1184.

[43] Testimony of Edwin Meese III, pp. 1413–14.

[44] Ibid., p. 1414. Richardson explained these notes as follows: "Was this an Israeli suggestion to sweeten the pot? It was discussed with the Israelis to how they could help generally, and that's North and Rabin. Don't recall asking them. Thought the Israelis offered" (Richardson deposition, Appendix B: Vol. 23, p. 323).

they went beyond the evidence or their own sources into a journalistic no-man's-land.

This is not the only distortion in this account of North's climactic interview on the diversion memo. But this one is all the more gratuitous, because their note refers to North's public testimony. In it he had merely credited Amiram Nir with the original proposal to build up "residuals" but with no reference to transferring them to the Nicaraguan Contras—a refinement that had allegedly come from Manucher Ghorbanifar. They thus made North say something in contradiction to his own testimony as well as in disregard of their own professed sources.

3. Sometimes Mayer and McManus create dialogue with no basis at all in their sources. One example is what President Reagan is supposed to have said to North in a telephone call made soon after Meese's press conference announcing North's downfall.

> "Ollie," the president said, "you're a national hero." Then he added the best consolation he knew: "This is going to make a great movie one day."[45]

The note leads one to North's testimony. There one finds that North said "he told me words to the effect 'I just didn't know.'"[46] That is all; no national hero, no movie.

North's two aides, Lieutenant Colonel Robert Earl and Lieutenant Commander Craig P. Coy, had other secondhand versions of the President's telephone call. Earl said that North had told them the President had said to him "that he, the President, recognized or that it was important that he, the President, not know—words to that effect."[47] Coy could only recall that the President "had in fact called and said he was sorry he had to let Ollie go, but he had to—something along those lines."[48]

The Mayer-McManus reference to the "great movie" presents a different kind of problem. It comes from an article by Shirley Christian in *The New York Times* of November 30, 1986. She wrote about North's life after the eruption of the Iran-Contra scandal, about which she has this sentence:

---

[45] *Landslide*, p. 351.
[46] North testimony, p. 246.
[47] Earl deposition, Appendix B: Vol. 9, p. 895.
[48] Coy deposition, Appendix B: Vol. 7, p. 1094.

They [friends] said he was also heartened by a telephone call of gratitude from Mr. Reagan, who, according to one acquaintance, began the conversation by suggesting that the revelations of recent days would make a great movie.

This remark comes from a reporter who cites an unnamed acquaintance about what the President supposedly said to North on the telephone days earlier.

Is it legitimate to make out of this a direct quotation, "This is going to make a great movie one day," and tack it on to "you're a national hero," as if Mayer and McManus knew that one remark actually followed the other? Is it legitimate to give a source note that is entirely misleading?

The source note for this passage reads: "Ollie, you're a national hero: North testimony, July 7, 9, 1987."[49] Even this is spurious. North had merely testified: "he told me words to the effect 'I just didn't know.' " That's all there is in North's testimony about the telephone call.

The words "national hero" come from a telephone interview with the President by Hugh Sidey of *Time* magazine.[50] Fawn Hall had testified to a somewhat different version—that North had told her the President had called him "an American hero."[51]

Mayer-McManus's source note would lead readers to believe that both the "national hero" and "great movie" remarks appear in North's testimony. In short, the "national hero," the "great movie," and the source note were all dubious concoctions. Though Mayer and McManus had assured the reader that "no dialogue has been reconstructed from secondhand sources," the "national hero" remark was reconstructed from a wrongly attributed secondhand source, and the "great movie" bit was reconstructed from a thirdhand source.

Yet Mayer-McManus boast of six hundred source notes. Whenever I was curious about something in their book, I rarely found a note. I was curious about the "national hero"–"great movie" paragraph and found the wrong note for the first and no note for the second. Source notes were evidently meant to imply that the authors were doing a serious work of history; such notes should not have been

---

[49] *Landslide*, p. 435.

[50] *Time*, December 8, 1986. The interview by telephone occurred on November 26, 1986.

[51] Hall testimony, p. 502.

used to cover up work that is in large part fictionalized journalism or factitious popular history.

This sort of treatment raises disturbing questions. Is such dialogue justified by any acceptable code of journalistic ethics? Should even popular history be written this way? Should journalism or popular history be fictionalized? Should any real person in a real event be made to say positively what is only alluded to or merely hinted at in the sources? Does it make no difference who said what—whether, for example, North himself said something or someone else said that he had said it?

These methods invite unacceptable abuses. Yet more and more journalistic books have adopted this style of dialogue. It is time for publishers, editors, writers, reviewers, and readers to examine their consciences and decide whether they approve of it.

(*The New York Review of Books*, January 19, 1989)

Neoconservative History

1

MYTHS ARE notoriously hardy. They can flourish, subside, and flourish again. One of the hardiest myths in modern American history is associated with the Yalta Conference toward the end of World War II. It originally arose during the Truman Administration, when Yalta was made into a code word for treason. The Republican Party's platform of 1952 went so far as to denounce the Yalta agreements on the ground that they had secretly aided "Communist enslavements." That there was nothing secret about them after the full text was published in March 1947 and that they were intended to prevent Communist enslavements made no difference to the platform writers. The guilt for this treasonable sellout of Eastern Europe was attributed to one man, Franklin Delano Roosevelt, and through him to the Democratic Party in particular and to liberals in general. The accusation envenomed American politics throughout the McCarthy period but seemed to be spent by the late 1950s.

Now it has returned. It has just been put forward in one form or another not once but three times by three different writers in the pages of the November 1985 issue of *Commentary*, its fortieth anniversary issue. A related version has also come to the surface in the recently published diaries of John Colville, Churchill's wartime private secretary and a contributor to the September 1985 issue of *Commentary*. I came across these reincarnations in casual reading;

no doubt more intensive research would turn up others, but these are enough to indicate a resurgence of an ominous mythology.

This phenomenon is worth examining for its own sake, because a nation should know its own past, and because Yalta-and-Roosevelt baiting is a form of retroactive politics that tells us something about the present.

The first specimen in the November 1985 *Commentary* was contributed by Lionel Abel, whose recent book was aptly entitled *The Intellectual Follies*. He based himself on a single article by Colville in the following way:

> And Roosevelt was personally responsible for terrible foreign-policy decisions (described in these pages only two months ago by John Colville in his article, "How the West Lost the Peace in 1945") which gave the Soviet Union control of Eastern Europe.

Colville in turn had placed the giveaway at Yalta in February 1945 and had specifically named Poland as the victim:

> After long discussions and much argument [at Yalta] it was agreed that some non-Communist Poles should be invited to join the [Polish] government—though they would be but a minority—and that "free and unfettered elections," in which all except the fascist parties should be allowed to put forward candidates, would be held within a few months. The British delegation was not content with the vagueness of the Soviet promises or the design of the proposed Polish government; but since the Soviets and Americans were in agreement, Churchill and Eden had to give way, though they knew there would be trouble in the House of Commons.

Here we have two enduring elements of the Yalta myth—that vague Soviet promises, rather than the breach of not-so-vague promises, were responsible for the subsequent fate of Poland, and that the Americans, not the British, bear the burden of guilt. Colville does not hold Roosevelt "personally responsible" and does not use any such crass expression as that Roosevelt "gave the Soviet Union control of Eastern Europe." Abel's embellishment of Colville's version is a good example of how these stories can go from bad to worse in the telling.

The next appearance of another form of the myth comes from a more serious source, Ambassador and now again Professor Jeane J. Kirkpatrick. Yalta was where it was decided to give the Soviet Union three votes in the General Assembly of the future United Nations. In the November *Commentary*, Kirkpatrick deals with it this way:

Founding the UN also required falsifying the relations between the Soviet Union and those two "autonomous Soviet Socialist republics," the Ukraine and Byelorussia. The Charter required that members be independent states. The Ukraine and Byelorussia were neither autonomous nor republics. Why did the United States and its democratic allies accept this falsification? Presumably, the reason was that they could not bear to face the fact that even after this most recent, most terrible war, there remained a powerful, repressive, expansionist dictatorship to cope with.

Nothing in the Soviet past justified optimism concerning its future behavior. Winston Churchill knew this, Franklin D. Roosevelt should have.

Kirkpatrick's sense of history here is—to be charitable—defective. The decision on the Ukraine and Byelorussia memberships was made before there was a UN and before it had a charter. The reason for the decision could not have had anything to do with whatever remained *after* "this most recent, most terrible war." The war was not yet over; fighting remained even against Germany; the last hard phase of the battle against Japan, with the possible entrance of the Soviet Union into the Far Eastern war, was still ahead; the atomic bomb had not even been tested; American military planners were still counting on a "most terrible war" to come. One must try to put oneself back into the real world of Churchill and Roosevelt at the time of Yalta before judging either of them so loftily.

If Kirkpatrick's history is bad, her attribution of motives is worse. Her differentiation between Churchill and Roosevelt is, as we shall see, as wrongheaded as can be. The mystery is how a former UN ambassador could get the whole story topsy-turvy.

But she is not the only one who has the allocation of the three Soviet seats in the UN all wrong. Another is John Colville in his recently published book, *The Fringes of Power*, made up largely of his wartime diaries. Colville was not at Yalta; the British Foreign Secretary, Anthony Eden, was. In an entry dated February 19, 1945, Colville tells about a conversation with Eden:

> The PM had been very persuasive about the Dumbarton Oaks compromise (voting in the Security Council) and the Russians would have been quite happy to agree to none of their constituent states belonging to the Assembly, had not the Americans foolishly acquiesced. Finally the Americans had been very weak.[1]

---

[1] John Colville, *The Fringes of Power: 10 Downing Street Diaries, 1939–1955* (Norton, 1985), p. 560.

Since this is apparently attributed to Eden, there is no telling what Colville knew. Nevertheless, Colville should have known—or learned—by the time his diaries were prepared for publication that there was no truth to this story. Colville's book has footnotes in which he frequently explains or comments on the text; he has no footnote on this one and this would lead the reader to believe that his source is trustworthy.

In any case, Kirkpatrick and Colville have put into circulation the same fable—that Churchill and the British opposed the allocation of Soviet seats in the United Nations, while Roosevelt and the Americans for reasons of undue optimism or weakness were responsible for it. Kirkpatrick writes so loosely that she first accuses "the United States and its democratic allies," which would include Great Britain, of accepting the falsification and then suggests that Churchill knew better than Roosevelt. Either way, she completely muddles what actually happened.

The third exhibit from *Commentary*, by Professor Robert Nisbet, shows how closely interwoven are the past and present in anti-Roosevelt, pro-Churchill retrospection. He does not mention Yalta specifically, but it would be the prime test of his indictment of Roosevelt. His starting point is in the past:

> The recently published correspondence between Churchill and Roosevelt must make for bitter reading in some quarters. All that we had known in a general sort of way about Roosevelt's strong disposition to trust Stalin, even over Churchill's cautionary advice, is detailed richly in these letters. Roosevelt's credulity toward Stalin and his sometimes rather pathetic ignorance of political history and geopolitics were joined unfortunately to a complacent certainty that Stalin wanted only one thing out of the war: world peace and democracy.

Nisbet then moves into the present:

> In many walks of life do we find alive and well the institutionalization of Roosevelt's unwavering faith in the Soviet Union.

There is nothing—I repeat *nothing*—in the recently published correspondence between Churchill and Roosevelt that shows Roosevelt's strong disposition to trust Stalin, or his credulity toward Stalin, or his complacent certainty about the only thing that Stalin wanted, or his unwavering faith in the Soviet Union, or that Churchill gave Roosevelt "cautionary advice" about not trusting Stalin. I have read and reread this correspondence without finding any of these things.

All these charges against Roosevelt have been invented by Nisbet; they are not in the correspondence. Thus for the third time in this little anti-Roosevelt anthology, Churchill is played off against Roosevelt in order to make Roosevelt appear to be an "unwavering" stooge of the Soviet Union.

If such misrepresentation is still possible in'1985, forty years after Yalta, it is time to set the record straight again. But there would be no urgent need for such an effort if history were not again being made to serve current political extremism. Did Roosevelt personally give the Soviet Union control of Eastern Europe? Why were three seats in the United Nations allotted to the Soviet Union? Did Churchill know so much better than Roosevelt? Before turning to the present political climate in which these questions have been raised, we need to clear up the past.

2

Franklin D. Roosevelt did not give the Soviet Union control of Eastern Europe; the Red Army did. By the time of Yalta, when the last diplomatic effort was made to stave off total control, the Red Army occupied most of Poland and Eastern Europe. But diplomacy can rarely save what is lost by force of arms. Both Churchill and Roosevelt failed not because they did not want to succeed but for lack of force at the right place at the right time. To accuse one of them, Roosevelt, of in effect doing whatever Stalin wanted him to do is grotesquely false.

If Stalin had any reason to believe that he could take Eastern Europe with impunity, he owed it in the first place to Churchill. Churchill had made a preliminary deal with Stalin in May 1944; they agreed that the Soviet Union would "take the lead" in Romania in return for letting the British "take the lead" in Greece.[2] At a meeting in Moscow in October 1944, Churchill proposed a more far-reaching arrangement: a division of power in percentages—for the Soviets, 90 percent in Romania, 75 percent in Bulgaria, 50 percent in Hungary and Yugoslavia, in exchange for 90 percent for Great Britain in Greece. These figures implied that Churchill envisaged a Soviet

---

[2] *Churchill and Roosevelt: The Complete Correspondence*, edited with a commentary by Warren F. Kimball (Princeton University Press, 1985), Vol. 3, pp. 137, 153. This arrangement was first opposed by Roosevelt, who later agreed to it for a three-month trial period after renewed pressure by Churchill (pp. 177, 181–82).

sphere of influence in Eastern Europe in exchange for a British sphere of influence in the Mediterranean area. When Churchill had reported "the system of percentage" to his colleagues in London, he had tried to pass it off as a way for both the British and Soviet governments to "reveal their minds to each other." Stalin had revealed his mind by immediately accepting the deal.[3]

This was far more than a mind-revealing exercise. It is less well known that the two Foreign Ministers, Eden and Molotov, haggled over the percentages the following day. Molotov wanted 75 percent in Hungary, Bulgaria, and Yugoslavia, then 90 percent in Bulgaria and 50 percent in Yugoslavia. Eden agreed to 75 percent for the Soviets in Hungary, 80 percent in Bulgaria, 50 percent in Yugoslavia. The two haggled some more the next day. Churchill described the percentages as a "guide" for the British and Soviet governments.[4] In fact, they guided Churchill's diplomacy right through and after Yalta. Churchill, as Eden's latest biographer has noted, "remained convinced that the British should try to hold the Soviets to the 'percentages' arrangements of the previous October even at the cost of condoning Stalin's breaches of the Yalta Declaration in the Soviet sphere-of-influence."[5]

There would be no need to rake up these old embarrassments if Churchill were not now being held up as the one who knew better what Roosevelt should have known. At this late stage of the war, Roosevelt had nothing to do with this open invitation to Stalin to take over most of Eastern Europe. No doubt Churchill had not

[3] In his review of the Churchill-Roosevelt correspondence in *The New York Review of Books*, February 14, 1985, Martin Gilbert, Churchill's distinguished biographer, reversed the roles played by Churchill and Stalin in what Gilbert called the "notorious 'percentages agreement.' " He described it as "that piece of paper on which, at Churchill's suggestion, Stalin marked his 'percentages' " and which was "in fact Churchill's belated attempt to find out from Stalin just what degree of influence the Soviet leader imagined Russia would have in Eastern Europe, country by country. Stalin's jottings about the countries he expected to control revealed an ambitious tyrant, but a tyrant whose armies were gaining every day by military conquest the 'percentages' which he had so brazenly committed to paper." It has been known at least since the sixth and last volume of Churchill's memoirs that it was Churchill who had written the percentages "on a half-sheet of paper" and had "pushed this across to Stalin, who by then had heard the translation. There was a slight pause. Then he took his blue pencil and made a large tick on it, and passed it back to us" (*Triumph and Tragedy* [Houghton Mifflin, 1953], p. 227). Such are the tricks of memory in this seemingly treacherous field.

[4] Sir Llewellyn Woodward, *British Foreign Policy in the Second World War* (London: Her Majesty's Stationery Office, 1971), Vol. 3, pp. 150–53.

[5] David Carlton, *Anthony Eden* (London: Allen Lane, 1981), p. 253. The reference here is to Romania.

counted on the brutality with which the Soviets would impose their "predominance"—another word that Churchill used—in Romania, Bulgaria, and Hungary. But then Churchill cannot be held up as a model for Roosevelt.

Poland was a special case, though it is hard to believe that it could have stayed out of the Soviet sphere if the rest of Eastern Europe went the way of the Churchill-Stalin deal. If Professor Nisbet were right, Roosevelt should have shown a "strong disposition to trust Stalin" and an "unwavering faith in the Soviet Union" precisely on the issue of Poland. Roosevelt did nothing of the kind.

The trouble in Poland was that the Soviets had already installed a puppet provisional government in Lublin, while the British and Americans had previously recognized another Polish provisional government in London. Roosevelt had tried before Yalta to get Stalin to postpone Soviet recognition of the Lublin Poles until they could meet and discuss the problem. Stalin refused. Roosevelt replied that he was "disturbed and deeply disappointed" by Stalin's action.[6] So far, no trust and no faith.

The Polish issue took up more time than anything else at Yalta. At no point did Churchill or Roosevelt agree to the Soviet plan to put the "Lublin Government" in power. With the Red Army in most of Poland, they had few cards to play, the only one of consequence being their refusal to rubber-stamp the Soviet design. If words had counted, they did not do at all badly. They arrived at a declaration on Poland which, while not foolproof, would have been satisfactory if the Soviets had lived up to it. It provided for a "new government" to be formed by reorganizing the Soviet-sponsored provisional government "with the inclusion of democratic leaders from Poland itself and from Poles abroad." The new government was pledged "to the holding of free and unfettered elections as soon as possible on the basis of universal suffrage and secret ballot." Stalin had said that this election could be held in no more than a month, in which case the new provisional government would have been short-lived.[7]

---

[6] *Stalin's Correspondence with Roosevelt and Truman, 1941–1945* (Capricorn Books, 1965), pp. 175, 182. This is a reprint of the edition originally published in Moscow by the Soviet publishing house in 1957. It is mystifying why this is the only extant version of the complete correspondence, even though some of the documents were available in the Soviet Union in Russian translation only and lack the original English texts.

[7] The full record is in *Foreign Relations of the United States: The Conferences at Malta and Yalta, 1945* (Government Printing Office, 1955).

On paper, neither side had its own way. Roosevelt was willing to fudge the issue of the new provisional government; Stalin was willing to concede the matter of early free elections. The combination might have extricated Poland if Stalin had seen it to be in his interests to make it work. In the end, words hardly mattered. The Soviets ignored both the promised reorganization of the provisional government and the commitment to free elections. Yalta was a dividing line, not because of what happened at the meeting there, but because of what happened after it. Brute power decided, not fair words. The trouble with the argument over Yalta is that it is too much about words and not enough about power.

After Yalta, however, a difference emerged between Churchill and Roosevelt. It is hard to tell what Nisbet has in mind, but if there were any truth in the story of Roosevelt's trust and faith in Stalin, it should have come out during their disagreement. Between February 23 and March 8, 1945, an Anglo-American-Soviet commission met to put the Polish agreement into effect. Only then did it become clear to Churchill that the Soviets were determined to have their own way in Poland, in violation of both the letter and the spirit of the agreement. On March 8, Churchill sent Roosevelt a message of alarm and proposed that both countries should send a protest to Stalin.

This cable has been described by Professor Warren F. Kimball, the editor of the Churchill-Roosevelt correspondence, as marking "a British reversal on Eastern Europe." It was a reversal in the sense that Churchill had publicly expressed more confidence in Stalin's good faith than Roosevelt had ever done.[8] Churchill, as Professor Kimball puts it, "was playing a tricky game" of pressing Roosevelt to protest over Poland, while Churchill himself was rebuking Eden for wanting to protest the Soviets' oppressive behavior in Romania.[9] Romania was different, because Churchill's deal with Stalin had made British interests in Greece depend on giving the Soviets a free hand in Romania. One of the reasons Churchill resented being "defrauded" by Stalin on Poland was, as he informed Roosevelt, that

---

[8] Winston Churchill, House of Commons, February 27, 1945:

> The impression I brought back from the Crimea, and from all my other contacts, is that Marshal Stalin and the Soviet leaders wish to live in honourable friendship and equality with the Western democracies. I feel also that their word is their bond. I know of no Government which stands to its obligations, even in its own despite, more solidly than the Russian Soviet Government.

[9] *Churchill and Roosevelt: The Complete Correspondence*, Vol. 3, pp. 545–47.

he had "advised critics of the Yalta settlement to trust Stalin."[10] If Roosevelt had permitted himself to be "defrauded," Churchill could not claim to have been any the wiser. In effect, Churchill, having invited the Soviets to predominate in much of Eastern Europe, was appalled at the prospect as soon as the Red Army began to turn it into a reality.

Roosevelt held back. Now was the time, according to the myth makers, when Roosevelt should have shown his trust and faith in Stalin. But he disagreed with Churchill on altogether different grounds. On March 11, 1945, a month after Yalta, Roosevelt wrote to Churchill: "I can assure you that our objectives are identical, namely, to bring about a cessation on the part of the Lublin Poles of the measures directed against their political opponents in Poland." The difference between himself and Churchill was tactical. Roosevelt thought that they should recommend "a general political truce" between the Lublin Poles and their opponents instead of complaining immediately to the Soviet government. As Professor Kimball sums up the situation, "Roosevelt and his advisers avoided making an appeal to Stalin lest the Soviet Premier give the wrong answer and thus force a confrontation or a retreat."

That was the rub—the British and Americans had nothing more than words to back up a confrontation. Again and again Roosevelt assured Churchill that the difference was over tactics, not policy. With this view Churchill agreed. In any case, the tactical difference was over by the end of March. Both Churchill and Roosevelt addressed strong, coordinated protests to Stalin, Roosevelt on April 1, 1945, Churchill immediately afterward.[11] Roosevelt died twelve days later.

During this entire period, when it was most likely to have happened, Churchill never cautioned Roosevelt not to trust Stalin. There is no such Churchillian "cautionary advice" in the entire correspondence. One begins to wonder whether Nisbet really read the correspondence as carefully as he pretends to have done.

The Western Allies did not give away anything at Yalta that they actually had; they did get some promissory notes which they could not cash in once Stalin decided to stop payment. They still hoped

---

[10] Churchill to Roosevelt (March 27, 1945), in ibid., p. 588.

[11] The entire sequence can be followed in ibid., pp. 545–602, after which Churchill wrote to Roosevelt: "I am delighted with our being in such perfect step."

against hope—Churchill as well as Roosevelt—to find some way to coexist peacefully, a hope that nourished illusions and compromises. But illusions and compromises were not born at Yalta; they had been fostered throughout the war in both liberal and conservative circles; they helped to sustain morale, when the British-American forces, even after the establishment of the second front on the Continent, were engaging only one third of the total German forces. Little or nothing would have changed if the break with the Soviet Union had come at Yalta instead of soon afterward; as long as the Western Allies could not contest Soviet power on the ground in Eastern Europe, they could do no more than get paper promises and respond with paper protests. It is easy enough now to scoff at the Yalta illusions; it was not so easy to give them up then. The illusions, moreover, were about the Soviet Union, not about the merit—at least as far as the plain meaning of the words—of the Yalta agreements.[12]

If Roosevelt and Churchill were wrong to hope for postwar co-operation with the Soviet Union, they had a lot of company. How hard it was to give up wishful thinking can be seen from the case of John Foster Dulles, no liberal, no Democrat, no trusting soul. In a speech on March 17, 1945, at this very juncture, he said:

> Many do not like the sample of reality which Yalta produced. But that is because the collaborators are themselves imperfect. Their defects will not be removed by breaking up the collaboration. On the contrary, that would intensify the defects.[13]

At a press conference on November 24, 1953, he remarked that, at the end of the war, "those in charge of our foreign policy at the time

[12] The merit of the agreement on Poland was most recently recognized by a leader of the Solidarity movement, Jacek Kuron, in an interview with Tamar Jacoby, deputy editor of the *New York Times* Op-Ed page, in an article in *The New Republic*, December 23, 1985:

> Kuron insists that what he wants is "not revising but renewing Yalta"—reviving at least some of the demands that the West put to Moscow in 1945. He admits that it might not be possible today to insist on free elections in Poland. But he believes that other demands, for economic reform and genuinely free trade unions, could now be made to stick because "there are political forces here within the country now that can fight for these conditions and defend them." What he envisions is nothing short of democratization, induced by the West, in the heart of Eastern Europe—and he apparently doesn't see much contradiction in either this or the original Yalta for-mulation, calling for free elections within the Soviet sphere of influence.

If Kuron's view prevails, Yalta may someday represent a historical weapon against the Soviet oppression of Poland, rather than the sellout it is supposed to have been.

[13] "From Yalta to San Francisco," delivered at the Foreign Policy Association in New York (typescript in the "Dulles Papers," Seeley G. Mudd Library, Princeton University).

seemed to have assumed—*many of us did*—that we were entering into an era of lasting peace and that the Soviet Union would not be a threat" (*emphasis added*).[14] And toward the end of the 1950s, Dulles confided to Andrew H. Berding, then assistant secretary of state for Public Affairs:

> The general impression is that the Yalta agreement was a mistake. I don't feel so categorical about this. In 1945 we still had the hope that the Russians would cooperate with us. Furthermore, since the Russians were already in occupation of the Balkans, all we could hope for was their promise that the peoples of the Eastern European countries could have governments of their own choosing.[15]

Not so long ago, Professor Kirkpatrick herself defended the Yalta agreements from the charge of having sold out Eastern Europe and Poland.[16] When an old Republican like Dulles and a new Republican like Kirkpatrick could see the rationale of Roosevelt's actions at Yalta, the present defamatory fury requires an extrahistorical explanation. The reason must have less to do with the past than with the present.

Ironically, Stalin succeeded in scoring a double triumph after Yalta. First, he took over Poland without a new, reorganized provisional government and without "free and unfettered elections as soon as possible on the basis of universal suffrage and secret ballot." Then he managed to get the blame shifted from himself to Franklin D. Roosevelt. For the second half of his triumph he needed the collaboration of Americans, some of whom knew no better and some of whom should by now know better.

---

[14] Typescript in "Dulles Papers."

[15] Andrew H. Berding, *Dulles on Diplomacy* (D. Van Nostrand, 1965), pp. 22–23. These sentiments did not prevent Dulles from helping to draft the 1952 Republican platform denouncing Yalta.

[16] In *The Reagan Phenomenon—and Other Speeches on Foreign Policy* (American Enterprise Institute, 1983), pp. 176–77:

> Today, in the shadow of the Soviet-ordered repression in Poland, it is easy to forget that Yalta reaffirmed the principles of the Atlantic Charter, recognizing "the right of all people to choose the form of government under which they will live," and, in the case of Poland specifically, pledged that "free and unfettered elections" would be held "as soon as possible on the basis of universal suffrage and secret ballot." Roosevelt and Churchill no doubt took these words very seriously. But Stalin, who once wrote that "good words are a mask for the concealment of bad deeds," clearly did not. A Soviet puppet regime was already in place in Warsaw. The Red Army had occupied all of Eastern Europe, with the exception of most of Czechoslovakia. Words and dreams could neither conceal nor change this reality.

3

There is something peculiarly shameful about the idea that Roosevelt gave away Eastern Europe. But putting the blame on him for the three Soviet seats in the United Nations is merely ludicrous. Again, it is Churchill who is being mistaken for Roosevelt.

The subject of membership in the future United Nations first came up at the Dumbarton Oaks conference in August 1944. The Soviets unexpectedly proposed that the sixteen individual Soviet "republics" be made full members of the UN. The demand was not as outrageous as it may seem today. It was explained by Ambassador Charles E. Bohlen, the wartime interpreter and adviser: "The Soviets knew they would be virtually alone in the United Nations, that their ideological system provided little common ground with other countries." Times have changed; it is again necessary to try to put oneself back into a very different period. The Americans flatly opposed the Soviet request. "President Roosevelt went so far as to tell members of Congress that if the Russians persisted in this proposal, he would counter with a demand that the forty-eight states of the United States be members."[17]

The dispute was resolved at Yalta. The Soviets decided to cut down the number from sixteen to two or three, eventually two more, the Ukraine and Byelorussia. Roosevelt initially objected even to this number. But Churchill for his own reasons made an eloquent plea in support of the Soviet request.[18] With some reluctance, Roo-

---

[17] Charles E. Bohlen, *Witness to History* (Norton, 1973), pp. 159–60.

[18] In *Foreign Relations of the United States: The Conferences at Malta and Yalta, 1945*, p. 714:

> This is why, Mr. President, the Prime Minister said, he had great sympathy with the Soviet request. His heart went out to mighty Russia which though bleeding was beating down the tyrants in her path. He said he could understand their point of view, as they were represented by only one voice in comparison with the British organization which had a smaller population, if only white people were considered.

Even so knowledgeable a historian as Professor Adam B. Ulam has perpetuated the myth that Churchill, "having very largely accepted Roosevelt's leadership when it came to dealing with Russia, felt constrained, even if groaning inwardly, to go along with the president" in acceding to Stalin's wish for three Soviet seats in the UN ("Forty Years After Yalta," *The New Republic*, February 11, 1985, p. 20). Professor Ulam is wrong here on two counts: Churchill was quite independent when it came to dealing with Russia, as the "percentages deal" and his disagreement with Roosevelt soon after the Yalta Conference showed; and it was Roosevelt who in this case went along with the Prime Minister, even if groaning inwardly.

sevelt went along with Stalin and Churchill, though he later regretted that the Soviet Union would get three votes in the General Assembly, Great Britain with its dominions six votes, and the United States only one. Roosevelt soon changed his mind and actually wrote Stalin and Churchill requesting three votes for the United States, to which they agreed. When the story was leaked to the papers, it was subjected to such ridicule that the idea was dropped. Since substantive decisions could be made only in the Security Council, in which each of the three powers had a veto, the votes in the General Assembly were not considered all that important.

Why was Churchill so willing to let the Soviets have their way? He explained the reason in a contemporary letter to Deputy Prime Minister Clement Attlee:

> For us to have four or five members, six if India is included, when Russia has only one is asking a great deal of an Assembly of this kind. In view of other important concessions by them which are achieved or pending I should like to be able to make a friendly gesture to Russia in this matter. That they should have two besides their chief is not much to ask, and we will be in a strong position, in my judgment, because we shall not be the only multiple voter in the field.[19]

Thus Kirkpatrick and Colville have the whole story upside down. Churchill, not Roosevelt, made possible the deal that gave the Soviets three members in the United Nations. There was no "falsification" which the United States and its democratic allies accepted, as Kirkpatrick alleges. Above all, her presumption of why they were parties to a "falsification" is itself most presumptuous. The reason had nothing to do with their being unable to face the fact that there remained "a powerful, repressive, expansionist dictatorship to cope with." It had nothing to do with whether Churchill knew and Roosevelt should have known that "nothing in the Soviet past justified optimism concerning its future behavior." The reason had everything to do with a temporary coincidence of interests on the part of both Stalin and Churchill to get more than one vote in the nascent UN.

We are now in a better position to assess the latter-day glorification of Churchill and denigration of Roosevelt. The wonder is not that they sometimes disagreed but that they worked together so well for so long, given the different traditions and interests of their countries.

[19] *Triumph and Tragedy*, pp. 359–60.

They were both giants in their time, whatever their shortcomings. I am inclined to think that Churchill was right about Roosevelt's "truce plan" in the period of their disagreement after Yalta, but the issue itself came up too late and would have changed too little to count for much. What is unforgivable is the ignorance and effrontery of those who now accuse one of them of virtual betrayal or outright falsification.

4

What in the present has provoked this abuse of the past?

The main source, I suspect, is the influence of the so-called neo-conservative ideology. The latest pronunciamento from that front on American foreign policy has made "liberal internationalism" the enemy. In this view, the era of liberal internationalism is fortunately coming to an end. No one represents this era more conspicuously than Franklin D. Roosevelt, who inaugurated it in our time. For this reason he is being belittled and his reputation besmirched.

"Global unilateralism" has been presented by Irving Kristol, the reputed "godfather" and "standard-bearer" of the new creed, as the neoconservative alternative to "liberal internationalism." His new order would require a total break with all our allies and the abandonment by the United States of NATO, the United Nations, and the Organization of American States. He wants to get rid of allies, because they are "very effective hindrances to American action."[20] This is another myth; the United States has not been hindered by NATO or the UN from doing anything it really wanted to do—not in Korea, not in Vietnam or Grenada or Central America or anywhere. Others have also had reservations about NATO's strategy and the UN's behavior. There is no law that says these organizations may not be modified or reformed to reflect the conditions of today rather than those in existence immediately after World War II. But Kristol is engaged in a throw-out-the-baby-with-the-bathwater op-

---

[20] Irving Kristol, "Foreign Policy in an Age of Ideology," *The National Interest*, No. 1 (Fall 1985), pp. 6–15.

Kristol is uncharacteristically squeamish in his avowal of "global unilateralism." After demanding the dismantling of NATO, the UN, and the OAS, as well as the virtually defunct Southeast Asia Treaty Organization, he coyly adds: "Whether the United States will then move all the way to what has been called 'global unilateralism' depends on the reaction among America's allies"—after he has just written them off as allies.

eration. It is so extreme that even his friend Jeane Kirkpatrick cannot go along with it.[21] If the Soviet Union has one governing objective in Europe it is the destruction of NATO. "Global unilateralism" is another way of doing it.

The world according to Kristol is a world in the grip of a "conflict of ideologies." The ideologies, however, do not seem to be in very good shape for a final conflict. They were in Kristol's view better off after 1945, when they were clearly identifiable as "liberal internationalism and Marxism-Leninism." But now both are said to be "floundering," each in its own way.

The "liberal internationalism" of the United States was allegedly "mortally wounded" in Vietnam. There is now, in Kristol's opinion, only "a tentative, fumbling search" for a new American ideology. Just what is taking its place is far from clear. Unfortunately, the "natural and instinctive attitude" of most Americans is said to be some version of isolationism. A liberal-capitalist ideology which aspires to be "universal" would seem to have the wrong people as its chosen instrument. But there is also better news. The same American people, in their post-Vietnam phase, wish the United States to "reassert its proprietary claim to the future." One might imagine from this that the future is a piece of property which should belong exclusively to the United States. If so, the ideological conflict may be not only with the Soviet Union but with any country that is selfish enough to want a piece of the future for and by itself.

The Soviet ideology is supposedly floundering for a different reason. We are assured that Marxism-Leninism is dead in the Soviet Union and in every other Communist nation. We are also told that the Soviet system "works" in foreign affairs only because it rests on Soviet military power and that this power alone legitimates the Soviet system abroad. Without such military power, "the Soviet leadership is under threat of being de-legitimated." Nevertheless, despite the

---

[21] "NATO has been a great success. It remains one. It was never intended to be an all-purpose instrument. It should, therefore, not be criticized for failing to be one" (*The Reagan Phenomenon*, p. 181).

More useful advice: "The dynamics of the American political system precludes the successful practice of purist politics and guarantees chronic frustration to all persons whose public policy preferences deviate significantly from the status quo. That includes most of us some of the time and some of us most of the time. The Reagan administration is no more able than any other to escape the powerful moderating, aggregating, consensus-building pressures that the American system puts on our governors. And that, as always, is a good thing for the United States" (p. 218).

internal bankruptcy of Marxism-Leninism and its total dependence abroad on military power, Soviet ideology is still "messianic."

How an ideology can be "messianic," if no one within the Soviet Union believes in it anymore, and it is carried abroad solely with guns, is a mystery that Kristol never clears up. A "messianic" ideology without true believers is something new under the sun. It may well be that Marxism-Leninism or whatever passes for it in such advanced proletarian nations as Ethiopia and South Yemen possesses an attractiveness of its own for military dictatorships that wish to pass themselves off as "progressive" or "revolutionary," but Soviet messianism has little to do with it. Kristol seems to need a Soviet messianism in order to convert the United States to a corresponding capitalist messianism.

There surely are ideological elements in the Soviet-American conflict, but they are precisely those elements that could be pursued most peacefully. Kristol and cohorts have something more in mind. Their version of ideological conflict shades into a real, ordinary, bloodletting war—anything up to nuclear devastation, which is the only concession Kristol makes to stopping short of mutual catastrophe. We are instructed to be "not at all risk-averse." We are also assured that "in the years ahead, the United States will be far less inhibited in its use of military power." If the Soviet Union does not convert "its secular, political messianism into a stable orthodoxy," whatever the latter may mean, global conflict will likely be "political, economic, and military, though always short of nuclear war," as if an impenetrable barrier could be built between nuclear and other types of war. In any case Kristol's "war of ideology" is not likely to be purely ideological.

This neoconservatism is not merely a hopeless muddle; it is also misnamed. We are probably stuck with the term, but it has little or nothing to do with traditional conservatism, particularly in foreign policy; it is a new concoction, much closer to other types of political extremism. We have had isolationists; we have had interventionists; we have never had isolationists who were also interventionists. This abnormal crossbreeding of isolationism and interventionism has produced the new species of "global unilateralists." They are global in their interventionism and unilateral in the way they wish to go about it. In the past, isolationists did not want us to intervene and interventionists did not want us to be isolated.

Though the enemy is ostensibly Communism and the Soviet Union, what really stirs the "neo" to a sort of holy wrath is anything that can be blamed on liberals. There is not much he can do about getting at the Soviet Union, but homegrown liberals are readily available as targets of his rancor. It is *de rigueur* for a "neo" who was formerly a liberal to be particularly unforgiving in his anathemas upon liberals. Against this enemy the "neo" goes into battle as if in a civil war, with more than a hint that those who differ are really serving the enemy. A disagreement over policy comes to resemble a quasi-religious war rather than a legitimate secular dispute. Indeed, Kristol wishes us to believe that "in our own era, the distinction between religious ideas and political ideas is blurred."

The remaking of history plays a large part in this apocalyptic drama of good and evil because the older "neo" has repented and recanted transgressions that he committed as a liberal or leftist. No one raises his blood pressure more than the liberal with whom he once shared the same views—about the Vietnam War, for example—but who has stubbornly refused to admit grievous error and recant publicly. The present frustrates "neos" because it resists their unconstrained adventurism; only in historical reinterpretations can they indulge themselves in ideological imperatives and infallible hindsights. Thus their treatment of history is peculiarly guilt-ridden, with the guilt often displaced onto others.

Foreign policy is actually not the best place to distinguish between American liberals and conservatives. The line between them can be drawn more clearly in domestic policy—and then not always. In the past, there have been interventionist conservatives and interventionist liberals, isolationist conservatives and isolationist liberals. In foreign policy, Presidents have not been liberal or conservative so much as isolationist or interventionist. Presidents have sacrificed their liberal domestic policies for the sake of foreign interventionism. Lyndon Johnson was such a case; he did not intervene in Vietnam on such a large scale because he was a liberal; liberals and Democrats were on both sides of the war. Johnson also knew that the Republicans would have pilloried him if he could have been accused of "giving away Vietnam," just as Truman and Acheson had been pilloried for "giving away China," and as Roosevelt even to this day is being pilloried for having "given away Eastern Europe."

The irony in all this is that, if it were not for "liberal internationalism," Nazi Germany would in all probability still be astride all of Europe, and the United States would have had no credible ideology for trying to prevent the Soviet Union from doing the same thing.

(*The New York Review of Books*, April 24, 1986)

The Mystery of
Max Eitingon

1

DR. MAX EITINGON was one of Sigmund Freud's most devoted and valued colleagues. In 1907, he came from Switzerland, where he was studying, to see Freud—the first, as Freud later put it, "to reach the lonely man" from another country.[1] Freud did not take to him immediately, but once convinced of Eitingon's dedication he received him into his inner circle.[2] In 1919, Freud himself proposed Eitingon as a member of that strange "secret council composed of the best and most trustworthy among our men."[3] By 1922, after an association of almost a decade and a half, Freud wrote to him that his acceptance in Freud's inner circle had not come easily but "ever since [I] have allowed you to render me every kind of service, imposed on you every kind of task."[4] Since his death in 1943, Max Eitingon has gone down in the history of psychoanalysis as one of its commemorated "pioneers."[5]

[1] Ernst L. Freud, ed., *Letters to Sigmund Freud* (Basic Books, 1960), p. 300.

[2] In 1922, Freud wrote a letter to Eitingon in which he tried to make amends for his early effort to keep Eitingon "at bay" (Ibid., p. 337).

[3] Ernest Jones, *The Life and Work of Sigmund Freud* (Basic Books, 1955), Vol. 2, pp. 152–54. Hereafter, "Jones, *Freud*."

[4] *Letters to Sigmund Freud*, p. 337.

[5] See the chapter on Max Eitingon by Sidney L. Pomer in *Psychoanalytic Pioneers*, edited by Franz Alexander, Samuel Eisenstein, and Martin Grotjahn (Basic Books, 1966), pp. 51–62.

The New York Times Book Review of January 24, 1988, published an article by Stephen Schwartz, a Fellow at the Institute of Contemporary Studies in San Francisco, entitled "Intellectuals and Assassins—Annals of Stalin's Killerati." The chief intellectual member of the "killerati" in the article was Dr. Max Eitingon.

According to Schwartz, "Dr. Max Eitingon was instrumental in preparing the 1937 secret trial in which the highest leaders of the Soviet Army, including the chief army commissar and eight generals, fell before the Stalinist execution machine." Eitingon is said to have been drawn into the work of a "special unit [which] connived with Reinhard Heydrich of Hitler's intelligence service." Even more infamously, Eitingon was "involved in the murder of Ignace Reiss and the disappearance of General Miller" in 1937.

Max is also linked by Schwartz to his "brother," Leonid Eitingon, "considered to be the KGB's outstanding expert in operations against Russian anti-Communist exiles." A book cited by Schwartz is said to "declare flatly" that Dr. Max Eitingon served Leonid Eitingon in the plot to abduct the anti-Soviet General Yevgeni Miller in Paris in 1937. Among the crimes attributed to Leonid is the murder of Leon Trotsky in Mexico in 1940.

If all this is true, Dr. Max Eitingon is one of the most remarkable cases on record of a double life or personality. In one of his incarnations, he was a man who had seemingly devoted his entire life to the advancement of psychoanalysis. In the other, he had belonged to a "special unit" which had carried out some of Stalin's most murderous missions outside Russia.

I decided to devote myself to a detailed examination of the Eitingon aspect of Schwartz's article not only because one man's good name had been vilified. In this world, with all its crimes and evils, it is sometimes possible to redress a single wrong to a single person; I do not overestimate what good it can do, but the world must be an infinitely worse place if we remain silent in the face of a shameful injustice to a worthy man. I never knew Dr. Max Eitingon and have no personal stake in his reputation; he happened to embody a case of personal injustice and intellectual foul play.

But there was more to my interest. Schwartz's article in "the most influential book magazine in America," as *The New York Times Book Review* advertises itself, was an example of a type of journalistic misconduct that passes too often without challenge. I wanted to see whether I could make it into a case study of how one man's life can be besmirched by the misuse of sources and the abuse of references that belie what they are supposed to prove. The principle here was far more important than one man.

When I first read the *Times* article, it struck me as a mixture of the true, the half-true, and the improbable. The story of Dr. Max Eitingon seemed to be particularly suspicious, because no effort was made to explain how he could have lived his two lives at once. The KGB and its predecessors did not entrust the organization of these "killerati" missions to amateurs; they were set up by trained, seasoned professionals.

Leonid Eitingon was such a professional. But was it conceivable that Max was another, particularly if there was no evidence that he was the brother of Leonid except for the similarity of names? Schwartz's article is not about "Stalin's Killerati" in general. It is specifically about intellectuals who were also assassins. Max was an intellectual; Leonid was not. Therefore, the main burden of the article struck at Max rather than at Leonid, who was brought in on the ground that Max had allegedly served him.

The first question, then, is: Has an innocent man, Dr. Max Eitingon, been defamed? When I started out I did not know what the answer was, but I was interested in finding out. If he was not one of Stalin's killers, he deserved to be vindicated; if he was, the mystery of his double life was even more fascinating.

The second question is historical in nature. What was the evidence for this shocking assault on Dr. Max Eitingon's good name? What sources were used to make the story about him trustworthy? Did the article use its own sources fairly and accurately?

I intend to lay out the evidence and sources in the way that I have found them, with the help of the staff of *The New York Review of Books*.[6] I will begin by examining the evidence and sources presented by Stephen Schwartz in his article in *The New York Times Book Review*. I was not satisfied, however, with a merely critical approach, and have undertaken independent research in an effort to solve the mystery of Max Eitingon. If Schwartz did not have the answer, what was it and where could it be found? We should be much closer to the truth at the end of our journey.

---

[6] I could not have written this article without the help of Sylvia Lonergan, Neil Gordon, Henning Gutmann, Ann Kjellberg, Halyna Stelmach, and Fred Corney. I am also deeply indebted to Sarah Hirschman and Joseph Frank.

2

First, what do we know about Max Eitingon?

He was born in 1881 at Mohilev, Russia, the son of well-to-do Orthodox Jewish parents. The family moved to Galicia, then in Austria, where his father acquired Austrian nationality, though after World War I Max Eitingon opted for Polish nationality. When he was twelve, the family moved again, to Leipzig, Germany. He studied medicine, first at Marburg, Germany, and then at Zurich, Switzerland; from there he came to Vienna in 1907 with a severely disturbed patient whom he thought Freud might be able to help.[7]

Eitingon received his medical degree and moved to Berlin in 1909. For the next quarter of a century, he was the chief psychoanalytical figure in Berlin, the founder in 1920 of the Berlin Polyclinic, the first Freudian training institute. A decade later he was president of the International Psychoanalytical Association.

Eitingon was notable among those in Freud's inner circle as the only one with independent means. As long as he was able to do so, he used his money generously in behalf of the movement. Freud once wrote to him: "You really are the most reckless member of my family." Freud was referring to a loan in 1919 to himself of 2,000 marks, another of 1,000 to his sister-in-law, and financial assistance to his youngest son, Ernst.[8]

We happen to know a good deal about Eitingon's financial fortunes, thanks to Ernest Jones's biography of Freud. Psychoanalytic circles were made aware of Eitingon's wealth because of their dependence on his largesse or lack of it. We learn that the Berlin Polyclinic was made possible in 1920 by Eitingon's generosity. When the psychoanalytic publishing house was threatened financially that year, Eitingon "saved the situation a few months later by inducing a sympathetic brother-in-law in New York to make the *Verlag* the handsome donation of $5,000." In 1931, however, Jones records: "The family business from which Eitingon drew his income was in America, and the disastrous economic situation there had proved catastrophic for it. Before long Eitingon was for the first time in his life a poor man."[9]

---

[7] Pomer in *Psychoanalytic Pioneers*, p. 57; Jones, *Freud*, Vol. 2, p. 31.

[8] *Letters to Sigmund Freud*, p. 325.

[9] Jones, *Freud*, Vol. 3, pp. 20, 35, and 165.

Another misfortune struck Eitingon in 1932. He suffered from a cerebral thrombosis which left him with a paresis of the left arm. When Freud learned that Eitingon had to spend several weeks in bed, the tables were turned and Freud offered to come to his financial rescue with a loan of $1,000.[10]

Though Freud valued Eitingon highly, it was not for his intellectual contributions. As a memoir of Eitingon puts it, he was rather the "initiator, teacher, administrator, reporter [on activities in the movement] and thanks to a generous nature, quite often financial backer." He has been described by those who knew him later in Palestine as "calm, courteous, patient," and also as "shy, modest, and quietly reserved," traits probably intensified by the coronary thrombosis of 1932 and a more serious heart attack in 1938, after which his health began to fail and his hearing was seriously impaired. He was unprepossessing physically, short and portly, bespectacled, with a Chaplinesque mustache, and he struggled all his life with a speech impediment.[11]

Eitingon made his first visit to Jerusalem as early as 1910 and decided to move there for good after Hitler took power in 1933. He left Germany for Palestine at the end of 1933.[12] One of his first acts in Jerusalem was to found the Palestine Institute for Psychoanalysis.

In Palestine, he was fully occupied with his psychoanalytic mission. He had patients and students, held regular hours for receiving visitors, and even in his last months could not be deterred from coming daily for at least a short time to his institute. A co-worker of those years tells of the time Eitingon spent trying to obtain employment, opportunities to recuperate, money, "or

---

[10] Ibid., p. 168.

[11] This paragraph is based on Pomer, in *Psychoanalytic Pioneers*, pp. 52, 54, and 60; and the contributions by Arnold Zweig and Erich Gumbel in *Max Eitingon: In Memoriam* (Israel Psycho-Analytic Society, Jerusalem, 1950), pp. 11 and 27.

[12] Jones, *Freud*, Vol. 3, p. 183, gives the date of his departure from Berlin as the last day of 1933; Pomer in *Psychoanalytic Pioneers* states that he made a preliminary trip to Palestine in September 1933 and left Germany to settle there permanently on the last day of 1934 (p. 58). Jones is almost certainly right; there is a letter from Arnold Zweig to Freud of October 29, 1934, from Haifa, which mentions Eitingon (Ernst Freud, ed., *The Letters of Sigmund Freud and Arnold Zweig* [Harcourt, Brace and World, 1970], p. 95).

suitably interceding in certain quarters" for a large number of patients.[13]

In 1950, the now Israel Psycho-Analytic Society issued a volume entitled *Max Eitingon: In Memoriam* with contributions by Arnold Zweig, the novelist; Anna Freud; S. J. Agnon, the preeminent Hebrew poet; Marie Bonaparte, the distinguished French psychoanalyst; and many others. They portray a gentle, studious, cultivated person. The same sense of him is given by Ernest Jones, who knew him well.

It is possible to get a fairly clear impression of Max Eitingon's residence in Jerusalem from the letters between Arnold Zweig and Freud. Zweig lived in Haifa and saw Eitingon regularly. It appears from the correspondence that Eitingon stayed in Jerusalem throughout 1934 to 1938, with the exception of three annual trips between 1934 and 1937 to see Freud in Vienna and one trip to the Paris congress of the International Psychoanalytical Association and to see Freud in London in 1938. In 1936, Zweig wrote to Freud: "It is maddening that for the moment I cannot think of going into Jerusalem again to see the Eitingons. Theirs is the most delightful ménage in Jerusalem, and it is wonderful to have people so close who are so intimate with you and who carry out your work so faithfully." In the very year, 1937, when Max Eitingon is supposed to have been organizing the kidnapping of General Miller in Paris, Zweig mentions him twice, once in May, writing that "at Eitingon's suggestion I wrote down a joke that had been improvised by me for our meetings in Jerusalem," and again in October, when Zweig was in Trieste, saying that Eitingon had told him on the telephone that Freud was "really extremely well."[14] It hardly seems believable that the man who was reporting to Zweig on Freud was at about the same time busy arranging a kidnapping in Paris.

---

[13] Margarete Brandt in *Max Eitingon: In Memoriam*, p. 269. Pomer has described Eitingon's activities in Palestine:

> For Eitingon, the move to Israel [*sic*] was more than a wartime necessity: it was a natural consequence of his lifelong interest in Zionism. In him was deeply ingrained the devotion to those related to him, the reverence for tradition, and the genuine piety characteristic of the old patriarchal Jewish family. Every cultural Jewish activity drew him. The Bezalel Art Institute enjoyed his support, and he dedicated himself to the furtherance of the Hebrew University in Palestine. According to Gumbel, it was a fulfillment of his most profound aspirations that he could settle in Jerusalem and introduce psychoanalysis there [*Psychoanalytic Pioneers*, p. 59].

[14] *The Letters of Sigmund Freud and Arnold Zweig*, pp. 124, 142, and 149. Zweig mentions Eitingon twenty-three times in these letters, far more than anyone else with the exception of Anna Freud.

Schwartz's version of Eitingon's relationship with Freud betrays a glaring ignorance of the two men. His article says:

> From 1925 to 1937, Dr. Eitingon became Freud's factotum and shield against the world . . . He was a virtual social secretary to the old man.

Eitingon's service to Freud long antedated 1925. After 1933, Eitingon, living in Jerusalem, was hardly in a position to be Freud's "factotum and shield," let alone a "virtual social secretary." When this fatuity was pointed out by Peter Gay in a letter to *The New York Times Book Review* of March 6, 1988, Schwartz brazenly tried to cover his tracks:

> My answer is that Eitingon was rich enough to travel extensively and did so, as well as using the telephone. His role as a go-between is described in Ernst L. Freud's edition of "The Letters of Sigmund Freud and Arnold Zweig."

After 1931, Eitingon was not rich and did not travel extensively. There is in fact nothing in the Freud-Zweig letters to justify the notion that Eitingon was a "go-between." The closest to it that appears in the letters is that Eitingon on six occasions reported to Zweig on how Freud was getting along.[15] Inasmuch as these letters are easily available, Schwartz must have gambled that no one would ever check up on him.

I have given this brief sketch of Max Eitingon's life and work because almost all the facts I have been able to gather have a bearing on the problem of whether he was a member of "Stalin's Killerati." He appears to have devoted his entire life to the cause and practice of psychoanalysis. He would seem to have had few or even none of the attributes associated with professionals of the KGB or its predecessors OGPU and NKVD. He was known to have lost his financial support in 1931 and to have lived thereafter without the money to which he had previously been accustomed. He was apparently able to come to Paris once to attend a psychoanalytic convention in 1938, when in failing health. He never left Jerusalem again.

Yet this same man is supposed to have been instrumental in arranging the secret trial of Soviet generals in Moscow, the murder of Ignace Reiss in Switzerland, and the kidnapping of the White Russian general Yevgeni Miller in Paris, all in 1937.

---

[15] Ibid., pp. 111, 118, 128, 149, 160, and 171.

3

Now we can examine the evidence and sources given in the article by Stephen Schwartz in *The New York Times Book Review*.

Schwartz depends for his information about Max Eitingon on two books. One is *Chekisty: A History of the KGB* by John J. Dziak, a specialist on Soviet political and military affairs at the U.S. Defense Intelligence Agency.[16] The other is *High Treason* by Vitaly Rapoport and Yuri Alexeev, two Soviet dissidents, who are said to have "fully researched, documented and written" their book in the U.S.S.R.[17]

It is clear from both books that their authors had no firsthand knowledge or privileged information about Max Eitingon's activities. They know only as much as their sources told them, and they must be judged on the way they use these sources.

Let us start with Schwartz's allegation that there is "evidence" that Eitingon was instrumental in preparing the 1937 trial of Marshal Mikhail Tukhachevsky and seven other Soviet generals in 1937, who were accused of treasonous conspiracy with Nazi officials. What and where is the evidence?

It is not in Dziak's book; he never mentions Max Eitingon in connection with the Tukhachevsky affair. It is not in the book by Rapoport and Alexeev, who also do not mention Eitingon as having any relation to that affair. It is not in the versions of the episode by Victor Alexandrov and Robert Conquest, discussed by Rapoport and Alexeev.[18]

---

[16] Lexington Books, 1988.

[17] Duke University Press, 1985.

[18] Victor Alexandrov, *The Tukhachevsky Affair* (Prentice-Hall, 1964) and Robert Conquest, *The Great Terror* (Macmillan, 1968).

Immediately following the sentence about Eitingon's alleged role in the preparation of the trial, Schwartz writes: "As the historian Robert Conquest established, to contrive evidence against the generals the special unit connived with Reinhard Heydrich of Hitler's intelligence service." Conquest had "established" nothing of the sort. He mentions no "special unit" and merely gives one version that a double agent who worked for both the Soviet and German secret agencies, the former czarist General Skoblin, "appears to" have sent to Berlin an NKVD story, which came to the attention of the deputy Gestapo chief Reinhard Heydrich, about Tukhachevsky's alleged conspiracy with the German General Staff. But Conquest goes on to give "the most probable account" in which Skoblin does not figure at all (pp. 301–3). In neither case does Conquest "establish" anything, least of all the implication that Max Eitingon was somehow involved.

The real name of Victor Alexandrov, according to Natalie Grant, was "Perry." He was a friend of the foremost fabricator of "political fiction" in the guise of "authentic memoirs of key Soviet witnesses," Gregory Bessedovsky. Alexandrov-Perry himself is said to be the author of similar concoctions that once passed for the real thing in revelations about the Soviet Union. One of his books, *Khrushchev of the Ukraine*, made the State Department's list of recommended reading for its personnel (Natalie Grant, *Deception, a Tool of Soviet Foreign Policy* [The Nathan Hale Institute, 1987], p. 34).

Schwartz himself seems to have had difficulty believing his own story about Eitingon's instrumentality in the Tukhachevsky trial. Toward the end of his article, he presents a version that is very different from the first one. He now brings in the former czarist general Nikolai Skoblin, who was alleged to be a double agent involved in a plot with the deputy Gestapo chief Reinhard Heydrich to incriminate Tukhachevsky. It may be argued, Schwartz acknowledges, that Max Eitingon's participation in the NKVD's activities

> must have been slight, although without his involvement as the link to Skoblin the liquidation of the Soviet generals might not have been carried out so easily. And, not to put too fine a point on it, it is not pleasant to imagine an associate of Freud in league with a henchman of Heydrich.

We will get to this alleged "link to Skoblin" very shortly, but whatever it was, it could not have put Eitingon in a position to participate in the preparation of the secret trial of the Soviet generals. The Skoblin link, as we shall see, is tenuous enough; it becomes ludicrous by stretching it as far as the liquidation of Marshal Tukhachevsky.[19] It is surely not pleasant to imagine an associate of Freud in league with a henchman of Heydrich, but that is a problem of Schwartz's imagination.

Next we come to Schwartz's implication that Eitingon was part of a "special unit" involved in the murder of Ignace Reiss.

Reiss was a disaffected Soviet secret agent who was shot to death in Switzerland in September 1937. Again, Dziak says nothing about Max Eitingon in connection with this case. Rapoport and Alexeev say nothing. Walter Krivitsky, at that time still chief of Soviet military intelligence in Western Europe, who was a friend of Reiss and was alarmed by his murder, makes no such allusion.[20] Reiss's widow,

---

[19] To explain the alleged connection, if there is any at all, I must jump ahead, but the steps will soon be clarified. The connection would have to be based on the alleged relationship between Max Eitingon and Skoblin; Skoblin's role in the disappearance of General Miller; and the conjecture that the Miller affair was connected with the Tukhachevsky affair. This theory was first put forward by Walter Krivitsky in *In Stalin's Secret Service* (Harper and Brothers, 1939), pp. 237–40). Natalie Grant, however, writes that "there are serious grounds to disbelieve this story" of the tie between Skoblin's activities and the Tukhachevsky liquidation. She believes that the Tukhachevsky purge was conceived by Stalin much earlier and that no fabricated documents inspired by Skoblin were necessary for the Tukhachevsky operation (*Deception, a Tool of Soviet Foreign Policy*, pp. 28–30). If she is right, the alleged amalgam of Eitingon-Skoblin-Tukhachevsky falls of its own weight. In any case, Eitingon was dragged in by Schwartz without the slightest justification.

[20] *In Stalin's Secret Service*, pp. 252–64.

Elizabeth Poretsky (his name was originally Poretsky), wrote a book about his life and death without making the slightest reference to Eitingon.[21] If anyone could have exposed Eitingon's role in Reiss's murder, it would have been Krivitsky or Elizabeth Poretsky. I have looked through the literature on the Reiss assassination without finding the slightest hint of anything implicating Max Eitingon. This tie-up, too, is nonexistent.

We have here a buildup of at least three cases of Max Eitingon's alleged contributions to the "annals of Stalin's killerati." At least two have absolutely no foundation. If the three were to be believed, they would make Eitingon into a professional NKVD operator on the highest level, with little time or energy for anything else. But the third charge is the real Eitingon mystery, though not the way Schwartz tells it.

4

On September 22, 1937, General Yevgeni Karlovich Miller left his office at 29 rue du Colisée in Paris and never returned. Miller was the head of the Russian General Military Union, known as ROVS from the Russian name, the leading organization of émigré czarist veterans. His predecessor, General P. A. Kutyepov, had disappeared in somewhat similar circumstances in 1930. Miller's disappearance was a *cause célèbre* of the late 1930s.

No one had been charged in Kutyepov's case, but Miller's was different. He had taken the precaution of leaving a note to the effect that he was going to an appointment with his aide at ROVS, General Nikolai Skoblin, who had arranged a meeting with a German officer. After Miller disappeared, the incriminating letter was shown to Skoblin, and, apparently as a result, he also disappeared. It is believed that Skoblin was a double agent, working for both the Soviet and Nazi secret services, and that he was primarily responsible for Miller's fate.

Skoblin got away, but his wife, Nadezhda Plevitskaya, a popular singer of Russian folk songs, famous in her day, was less lucky. She was picked up by the French police and eventually put on trial in

---

[21] *Our Own People* (Oxford, 1969). In his reply to letters in *The New York Times Book Review* of March 6, 1988, Schwartz mentions this book without letting on that it has nothing to do with Dr. Max Eitingon.

December 1938. At the trial, an "M. Oetingen" (as the name appeared in *Le Temps*), "Oetington," "Eitington" (as it appears in other sources), or "Eitingon" was mentioned.[22] Virtually the entire case against Max Eitingon as a secret Soviet agent engaged in assassinations is actually based on his mention in this trial.

Let us now go back to Stephen Schwartz's treatment of the evidence of Max Eitingon's guilt in the disappearance of General Miller.

> In his book, *Chekisty: A History of the KGB* (D.C. Heath & Company), Mr. Dziak reports that one of the group's key agents in the kidnapping of General Miller was none other than a close personal associate of Sigmund Freud and a pillar of the psychoanalytic movement, Dr. Max Eitingon (sometimes misidentified as Mark), the brother of Leonid Eitingon.

We will leave for the time being the question of whether Max Eitingon had a brother named Leonid. Here is what Dziak says about Max Eitingon's role in the Miller affair:

> [Leonid] Eitingon was one of the more enigmatic figures of Stalin's state security. His father and brother were doctors in Europe, the brother Mark a psychiatrist and student of Sigmund Freud. Mark apparently was linked to General Skoblin and his wife Plevitskaya; he moved to Jerusalem two days before the kidnapping of General Miller . . .
>
> Plevitskaya's connection to Mark Eitingon apparently involved significant financial support, but whether the money came from the Eitingon family or from Soviet sources is unclear. (The Eitingon family at one time had been well-off but apparently lost much of its wealth in the depression.)[23]

That is all. It may be noticed that Dziak never uses the name *Max* Eitingon; he always refers to *Mark*. Dziak also never uses the name *Leonid*; he always refers to a *Naum*. The reason for this curious confusion of names is that Dziak uses as his source the book by Rapoport and Alexeev, who in their turn use a Russian source that makes the same transformation of names.[24] One would imagine that the difference in names would have presented a problem to Schwartz.

---

[22] *Oetington* is used in the account by Geoffrey Bailey, *The Conspirators* (Harper and Brothers, 1960), p. 347; and *Eitington* by Boris Prianishnikoff, *Nezrimaia pautina* ("An Invisible Web"), in Russian, privately printed, 1979, p. 353.

[23] Dziak, *Chekisty: A History of the KGB*, pp. 100–2.

[24] It is Boris Prianishnikoff's *Nezrimaia pautina*.

Instead, he covers up the mixup by blithely informing his readers that Dr. Max Eitingon was "sometimes misidentified as Mark."

There is no authority for this alleged misidentification. Schwartz's main sources, Dziak and Rapoport-Alexeev, if they were at all well informed, must have been aware of the existence of a Dr. Max Eitingon, a well-known figure in psychoanalytic history. Max never used the name of Mark. The misidentification, if there was one, itself demands an explanation that cannot be found in Dziak or Rapoport-Alexeev.

In any case, there is more trouble with Dziak's version. He has Mark's father a doctor in Europe. Max's father was not a doctor. Mark is supposed to have moved to Jerusalem two days after the kidnapping of General Miller. Max had moved to Jerusalem for good in 1933.

In a note, Dziak makes matters even less credible.

> There is considerable confusion over the activities of the two Eitingon brothers. Mark was linked to Nadezhda Plevitskaya and her husband General Skoblin. However, a Soviet dissident work has Naum as the one who probably recruited Plevitskaya in 1919 and directed the kidnappings of Generals Kutyepov and Miller.[25]

And what is this dissident Soviet work? None other than the book by Rapoport and Alexeev.

In fact, then, Dziak is hardly in a position to "report" with any independent authority that Dr. Max Eitingon was one of the "key agents in the kidnapping of General Miller."

We now come to Schwartz's other main source, *High Treason*, by Rapoport and Alexeev. This is how Schwartz works it into his article:

> In his book, Mr. Dziak concludes that it was Dr. Max Eitingon who recruited Skoblin and Plevitskaya into the special unit. That charge is supported by other historians. At the time of the kidnapping of General Miller, Dr. Eitingon decamped for Palestine, where he had previously established a psychoanalytic institute. The dissident Soviet historians Vitaly Rapoport and Yuri Alexeev declare flatly in their book, *High Treason* (Duke University Press), that Dr. Eitingon, serving his brother Leonid, was the control agent for Skoblin and Plevitskaya. Plevitskaya described him at her trial as her financial angel. Soon after Dr. Eitingon left Europe, so did his brother.

[25] Dziak, *Chekisty*, p. 199, note 79.

If we turn to Rapoport-Alexeev to see what kind of support they give Dziak, we find, as I have noted, that Rapoport-Alexeev never mention Max or Leonid Eitingon; they make the confusion of names all the worse by always referring to Mark and Naum *Ettingon*. But it is here that we approach the source of the story picked up and distorted by Schwartz.

This is from Rapoport-Alexeev:

> Most likely Skoblin had been recruited by the NKVD through his wife, the famous Russian singer Nadezhda Plevitskaya. Plevitskaya's superior in the NKVD was the legendary Naum Ettingon. Her contact and bagman was Ettingon's brother Mark.[26]

All this appears to be authoritative, even if it is about Mark, not Max, and about Ettingon, not Eitingon. It has, however, not the slightest authority of its own. A note after the first sentence tells us to go to the book by Boris Prianishnikoff, published in Russian under the title *The Invisible Web*, to learn about Skoblin and Plevitskaya. A note after the third sentence plaintively instructs us that "very little is known about the evil figure of N. Ettingon." It then sends the reader to a two-page appendix on Naum Ettingon, the alleged misidentification for Leonid.

This appendix begins with the equally discouraging words: "Information about Naum Iakovlevich Ettingon is laughably scarce." Nevertheless the authors go on for almost two pages with what they think they know about Mark and Naum. About Mark they say:

> Mark Ettingon was a psychiatrist, a student of Sigmund Freud, and a friend of Princess Maria [*sic*] Bonaparte. For many years he was a generous patron of Nadezhda Plevitskaya. She said at her trial that "he dressed me from head to foot." He financed the publication of her two autobiographical books. It is unlikely that he did so only for the love of Russian music. It is more likely that he acted as messenger and finance agent for his brother Naum.[27]

This, then, is the source of the story that Max Eitingon was "the control agent for Skoblin and Plevitskaya," as Schwartz put it, and that "Mark Ettingon" was the "messenger and finance agent for his brother Naum," as Rapoport and Alexeev have it. But Rapoport and Alexeev had merely surmised—"It is more likely"—that Mark

[26] Rapoport and Alexeev, *High Treason*, p. 259.
[27] Ibid., p. 391.

Ettingon had played such a role for his brother Naum. By the time this bit of pure speculation came out in Schwartz's version, Rapoport and Alexeev were made to declare "flatly" that Dr. Eitingon "was the control agent for Skoblin and Plevitskaya."

In fact, Rapoport and Alexeev make clear that they have been drawing on and embellishing the Russian book by Prianishnikoff which is the real source of their story, even to the use of the name Mark instead of Max, though they change Prianishnikoff's "Eitington" to their "Ettington." So far the core of the mystery is in Prianishnikoff's book.

5

Prianishnikoff's book is wholly the result of research in public libraries and private archives. His information about "Mark Eitington" comes from the trial of the singer and wife of General Skoblin, Nadezhda Plevitskaya, in Paris in December 1938. Prianishnikoff introduces the testimony of one witness, Leonid Raigorodsky, in the following way:

> Raigorodsky and the well-to-do M. Ya. Eitington, who was then living in Berlin, were married to two sisters. Both men admired the talented Plevitskaya. A close platonic relationship even developed between Eitington and Plevitskaya. In 1930, after the kidnapping of General Kutyepov, Plevitskaya's book, *My Road With A Song*, was published by the "Tair" publishers with a moving inscription: "Dedicated to my loving friend, M. Ya. Eitington."

The name "M. Ya. Eitington" should have been a signal that something was wrong in the identification with Max Eitingon. The latter's patronymic could not have been "Ya." No effort was apparently made to check on the name of Max Eitingon's father, which was Chaim. In addition, Raigorodsky and Max Eitingon were not married to two sisters. We will come to their relationship later; meanwhile, it is enough to note that Prianishnikoff was misled by references to Raigorodsky at the trial of Plevitskaya.

Plevitskaya herself testified about her friend Eitingon in Berlin. Prianishnikoff gives this exchange at her trial:

> *Q.* What was the source of income of you and your husband?
> *A.* I gave concerts, I made money, my concert performances paid very well, especially on my tour of the Baltic countries, Finland, and the Balkans.

Q. But we know that you lived above your means.

A. No, no. And whenever we were short of money, we could count on my friend Eitington's support. A wealthy man, he sent us money from Berlin. Just how much—I don't remember exactly. My husband knew about that; he was in charge of our family's finances.

Prianishnikoff soon tells us more about his Mark Eitington:

In Skoblin's office, among other papers, there were also letters addressed to Plevitskaya from Mark Eitington and members of his family. Eitington was that same patron who, in Plevitskaya's own words, supported the Skoblins during hard times. A well-to-do physician-psychiatrist, Eitington lived in Berlin and was financially connected to the Soviet fur trade; his brother sold furs and thus contributed to the USSR's amount of currency. In September 1937, he and his wife, the former actress of the Moscow Art Theater, arrived in Paris on business and stayed at the George V hotel. From the hotel he telephoned to Ozoir[-la-Ferrière, where the Skoblins had a house] and talked with the Skoblins. On September 20, at 6 AM, two days before Miller's disappearance, Eitington left for Florence, and then for Palestine. The Skoblins saw him off at the Lyons train station.

Eitington is identified as a "physician-psychiatrist," which would fit Eitingon. But he is put in Berlin again, which suggests that the reference is to Eitingon's Berlin period, not to any time after 1933. Moreover, Eitington is here made to leave for Palestine at this time, in 1937, as if to make his getaway, more than three years after Max Eitingon had already settled there.

We then get more of Plevitskaya's testimony, in Prianishnikoff's version:

Q. You used to receive money from M. Eitington. Who is he?

A. He is a very close friend, a scholar-psychiatrist. His wife is a former actress of the Moscow Art Theater.

Q. Were you intimately involved with Eitington?

A. I never sold myself. I accepted gifts from both of them. But whether my husband received any money, that I don't know.

Q. How can that be true? Didn't you yourself say that Eitington provided you with clothing?

A. No . . . I said that accidentally. Madame Eitington gave gifts to others too . . . I have never stained my womanly honor, and I have never received gifts for any intimate deeds. Whoever knows Eitington would never believe that there could have been any improper incidents.

We have from this testimony reason to believe that Plevitskaya knew an Eitington or Eitingon. We have nothing here or elsewhere in Plevitskaya's testimony to suggest that the relationship had anything to do with General Miller's disappearance.

A French financial auditor, M. Février, who went through Plevitskaya's accounts, testified, according to *Le Temps* of December 12, 1938: "The concerts, records and books of Plevitskaya amount to little; the generosity of M. Oetingen, psychiatrist of Jerusalem, is not verifiable."

That "psychiatrist of Jerusalem" could have referred only to Max Eitingon, whatever the confusion of names may have been. Février, however, had found no evidence of "generosity" in the Skoblin-Plevitskaya papers that were available in Paris.

We get much closer to Eitington or Eitingon in other testimony by Leonid Raigorodsky, as given by Prianishnikoff:

> *Q.* Where is Mr. Eitington now, your brother-in-law?
> *A.* He lives in Palestine.
> *Q.* Is it true that he used to clothe Plevitskaya from head to toe and gave Skoblin large sums of money?
> *A.* Mark Eitington is a rich man of independent means. How he helped Plevitskaya with money, I don't know. That money never passed my hands. But Eitington helped many people. His father founded a hospital in Leipzig, and a street is named in his honor. After his death he left his sons 20 million marks. Mark Eitington is a respected man, an esteemed scholar, a student of Freud, and a friend of Princess Marie Bonaparte. He is as clean as snow.
> *Q.* Is he not the one who, in London and Berlin, used to sell Soviet furs?
> *A.* It was not he, it was his brother. In this type of trade there is nothing reprehensible, but Mark had nothing to do with it.[28]

On close examination, Février and Raigorodsky tell us nothing about what we want to know about General Miller's disappearance and any part that Max Eitingon, Mark Eitington, or M. Oetingen may have played in it.

Raigorodsky in turn was asked personal questions about his brother-in-law, "M. Eitington," who certainly seems to be Max Eitingon. But otherwise he says nothing and knew nothing about the main issue—what did his brother-in-law have to do with General Miller's disappearance? Raigorodsky's statement that Eitington-Eitingon was a rich man could have referred only to years past, not

---

[28] These excerpts from Prianishnikoff's book come from pages 285, 289, 315, 352, and 353. I am indebted to Larissa Onyshkevych for the translation.

to the circumstances of 1938. He did not know anything about money given to Plevitskaya, which was the main reason for his testimony. Yet he knew that there was some sort of Soviet connection with the fur business, through a brother, although that was not quite right—he was a first cousin. He was right about the father's past connection with Leipzig. In the end, Raigorodsky merely testified that he knew Max Eitingon and he showed that he had a general, not altogether accurate, notion of his circumstances and background.

6

The next exhibit in the Eitingon dossier is not in any of the sources we have so far mentioned.

General Miller's followers in Paris published the *plaidoirie*, or argument, of the chief counsel for the Miller family, Maître Maurice Ribet.[29] He first sketched the relationship between General Skoblin and Plevitskaya. They had met in Russia during the civil war. Plevitskaya was then married to her second husband, an officer in the Soviet Army. Skoblin became her lover and then her third husband.

According to Ribet, they had been Soviet agents since 1927. But they were also double agents, for the Germans as well as the Soviets, and needed a cover to account for their livelihood. This cover was said to have been provided by Plevitskaya's earnings from her concerts. Yet a French auditor, M. Février, had found that her earnings could not have been enough to pay for their lavish style of life.

At this point Ribet introduced the name of Eitingon. It first appeared in a passage dealing with Plevitskaya's movements on the night of September 23, 1937, after the disappearance of her husband, General Skoblin, had alarmed her. Here, according to Ribet, is what happened next:

> The night of the twenty-third? You know where she passed it! First, she went to see her doctor who did not wish to keep her at his home and took her to that of the brother-in-law of M. Eitingon, who took her in and who, for fear of compromising himself, brought her the next morning to [the] Gallipoli [Association, made up of White Russian émigrés]. It is there, Messieurs, that [Commissaire] M. Roches took her in charge and turned her over to the police who have been holding her ever since.

[29] *L'Enlèvement du Général de Miller par le Général Skobline: Le Procès de la Plevitzkaia: Plaidoirie de Me. Maurice Ribet*, no date but probably 1939, 31 pages, no publisher listed.

The brother-in-law, as we have seen, was Leonid Raigorodsky. This was how, in this version, he was drawn into Plevitskaya's story—Plevitskaya's doctor had brought her to him. In any case, Raigorodsky turned her over to the police.

Next Ribet turned his attention to the Skoblin-Plevitskaya finances. How did they make up the difference? What were their mysterious "resources"?

Ribet now summoned up all his considerable powers of ridicule and scorn for the benefit of the jurors:

> Mysterious resources? Plevitskaya, Messieurs, has a fertile imagination; a man, a scholar, an old friend, a psychoanalyst, Dr. Eitingon, who lives in Jerusalem, came with the most honorable intentions to the assistance of her ménage; he considered his protégé as if she were a holy icon, dressed her "from head to foot" and from time to time made little payments to her.
>
> There is the explanation that has been offered to take advantage of your naïveté.

Ribet obviously thought that the Eitingon connection was a product of Plevitskaya's "fertile imagination" and had been concocted to cover up the real source of her apparent wealth. He went on:

> So you see that from this point of view everyone agrees with the expert, M. Février: there were mysterious resources. Where did the money come from? It has been impossible to discover the exact source. It comes, if we believe the avowal of the accused, in part from M. Eitingon. On the other hand it is said that Dr. Eitingon is an honorable man. I can affirm that there is a doctor who formerly lived in Berlin and who decided to leave for Jerusalem. He is the son and nephew of the Eitingons who settled themselves in London and Leipzig, and I can say that the activity of his father and his uncle consisted of selling, on behalf of the Soviets, "requisitioned" furs in Siberia, and when I say "requisitioned," you know that I am employing the Soviet word which is only a euphemism. Have they made a very great fortune? But all this is natural: the profit was all the greater since the furs did not cost anything.

After which Ribet summed up his view of Eitingon's role:

> I can say that Dr. Eitingon, if we do not have absolute proof that he is a Soviet agent, has a source of money which is clearly impure.

Thus Ribet cast doubt on the story that an M. Eitingon was the main source of Plevitskaya's mysterious financial resources. He denied that there was definite proof that this Eitingon was a Soviet agent. Finally, he settled for the general imputation that it was "impure" to do business in Soviet furs. On this reasoning, no one in France should have imported anything from the Soviet Union, since everything had been "requisitioned" by the Soviet state and there was no other way to do business with it. By 1937–38, moreover, Max Eitingon had been getting very little from his relatives in the fur business in New York, who were just beginning to recover from the crash earlier in the decade.

Ribet made one other significant allusion. He referred to a green Bible that Plevitskaya had asked for at her judicial examination. In this Bible, he charged, there was "a key to a cipher with which to translate certain secret letters."[30]

In his reply to letters in *The New York Times Book Review* of March 6, 1988, Stephen Schwartz alleges:

> According to French police files at the Hoover Institution in California, French officials discovered in Plevitskaya's home a Bible sent to her by Max Eitingon from Palestine, which the police concluded was used for encryption.

Police files are not the most reliable of historical sources; they are usually a mixture of fact, gossip, and speculation. Such files are even more suspect when they contain raw data from informants who never need to appear in public or face cross-examination.

The relevant portions of the file to which Schwartz alludes, and which I have examined, contain two references to the Bible in question. The mentality behind the first reference may be gathered from an introductory remark:

> It is, moreover, a constant rule in all countries that spies are recruited among the women of the theater, singers, stars, or demimondaines. Thus Troukhanova, the celebrated dancer and wife of Count Ignatieff (who went over to the Soviets), and friend of the singer Plevitskaya, had been a Bolshevik spy (which the latter denies).

The following is then based on the testimony of one Simenoff:

> To justify a part of her income, Plevitskaya claimed to have a patron in the person of Mr. Eitingon, who had lived in Berlin and was now settled in Jerusalem. This same Eitingon presented Plevitskaya with the famous Bible, which the prisoner so much demanded and which contained, it appears, the key to the cryptographic language used by Skoblin to correspond with his collaborators of the "interior line" [a

---

[30] Ibid., pp. 10, 16, 18, and 25.

special group headed by Skoblin within the émigré military organiza-
tion]. Now, Eitingon was a high Soviet functionary in Berlin, assigned
to sell off Siberian furs for the government of the USSR [Hearing,
Simenoff].

The second reference occurs in a summary of the information
gathered in the course of the police investigation. It states that the
investigators came to an early conviction that Plevitskaya knew all
about the political activity of her husband, General Skoblin. It then
goes on:

> Certain incidents during the search made at Ozoir-la-Ferrière, espe-
> cially the Bible which Plevitskaya insistently asked for and which—a
> fact established previously—furnished the key for the cryptography of
> the documents, certain letters written by various correspondents to
> Skoblin about which his wife has not yet been interrogated, in some
> way confirm the first impressions of the investigators.

The intelligence based on Simenoff is a typical jumble. It makes
Max Eitingon into a high Soviet functionary in Berlin who spent his
time selling furs for the Soviet Union. Ribet and the police intelligence summary did not see fit to mention Eitingon in connection
with the Bible. We are told that there was a cryptographic cipher in
the Bible, but not how it got there or who put it there.

In this case, however, Schwartz was right about a fact but wrong
about the source—and what it signifies. There is indeed reason to
believe that Max Eitingon had sent a Bible to Plevitskaya from
Palestine.

7

Plevitskaya was convicted of complicity in the disappearance of General Miller and given an unusually harsh sentence of twenty years at
hard labor. She died in prison at Rennes in 1940.

While awaiting trial in 1937–38, Plevitskaya wrote a so-called diary,
which is more like a collection of random memories.[31] Somehow it
found its way to the Rare Book and Manuscript Department of the
Columbia University Library. It consists of six notebooks of about
two hundred pages in her scribbled handwriting. Three pages are
devoted to "my friend Eitingon." She evidently set down her

---

[31] It is listed as the Nadeshda Plevitskaia Skoblin prison diaries (1937–38) in the Bakh-
meteff Archive, Filonenko Papers, in the Columbia University Library.

thoughts whether they made sentences or not and some words are virtually illegible. Nevertheless, the sense is unmistakable and helps to solve the mystery of Max Eitingon.

Here is the excerpt on Max Eitingon from Plevitskaya's diary in full:

Max Eitingon, a well-known psychoanalyst doctor, chairman of the international psychoanalyst society, personal friend of *Professor Freud*, son of a rich furrier, inherited everything after the death of his father. He does not *concern* himself with *politics*, does not subscribe to parties, especially to the Communist. *Scholarly, rich*. What does he need Communists for?

His wife is a former actress of the Moscow Art Theater. Both are cultured, art-loving—always helping artists. Our friendship lasted for fifteen years. They helped us materially.

The writer, I. S. Lukash, edited my memoir, *Dyozhkin Karagod*, and the second part *Moy put's pesney*.[32] The first book, "D.K.," begun in Paris was continued in Berlin in the Eitingons' apartment. M. Eitingon published "D.K.," paid for the printing—timing the gift for my fifteenth anniversary [of the beginning of her career].

Lukash used to come to the home of the Eitingons, and *knows* that they were not busy there with *politics* and *commerce*. Anyway the *content of my book* itself shows that an "admirer" or a "worker" of the Communists would not publish such memoirs which eulogize what came *before* the Bolsheviks.

When Hitler was enthroned in Germany, the Eitingons went to Palestine. From there they used to come to Europe, we saw each other. From Jerusalem they sent me a holy book, the *Bible*, which came up in court. The Eitingons knowing that it would give me special joy sent me the Bible. And through Dr. I. A. Goldenshtein they sent me an *icon of Nikolai the miracle worker*. They sent me holy water from *Jordan* and *candles* from the *Lord's sepulchre*. So where is Communism?

The writer *I. S. Lukash* could say what he saw at the home of the Eitingons in 1925.

Dr. I. A. Goldenshtein brought me the *icon* from Jerusalem in 1936. (My views and tastes have not changed since that time.)

The numerous *letters* of Mira Yakovlevna Eitingon show that the friendship continued and the help was also there whenever it was needed.

These rather artless jottings by a probably distraught woman in prison provide the missing link in the chain of circumstances that has

---

[32] The titles of the two books of memoirs put out by Plevitskaya, the first one in Berlin in 1925, the second in Paris in 1930.

led to the Eitingons. Plevitskaya came from a simple peasant background, her education was apparently limited, and her head was full of primitive religiosity.

It is clear that Plevitskaya knew the Eitingons in Berlin during the period when they were more affluent. This acquaintance is not surprising; the Eitingons were known for their hospitality and assistance to intellectuals and artists of all kinds. Plevitskaya was then a beautiful singer and something of a celebrity. She was so famous that when a book was put out in Moscow in 1970 about three of the most famous "stars of the Russian stage," she was one of them. At her trial, Plevitskaya seemed to hark back to her friendship with the Eitingons in Berlin, as if she remembered them best from that period.

One also gets the impression that Plevitskaya was closest to Mira, Max Eitingon's wife. They had most in common, one being a former actress and the other a singer; Plevitskaya significantly mentions the letters from Mira Yakovlevna Eitingon. It has been something of a mystery why Plevitskaya should have dedicated her 1930 book to "M. Ya. Eitingon," if she had intended to pay tribute to Max Eitingon. The answer seems to be that she was dedicating the book to Mira Yakovlevna and not to Max, who could not have used the patronymic "Ya."

Plevitskaya did something else of great significance in prison. After less than a year in the Central Prison at Rennes, she began to suffer from a heart ailment. Then an abscess in her left foot made it impossible for her to walk. She told her confessor, a half-Russian Orthodox priest, Father Gillet, that she wanted to speak with Commissaire Jean Belin of the Sûreté, the French police official who had originally investigated the Miller disappearance and Plevitskaya's role in it. Belin hurried to Rennes on May 10, the very day that the German Army invaded Holland and Belgium. In his memoirs, Belin related that he saw before him not the glamorous singer of old but "a miserable prisoner, emaciated, bent, shriveled, very meek." She spoke to him with difficulty. A nurse stood by and administered smelling salts whenever Plevitskaya grew faint.

Belin and Plevitskaya spoke for several hours. He tried to console her: "Why fatigue yourself? Your story is a story of the past, forgotten." She replied, "I beg you. I am going to die. Do not leave me. Tomorrow will perhaps be too late. I ask you to listen to me."

Plevitskaya admitted that she had lied at her trial by saying that she had known nothing about General Miller's abduction. She now confessed to Belin that Skoblin had told her on the night of September 21, 1937, after Miller's disappearance, that he had been responsible for having lured Miller to a house in Saint-Cloud where three men who spoke Russian and German equally well had given the general an injection.[33]

This was the substance of Plevitskaya's "confession." She did not confess that she had been an accomplice of Skoblin in the abduction of General Miller; she confessed that she had known that Skoblin had been guilty of luring him to his fate. Yet she was convicted as an accomplice. It made no sense to think that an accomplice would have not have been spirited away, as Skoblin was, and would instead have willingly gone to a French police station. Plevitskaya's behavior on September 21 and 22, 1937, had nothing in common with that of an accomplice.

Plevitskaya died in prison on September 21, 1940.[34] By this time the German Army had occupied Paris and the case of Plevitskaya had long been overtaken by far more tragic events. In retrospect, her sentence of twenty years at hard labor was a disgraceful miscarriage of French justice. As Commissaire Belin himself admitted: "We have no formal proof of Plevitskaya's complicity in that affair."[35] The French authorities had taken revenge on her only because they had been unable to get at the real criminal, her husband, Skoblin, whose admissions to her she had not given away at the trial. It would be an act of historical justice and mercy if her case were reopened in France, her name cleared of this crime, and a proper verdict rendered on a judicial, and even more a political, perversion.

And if Plevitskaya was not a Soviet agent, there is little point in making Max Eitingon into one through his relationship with her.

Something else makes one wonder at the charge against Dr. Max Eitingon. General Miller was abducted on September 21, 1937. The trial of Plevitskaya began on December 14, 1938. Between these two dates the French police had obviously been building a case against her. They had ransacked her home at Ozoir-la-Ferrière and had

---

[33] Jean Belin, *Trente ans de sûreté nationale* (Paris: Bibliothèque France-Soir, 1950), pp. 248–51.

[34] Marina Grey, *Le Général meurt à minuit* (Paris: Plon, 1981), p. 166. Chapters 17–19 of this book contain the best reexamination to date of the Miller case and Plevitskaya's role.

[35] Belin, *Trente ans de sûreté nationale*, p. 248.

found letters later used to incriminate Dr. Eitingon. Yet he had come to Paris to attend the congress of the International Psychoanalytical Association which had opened on August 1, 1938.[36] The police had had every opportunity to pick him up. Nevertheless, he had attended the congress unscathed and had then gone on to visit Freud in London for the last time. By this time the French authorities knew all there was to know about him as far as the evidence that came out at Plevitskaya's trial was concerned. One can only conclude that they were willing to use material making him suspect at the trial in which they themselves did not believe.

There was an even more tantalizing development at the end of 1938. The Sigmund Freud Archive at Wivenhoe, Colchester, England, contains six letters from Freud to Eitingon in that year, none from Eitingon to Freud. But the final letter of Freud to Eitingon, dated December 29, 1938, alludes to a previous letter from Eitingon in which he evidently referred to his involvement in Plevitskaya's trial that very month. The third paragraph of Freud's letter reads:

> What the affair with the Russian singer was, in which you found yourself involved, was not clear to me from your allusions. From the English newspapers, which did not mention your name, there remains in my memory only an unusually harsh punishment. It seems to have touched you deeply.[37]

Unfortunately, we will never know what allusions Eitingon had made to Freud about the "affair of the Russian singer." Efforts to locate Eitingon's letters to Freud in this period have been fruitless. It would appear that Eitingon had made the matter clear to Freud without having stirred up the latter's suspicions of any wrongdoing on Eitingon's part. If Eitingon had been the kind of Soviet agent that he has been described, it is hardly likely that he would have bothered to write to Freud about the affair and that his "involvement" in the trial would have been mentioned by Freud with such unconcern. If only we had Eitingon's previous letter, we might once and for all clear up the relationship with Plevitskaya. But such are the hazards of historical research.

[36] Emil Michael Johann Neiser, *Max Eitingon: Leben und Werk* (Mainz, 1978), p. 58; Pomer, in *Psychoanalytic Pioneers*, p. 60.

[37] I am indebted to Tom Roberts of the Sigmund Freud Copyrights for copies of the Freud-Eitingon letters of 1938.

It seems equally strange that a veteran Soviet agent would have put his name in a Bible sent to Plevitskaya with a secret cipher.[38] There is no telling who put the cipher in the book or why Plevitskaya would have drawn attention to it by asking for it in prison. If this cipher in the Bible is attributed to Eitingon, it would imply that he was running a secret Soviet ring from faraway Jerusalem—an aspect of the story that surely strains credibility. There is also no reason why Max and Mira Eitingon should have known of Skoblin, let alone of Plevitskaya, as secret Soviet agents. Jerusalem was not the best place in the 1930s to get Soviet émigré gossip in Paris.

There remains the question of Max Eitingon's alleged brother Leonid, who was almost certainly a high officer in the OGPU and later the NKVD. There is a considerable literature on Leonid, especially his role in the assassination of Trotsky. What is at issue here is whether there is any evidence that he was the brother of Max Eitingon.

Schwartz, following Dziak, makes the flat statement that Max and Leonid Eitingon were brothers, and, based on Rapoport-Alexeev, the additional assertion that Max, "serving his brother Leonid, was the control agent for Skoblin and Plevitskaya." So we again have to turn to their books to find out whether there is any truth in these allegations.

Dziak, as usual, made Max and Leonid Eitingon brothers on the authority of Rapoport and Alexeev.[39] They in turn made "Mark" the brother of "Naum"—their stand-ins for Max and Leonid—by referring to Prianishnikoff.[40] The testimony in Prianishnikoff's book from the trial of Plevitskaya never alludes to a link between "Mark Eitington" and a Naum or Leonid.

Thus Schwartz leads to Dziak, who leads to Rapoport-Alexeev, who lead to Prianishnikoff, who leads to nowhere. The only apparent reason for making Max Eitingon the brother of Leonid is that they had similar family names, as if every male with the name of Eitingon must have been a brother of Max.

A book by a French specialist in Soviet espionage, P. F. de Ville-

---

[38] At the trial, the translator who went through the coded correspondence found at the Skoblin-Plevitskaya residence testified that there was nothing in it related to the kidnapping of General Miller and that everything in it was of an "anti-Bolshevik tendency" (*Le Figaro*, December 13, 1938). The trial was full of such leads that seemed to go nowhere.

[39] Dziak, *Chekisty*, p. 100 and p. 199, note 79.

[40] Rapoport and Alexeev, *High Treason*, p. 259, note 9 (p. 411), and Appendix, p. 391.

marest, suggests that there had been some confusion, even among experts, between Max and Leonid Eitingon. Villemarest refers to a "Dr. Oettingen, an alleged importer of Soviet furs, via Leipzig, in Germany." After stating that this Oettingen "disappeared" two days after the kidnapping of General Miller, Villemarest identifies him as "a strange personage whom several witnesses will be sure to recognize the following year at the Soviet embassy bearing the features of the assistant military attaché, Leonid A. Eitingon." One wonders how much of the case against Max Eitingon has rested on this type of mistaken identity.[41]

8

There was a branch of Dr. Max Eitingon's family in America. Years ago I happened to know the head of the family. When I found myself embroiled in the Eitingon mystery, I decided to get in touch with the present generation of the family and learn as much as possible about the connection with Max Eitingon.

This is what I have learned:

There were three branches of the far-flung Eitingon family, descending from Moses Eitingon.[42]

One branch went back to Chaim Eitingon, originally the owner

---

[41] P. F. de Villemarest, *Les Pourvoyeurs du Goulag* (Geneva, 1978), p. 167. In his reply to Peter Gay in *The New York Times Book Review* of March 6, 1988, Stephen Schwartz referred to this very book. Either Schwartz had not really read it, or did not understand what was in it, or was guilty of more humbug.

[42]

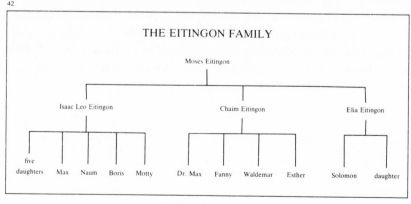

THE EITINGON FAMILY

Moses Eitingon

Isaac Leo Eitingon — Chaim Eitingon — Elia Eitingon

five daughters · Max · Naum · Boris · Motty · Dr. Max · Fanny · Waldemar · Esther · Solomon · daughter of a sugar beet factory in Russia. He left Russia in the late nineteenth century and moved to Leipzig, Germany, where he went into the fur business. He prospered to such an extent that he built a synagogue in 1923 and a Jewish hospital in Leipzig in 1928. Chaim had two daughters, Fanny and Esther, and two sons, Waldemar and Max. Waldemar came to New York, where he ran the American end of the business and died in 1920. His brother, Max, became the psychoanalyst Dr. Max Eitingon.

Another branch derived from Isaac Leo Eitingon, a banker in Russia. He had four sons, Max, Naum, Boris, and Motty. This other Max was a furrier in Leipzig, who then came to New York and worked in the family fur business. Naum and Boris went into the textile business in Lodz, Poland, where they stayed until 1939, when both families moved to New York or São Paulo, Brazil.

Motty Eitingon was the family's entrepreneur. In an article on the fur trade in *Fortune* magazine (January 1936), he was said to have had his property confiscated and to have been thrown in jail in Russia by the Bolsheviks in 1918. He escaped and moved the headquarters of the family's fur operation to New York. In 1923, he made a deal to purchase at least $3 million worth of Russian furs, with which he began to dominate the market. By 1930, he controlled the entire crop of the U.S. government's Alaska seal herd. The firm of Eitingon Schild, as it was called, for the first time seemed to control the fur market from fur pelts to manufacturer.

Motty was a speculator, a three-time millionaire who made and lost fortunes. His business suffered huge losses in the 1930s; the company was stricken from the New York Stock Exchange in 1940 because its assets had dwindled so much. He was the one who gave financial support to Dr. Max Eitingon, his first cousin, depending on how profitable his business was. After 1931, as Ernest Jones noted, Max Eitingon was far from rich, for one reason because Motty's business had fallen on hard times. Yet Motty bounced back after World War II; he was instrumental in putting up the first hotel at La Guardia Airport.

As for the third branch, which went back to Elia Eitingon, a son, Solomon, represented the family firm in India and Afghanistan for many years.

There was no Leonid in any known branch of the family. It is hard to say where Leonid Eitingon—if that is his real name—belongs.

There was family conjecture about his background, but there seems to be no way of knowing anything for sure about him until Soviet records can be consulted.[43]

Schwartz has also charged that the Eitingon companies "provided business cover for GPU operations" and that Dr. Max Eitingon had "fabricated" the losses of his American family businesses in 1931 in order "to hide a decision about allocation of funds by his Soviet masters."[44]

At this point, Schwartz crosses the line between distortion and defamation, not merely of Dr. Max Eitingon but of an entire family and the psychoanalytic movement. Schwartz is now in the grip of a runaway phobia that drives him to make increasingly shameful accusations to bolster his previous outrages. The implication here is that the Soviet masters provided the funds and instructed Dr. Max Eitingon to assist the Freudian movement financially until, in 1931, the funds were cut off and the instructions changed. The Soviet enmity toward psychoanalysis throughout this period was notorious; Schwartz has the Soviet Union providing its main financial support! This is no longer a denunciation of Dr. Max Eitingon; it is an indictment, through him, of the Freudian movement as wittingly or unwittingly a financial dependent of the Soviet Union. Whatever one may think of the psychoanalytic movement intellectually, no one has stooped so low as to besmirch it during some of its most creative years on this political ground.

What we know of Dr. Max Eitingon taken as a whole makes it virtually impossible to believe that he was the murderous Soviet agent that he has been made out to be. His life must be viewed in its entirety and the charge that he was a Stalinist killer fitted into it before a denunciation of such gravity is permissible. About all we

---

[43] I have been told by Mary Eitingon, the wife of Naum's late son, Leon, that there was a family story about Leonid Eitingon. The name of Leonid first came to the attention of the family as a result of a story in *Life* magazine (September 28, 1959) on the assassination of Leon Trotsky, which Leonid was said to have masterminded. At that time, members of the family wondered who this Leonid was, because they had never heard of him. The story came from Naum Eitingon that the property of Chaim Eitingon in Russia had been taken over by strangers when he left Russia at the turn of the century. Naum said that it was common for the new owners to take the name of the old one in order to establish their right to the property. Naum believed that Leonid's father might have appropriated Chaim Eitingon's property and had handed down the name to his son, for which reason the legitimate Eitingons had never known or heard of him before the appearance of the *Life* article. I have no way of checking this story, but no one has come up with a better one.

[44] *The New York Review of Books*, June 16, 1988, p. 51.

can say is that Max Eitingon and his wife knew Plevitskaya as a well-known singer in Berlin; that he helped her financially, as he helped many others when he was able to do so; that he saw her when he came to Paris; and that he sent her a Bible from Palestine. We also know that he devoted his life to psychoanalysis, that there is no evidence that he had any involvement in secret Soviet activities, that he did not have much money after 1931, and that his brother was not Leonid Eitingon.

Can these few circumstances from long ago conceivably justify the unequivocal assertions of Stephen Schwartz that Max Eitingon was "one of the [secret Soviet] group's key agents in the kidnapping of General Miller"; that he "recruited Skoblin and Plevitskaya," on the dubious authority of Dziak's book; that he was "the control agent for Skoblin and Plevitskaya," on the equally dubious authority of the Rapoport-Alexeev book; that he helped to prepare the liquidation of General Tukhachevsky and was involved in the murder of Ignace Reiss, on no authority at all?

There would appear to be a monstrous disparity between the gravity of the charges and the seriousness of the evidence. The least that can be said of this article is that it betrayed an unconscionable lack of scruple in its handling of the very sources on which it is based and in its failure to make use of all the evidence that might have been brought to bear on the case.

The mystery of Max Eitingon has now become the mystery of the publication of the article about him in *The New York Times Book Review*. The author systematically distorted and misrepresented the very sources on which he relied. The sources themselves cannot stand the test of critical examination. Other key sources were not consulted.

The article was not so much about intellectuals and assassins as it was an intellectual assassination of Max Eitingon, forty-five years after his death.

(*The New York Review of Books*, April 14, 1988)

Index